THE
Role of Theology and Bias
IN **Bible Translation**

THE
Role of Theology and Bias
IN **Bible Translation**

With a special look at the
New World Translation
of Jehovah's Witnesses

ROLF FURULI

ELIHU BOOKS
Huntington Beach, California

Published by:
Elihu Books
PO Box 3533
Huntington Beach, CA 92605-3533
www.elihubooks.com

The cover is a reproduction of a painting made by the Norwegian artist Arne
Paus. Because of its name, "Metamorphosis," it is used to illustrate translation,
which is a metamorphosis of language

Printed in the United States of America by
KNI, Anaheim, California

Publisher's Cataloging-in-Publication
(Provided by Quality Books, Inc.)

Furuli, Rolf.
    The role of theology and bias in Bible translation :
with a special look at the New World translation of
Jehovah's Witnesses / Rolf Furuli. -- 1st ed.
      p. cm.
    Includes bibliographical references and index
    LCCN: 98-74522
    ISBN: 0-9659814-4-4 (pbk.)
    ISBN: 0-9659814-9-5 (hardcover)

    1. Bible.--English--Versions--New World--
Criticism, interpretation, etc. 2. Bible--
Translating. I. Title.

BS195.N442F87 1999   220.5'2
                QBI99-67

TABLE OF CONTENTS

Table of Contents

PREFACE

I appreciate being able to use the painting named "Transformation," made by my close friend Arne Paus, for the cover. The boy in the picture is using a waterwheel which transforms water energy into electrical energy. This serves as a fine illustration for translation, which is also a kind of transformation.

The style of the picture represents what is called "New Romanticism." Even though its form of expression is not photographic, it beautifully and accurately reproduces the details of nature. This may serve as an illustration for a similar "genre" inside the discipline of applied linguistics, namely, that of literal translation, which does not attempt to reproduce each word from the source language; rather, it attempts to accurately convey the message. Just as not all appreciate the style of "New Romanticism," not everyone appreciates literal Bible translation.

To help the reader get a thorough understanding of the issues addressed in this book, Chapters 1, 2, and 3 approach the subject from a linguistic point of view, introducing the readers to the problems and practices involved in Bible translation. In Chapters 4, 5, and 6 we approach the subject from a philological point of view, using both the conclusions drawn in the first three chapters, as well as other relevant material to help articulate just how theology and bias influence Bible translation. Chapter 7 contains some suggestions for further study, and contains some concluding thoughts on the subjects discussed.

Textual questions are not discussed in detail in this book, but the Masoretic text of the OT, and the NT editions of Westcott and Hort, Nestle, and the United Bible Societies are accepted as reliable textual witnesses. Scripture quotations, unless otherwise indicated, are from the 1984 Reference Edition of the *New World Translation of the Holy Scriptures*.

ACKNOWLEDGEMENTS

I would like to express my appreciation to those who have given support and assistance in connection with the writing of this book. Dan-Åke Mattson and Pål-Espen Tørisen have given assistance from the beginning. They read each chapter when it was finished, giving criticism and valuable suggestions along the way. Pål-Espen has also made the illustrations, and Brandon Kruper helped enhance their quality.

I have also received sound advice from colleagues at the University of Oslo and others with whom I have consulted. Øivind Tjelland, Tony Byatt, Al Kidd and Wes Williams have reviewed the final draft, and because of their notes several improvements have been made.

I am particularly indebted to Greg Stafford, because he, in addition to providing helpful criticism and suggestions of a high quality, has also worked hard to help me improve the English style and idiom of the text, and to give the book a fine layout.

My wife Anne-Sissel has been of great encouragement from the start, and she has made valuable suggestions. I wish to acknowledge that without the help of all the aforementioned this book would not have become what it is, and I express my deep gratitude to each of them.

INTRODUCTION

When we open an English version of the Bible and read a portion of it, can we be sure that the message we are getting is the one intended by the author? The question is important, both for those believing that the Bible is inspired by God, and for those who believe that his words may or may not be found in the Bible—because the word of God should not be tampered with. The Bible itself shows the importance of details and nuances in the text, even in what is only implied. As an example, Jesus found evidence for the resurrection of the dead in the "tense" of a verb of Luke 20:37[1]; a past meaning would prove nothing, but a present meaning would imply that a resurrection of the dead would occur.

To answer the opening question in the above paragraph, we need to know something about the making of the text of the English Bible, and this is a contribution in that direction; it is a book about Bible translation. It is primarily written for the student of the Bible who wants to come as close as possible to the original text through the help of his or her mother tongue. A considerable part of the material is seen through the eyes of the Bible translator, something which is an advantage both for the student and for the translator who wants to arrange the text to serve the interests of the Bible student.

The book throws light on the unconscious forces and inclinations influencing the Bible translator, gives an outline of the principles and the process of Bible translation, and—this is somewhat new—suggests a theoretical foundation for a *literal* Bible translation based on modern linguistic principles. The conclusion drawn is as follows: Only by the help of a literal

---

[1] In the clause in Exodus 3:6 to which Jesus is referring, there is no verb. A clause without a verb is called a nominal clause and is very common in Hebrew. In such clauses the auxiliary verb "to be" is implied, usually with present meaning, thus the meaning of the clause is "I *am* the God of Abraham, Isaac and Jacob," not "I *was* the God of Abraham, Isaac and Jacob."

translation can the reader, with a good measure of certainty, know that he or she is getting the original message of the Bible.

Some persons believe that a good knowledge of the original languages is all that is necessary to translate the Bible. But this is a gross misunderstanding. Not everyone has heard, for instance, about the discipline of sociosemiotics, let alone its importance for Bible translation. Yet, two distinguished Bible translators believe "some important insights from sociosemiotics, which have provided a new approach to the issue of meaning, not merely for words, but also for syntax and rhetoric," are justification for writing a new book on Bible translation.[2] Additionally, there are several other scientific disciplines, such as linguistics, communication theory, psychology, anthropology, theology and history, fields of study in which the Bible translator must have some knowledge if he or she is going to provide us with an accurate or even adequate translation of the Bible. The truth is, the influence of these disciplines upon the translator and his or her view of translation principles may produce very different results.

Another factor influencing Bible translators is their own mind. All of us have a *horizon of understanding* which can be defined as "the totality of concepts and attitudes that we have at a given moment, conscious and unconscious, toward which our attention is not directed."[3] From childhood, all of us are made to abide amidst an intellectual landscape shaped by our parents, teachers, friends, and the authors of messages conveyed through the press and other media. As time goes by, we develop preferences, we formulate certain beliefs, and we build our life around a set of values. In a way, we are like computers into which software programs are continually being added; hence, the performance of a computer may continually change. When we make decisions or undertake evaluations, as translators do all

---

[2] J. de Waard and E. A. Nida, *From One Language* (Nashville: Thomas Nelson Publishers, 1986), p. vii. Sociosemiotics is the discipline where one studies how signs and symbols, including the symbols of language, function as a means of communication between persons and groups in different situations.

[3] Dagfinn Føllesdal, Lars Walløe, Jon Elster, *Argumentasjonsteori, språk og vitenskapsfilosofi* (Oslo: Universitetforlaget, 1986), p. 101.

the time, our mental "programs" are activated, and our *horizon of understanding* exerts an influence on the decisions just as much as intelligence and logic.[4] It follows that it is impossible for a human being to be completely objective; therefore, it is understandable for us to be concerned about the role of bias in Bible translation.

It is obvious that, aside from knowledge of languages, the most crucial factor influencing a translator is personal theology. Bible translators believe in something, often strongly so, and their beliefs must necessarily be reflected in their translations. "Neutral" translations do not exist and are not even desirable. Translation *is* interpretation, and the interpreter's theological view of a passage or a discourse is an important factor because it is certainly present with many other factors when a text is translated. Therefore, I will discuss the legitimate role of theology in translation.

The intended audience probably exerts the strongest influence on the nature of a translation. The translator must ask: For whom am I translating? For experts? For the general public? For young persons? For children? Obviously the nature of a translation will be different depending on who is the target group. The modern theory of Bible translation focuses on the general reader.[5] Every effort is made to process the text so thoroughly that anyone in the target group, even those without much formal education will be able to understand the text. But this quest to make the text an easy read for everyone may also create problems.

We can illustrate this dilemma by an analogy from medicine. Some decades ago the physician or the surgeon had

---

[4] It may have been this situation Paul had in mind when he admonished the Ephesians to "be made new in the *force actuating YOUR mind*." (NWT, 4:23) Before they became Christians the world had exerted an influence upon them; it shaped their thinking. After becoming believers, a new force, namely the influence of the Christian faith and fellowship, should transform their minds.

[5] Or, rather, on the one hearing the text read. Nida and Taber believe that a person's acquaintance with the Bible comes more from hearing the text read aloud in church than from personal Bible reading, and therefore an "oral" language has priority over a written language (E. A. Nida and C. R. Taber, *The Theory and Practice of Translation* [Leiden: Brill, 1974], p. 14).

the final word as to treatment, and it was expected that the patient would accept anything they decided. Today we have the principle of "informed consent." It implies that the doctor uses his specialized medical knowledge to explain the situation, and based on this information the patient chooses the kind of treatment he or she wants.

In the same way, the translator used to have the final say, and the reader had to accept the translated text without having any means to control the translator's linguistic knowledge or his or her theology and bias. This author believes that, to the greatest possible extent, readers of the Bible should have *the possibility* of "informed consent" and be given the tools to make "informed choices." This is possible only with a concordant or literal translation. While idiomatic translations serve a great need, they should not be the only translations available.[6]

The Bible translation chosen as the object of study in this book is *The New World Translation*. As of 1996, 91 million copies have been printed in 16 languages.[7] It is quite different from the mainline translations in its dynamic renderings of Greek and Hebrew verbs, in its many novel renderings of traditional and familiar terms, and in its renderings of passages traditionally used as evidence for the trinity doctrine. It is extremely literal, closely following the sentence structure of Hebrew and Greek, but at the same time has several elegant, idiomatic renderings. The quality of the translation, however, is widely disputed. Thus we have an ideal situation for study: A modern, literal Bible translation that, more than any other translation, is accused of being dogmatic, biased and at times even dishonest. A study of this translation and of the criticisms brought against it,[8] will

---

[6] All modern Bible study aids may help the student who is interested in coming closer to the original text, but the idiomatic translations really constitute an obstacle in reaching this goal.

[7] Unless otherwise indicated, the 1984 revised edition of the NWT will be used when .English translations of Bible passages are given. Different editions of this translation have been published by the Watchtower Bible and Tract Society of New York, Inc. The New Testament portion has been translated into an additional 13 languages.

[8] The basic objections of three books critical of the NWT are discussed: R. H. Countess, *The Jehovah's Witnesses' New Testament* (Phillipsburg: Presbyterian and Reformed, 1982); R. M. Bowman, Jr., *Jehovah's Witnesses, Jesus Christ, and*

throw light on how theology and bias influence Bible translation and on the reader's dependence upon the translators.

In the course of the book we will give special attention to the following questions:

- What should be the basic unit of translation? What is the interplay between the word and the context? What is the difference between *word, meaning, concept* and *reference* ?

- At which stage of the translation process may the reader have a share? How does theology and bias influence the renderings of particular passages?

- Is the use of the trinity doctrine as a translation principle an anachronism? What does the origin of the doctrine teach us in this respect?

- What roles do bias and theology play in the NWT? Does this translation follow its own translation principles? What is the linguistic foundation for its most disputed renderings?

- How can the students of the Bible make the most of their Bible study? What tools can they use?

This book takes a philological and linguistic approach to the issues, rather than a theological one. This means that the role played by theology and bias in Bible translation is not judged in the light of some full-blown theological system, but in the light of the lexical semantics, grammar, and the syntax of the original languages, as well as in the light of translation theory, psycholinguistics, patristics and church history. Theological considerations are made, but they are reduced to a minimum.[8]

---

the *Gospel of John* (Grand Rapids: Baker, 1990); and S. Kubo and W. F. Specht, *So Many Versions?* Revised and Enlarged Edition (Grand Rapids; Zondervan, 1983).

[8] Any work will, to a certain extent, be colored by the author's theology, and this is of course also the case with this book.

Let us prepare, then, for a reading session by keeping in mind the following expansion of the opening question: How can a general or lay reader who does not know the original languages assess the effects on the message of the original text after it has undergone translation into his vernacular? Also, how can a translator prepare his translation with the interests of the readers in view?

ABBREVIATIONS

I have tried to use as few abbreviations as possible, so everyone reading this publication will feel comfortable in not having to decipher too many unfamiliar signs and symbols. However, I have chosen to abbreviate certain items, including the following:

ASV	*American Standard Version*, 1901.
BAGD	W. Bauer, W. F. Arndt, F. W. Gingrich and F. W. Danker, *Greek English Lexicon of the New Testament and Other Early Christian Literature.*
BCE	Before our Common Era
BDB	Brown, Driver, Briggs, *Hebrew-English Lexicon*
CE	Common Era
GNB	*Good News Bible* (American Bible Society, 1976)
KIT	*Kingdom Interlinear Translation* (Watchtower Bible and Tract Society, 1985)
KJV	*King James Version*
LXX	Septuagint
NAB	*New American Bible* (Thomas Nelson, 1983)
NASB	*New American Standard Bible* (The Lockman Foundation, 1988)
NEB	*New English Bible* (Oxford, 1970)
NIDNTT	*New International Dictionary of New Testament Theology* in 4 volumes, (Zondervan) Colin Brown, ed.
NIV	*New International Version* (International Bible Society, 1984)
NJB	*New Jerusalem Bible* (Doubleday, 1985)
NKJV	*New King James Version* (Thomas Nelson, 1982)
NPNF	*Nicene and Post-Nicene Fathers* (Eerdmans' reprint series)
NRSV	*New Revised Standard Version* (National Council of the Churches of Christ, 1989)
NT	New Testament
NWT	*New World Translation* (Watchtower Bible and Tract Society, 1984 [REF])
NWTNT	*New World Translation of the Christian Greek Scriptures* (1950)
NWTREF	*New World Translation*, Reference Edition (1984)

OT   Old Testament

RSV   *Revised Standard Version* (National Council of the Churches of Christ, 1971)

TWCNT   *Twentieth Century New Testament*

TDNT   *Theological Dictionary of the New Testament* in 10 volumes, (Eerdmans) Gerhard Kittel, ed.

TDOT   *Theological Dictionary of the Old Testament* in several volumes, (Eerdmans), G. J. Botterwick, H. Ringgren and others, eds.

TEV   *Today's English Version* (American Bible Society, 1992)

YNG   *Young's Literal Translation* (1898)

CHAPTER 1

WORDS AND MEANING

Translation is a science, a skill, and an art. It is a science because its methodology can be studied and described systematically by others. It is a skill because experience makes better translators. It is an art because all the fine shades of communication cannot be conveyed effectively without having the mind of an artist. It is safe to conclude that, just as all persons cannot be good artists, not all persons can be good translators. Translation, therefore, has both an objective and a subjective side.

What, then, is translation? One well-known textbook on the subject of translation gives the following definition: "Translating consists in reproducing in the receptor language the closest natural equivalent of the source-language message; first in terms of meaning and secondly in terms of style."[1]

From this, three important points can be inferred: First, translation is *communication* where the message is more important than translating single words. Second, focus is on the receptor of the message, and third, idiomatic and literal translations take care of the interests of the receptors in completely different ways. Let us take a closer look at what this involves. The words of 2 John 1:11 help to illustrate that communicating the *the message* is more important than conveying the lexical meaning of words, "For he that says a greeting to him is a sharer in his wicked works." The Greek words in this verse are translated quite similarly both in idiomatic and in literal translations as "saying a greeting to him." To "say a greeting" is in this situation the closest natural equivalent in English to the Greek infinitive *chairein*. However,

---

[1] E. A. Nida and C. R. Taber, *The Theory and Practice of Translation* (Leiden: Brill, 1974), p. 77. Look at the "Explanation of words" on pp. 314 and 315. Here you will find the meaning of "source language," "target language" and the "closest natural equivalent." If in the course of reading you find a word you do not understand, it might be found in this list.

if we were seeking a *lexical* (word for word) equivalent we should have translated, "saying that he should rejoice," because "to rejoice," "to be glad" is the sense of the *word chairein.* However, a lexical equivalent would not convey the message.

To understand how different translations affect the receptor, we must answer these questions: "What is the basic translation unit?" "Is it the *word* or must we seek another unit?" "How literal should we make the translation?" These are the most fundamental questions affecting translation. Among translators not working on the Bible there are different viewpoints as to the role of the word. On one side we have the Paris school[2] with the slogan: "Take care of the meaning and the words will take care of themselves." To put it differently, the words themselves have little or no importance for the translator. On the other hand, we find translators like Peter Newmark who states: "Many translators say you should never translate words, you translate sentences or ideas or messages. I think they are fooling themselves. The SL (source language) texts consist of words, that is all that is there, on the page."[3]

What, then, is the view of Bible translators? In the 19th and first part of the 20th century many Bible translations were literal, but in the last few decades mostly idiomatic translations have been produced. Why has this change come about? It is because the theoretical foundation of Bible translation has changed, bringing it more in line with the thoughts of the Paris school. This, however, has affected the relationship between the translators and the receptors. The new idiomatic Bible translations communicate meaning to the receptors in a much better way than did the older, more literal ones, and even when they are read aloud the meaning usually can easily be grasped. But this has its price: The receptors' dependence upon the translators has increased. Therefore, in the interest of those

---

[2] École Supérieure d'Interprétes et de Traducteurs, Sorbonne Nouvelle, Paris III, represented by Danica Seleskovitch, *Sense and Language* (1978), and Jean Delisle, *Translation: An Interpretative Approach* (Translation Studies 8; Ottawa: University of Ottawa Press, 1988).

[3] P. Newmark, *A Textbook of Translation* (New York: Prentice Hall, 1988), p. 36. Newmark's book was awarded the British Association of Applied Linguistics prize in 1988.

wanting to work with the biblical text on their own, there is also a need for modern, literal translations. "Informed choices" can best be achieved this way. To get a better understanding of this we will take a look at the nature of the word.

CHARACTERISTICS OF WORDS

In our use of words in everyday speech, the meaning comes to us automatically, and we seldom reflect on *how* words convey this meaning. If we did, we might have discovered several interesting characteristics of the words we use and how meaning is achieved.

Let us begin this study of words with the observation that apart from onomatopoeia (words mimicking particular sounds), the relation between the form of a word and its meaning is an arbitrary one. There is no particular reason why, for instance, c-o-w means an animal from which we get milk and b-r-e-a-d means a particular kind of food made from cereals. The meaning we ascribe to combinations of letters or sounds comes from a linguistic *convention*, which we are taught from childhood, and not from logic. Keeping this in mind we may better understand the thoughts behind the famous cliché, "Words do not have meanings; meanings have words."

Plato and some of his contemporaries believed that words had an intrinsic meaning connected with their sounds, and the central principle behind the study of biblical words down to the 20th century was that each word form retained a basic meaning rooted in its etymology, and that the multiple senses of a word, seen in different contexts, could be traced back to this one fundamental meaning. All the literal Bible translations of the 19th and first half of the 20th century were made on the basis of this "etymological approach." Recently, H. P. Scanlin said that "at present one may confidently say that linguists generally no longer uphold the etymological approach."[4] But J. P. Louw

---

[4] H. P. Scanlin, "The Study of Semantics in General Linguistics," in *Linguistics and Biblical Hebrew*, ed. W. R. Bodine (Winona Lake, Indiana: Eisenbrauns, 1992), p. 134. "Etymology" involves studying the different elements of a word,

lamented that "the legacy of centuries seems to hold the ground, not only among people in general, but also among scholars engaged in various hermeneutic activities."[5]

What, then, was wrong with the traditional model, and is the present approach better? For one thing, etymology is tricky business. It is very difficult to follow a word backwards through time and ascertain how the use of it has changed. At what point in history can we, for example, pause and be sure that we have found the *fundamental* meaning of the word?

An illustration of this problem can be found in Genesis 2:23. Here it is said that the woman was called *'isha* because she was taken from *'ish*, the man, "This one will be called woman, because from man this one was taken." The etymology is explicitly stated, and it seems to fit well, but most scholars do not accept it because the letters of the plural forms of the Hebrew words seem to contradict it.[6]

In addition to the difficulty in finding an original meaning, words often have "fuzzy edges." This indicates that the meaning attached to a word may be quite fluid, and there often is no clear point at which one word ends and another begins. Look at the following figure.

---

its use, changes in form and meaning, and tracing its transmission from one language to another in hopes of determining the word's origin and historical development.

[5] J. P. Louw, *Semantics of New Testament Greek* (Chico, CA: Scholars Press, 1982), p. 23.

[6] Compare N. P. Bratsiotis, "אִשָּׁה," TDOT 1 (Grand Rapids: Eerdmans, 1974), p. 222.

Figure 1.1
The Fuzzy Edges of Words

Where does the sense "cup" end and "bowl" begin? And at which point is the figure a "vase"?[7]

When we work with different languages we find additional problems related to the meaning of words. When quite definite meanings are attached to words in one language, we often find that they do not match exactly with the meanings attached to similar words in another language; their range of meaning is somewhat different. Look at the figure below. It illustrates the range of meaning between the words "tree" and "forest" in four languages.[8]

---

[7] The "fuzzy edges" are not found only in cases of quite similar words, but in almost all words. Or, rather, the concepts they signal are fuzzy. This will be elucidated later, but we should keep in mind that each word/concept that is stored in our mind has a central core which is rather easy to discern. However, as we approach the edges of the concept they become more difficult to discern. In many instances the concept is so extensive that it is impossible to make a list of all that it encompasses. One such example is the concept signaled by the word "culture." Just try and articulate the meaning of this word!

[8] The comparison is based on a figure by the Danish linguist L. Hjelmslev, who is quoted in Lomheim, *Omsetjingsteori* (Oslo: Universitetsforlaget, 1995), p. 27.

Figure 1.2

"Tree" and "Forest" in Three Languages

træ	Baum	arbre
	Holz	bois
skov	Wald	forêt

In spite of all these semantic ambiguities, we have few problems using words to communicate with other speakers of our native language, even to convey the finest nuances and details of our thoughts and plans. This is because words, used in the act of communication, are not treated alone, but as entities interacting with each other. The word "degree" may, for instance, have several meanings, but in a context with the word "heat" it likely refers to temperature, and whether Fahrenheit or centigrade is meant depends on what is common where the communication occurs. Syntax may also be a decisive factor as to the sense of words. In the sentences "Here is water" and "He will water" the word "water" has the same form. In the first sentence, however, it is the subject and in the second it is a part of the predicate. A difference in meaning is evident.

The fact that words behave differently in relation to other words, than when standing alone, has given rise to the "semantic domain" approach to word meaning with this central principle: "a word does not have meaning without a context, it only has possibilities of meaning."[9] Those translators using this approach in word studies are interested in similarities and contrasts in the meaning of *related* words (for example, the

---

[9] Louw, *Semantics of New Testament Greek*, p. 40.

Greek words *philia* and *agapē*, which are both connected with the English word "love"), rather than in the etymology of these words. No one disputes that the context helps make visible the meaning of words, but the crucial question is whether meaning can be ascribed to words standing alone. Or, to put it differently, must we completely discard the "etymological model" for the benefit of the "semantic domain model"?

WORDS AND COMMUNICATION

When people communicate and exchange information, they do not use single words, but clauses and sentences consisting of many words. The reason is that single words do not communicate, or at least do so in a much more restricted way than ordered words in a discourse.

This is excellently illustrated by the difference between the interlinear translation on one hand and the idiomatic and literal translations on the other. In the interlinear translation a word (the lexical equivalent in the receptor language) is placed beneath the source-language word: the context is completely ignored. Thus little communication is conveyed, only single words; and it can hardly be called a translation at all in the normal sense of the word.[10] Therefore we usually find a running translation beside the interlinear text. The translators of the literal translation (and of course of the idiomatic ones) treat the words in relation to each other in a living context in order to create mental images in the minds of the readers. Thus there is a much greater difference between the interlinear translation and the literal translation than between the literal and the idiomatic translation. But from this does it follow that words do not have meaning?

---

[10] Interlinear bibles, however, are gold mines for those wanting accurate knowledge of the Bible. de Waard and Nida, *From one Language to Another*, p. 40, say, "An interlinear translation (usually with an accompanying literal rendering in intelligible syntactic order) may be valuable to ethnologists, linguists, and philologists, who are interested in the original structure or literary devices without themselves having to learn the language in question."

With regard to the individual letters of the word, it is clear that they do not carry any meaning in themselves, but if the belief that "a word does not have meaning without a context" is true, in a strict sense, then words also do not exist as single semantic entities. However, this seems to be contradicted by what has actually been found.

The goal of the discipline of psycholinguistics is to describe the way our mind works as regards language and communication. In studying persons with brain damage, speech disorders, slips of the tongue (by normal persons) and through different experiments inside the frame of theoretical linguistics, we have a better understanding of how verbal information is structured in the brain.

To be able to use a word, humans must know three things: its meaning, its role in the sentence and what it sounds like. There is absolutely no reason to believe that information covering these three areas is stored in the brain as sentences or as words in context, but as one psycholinguist says, "The large number of words known by humans, and the speed by which they can be located, point to the existence of a highly organized mental lexicon."[11] If this is true, then it becomes quite obvious that words are independent entities which have individual meaning.

This does not mean, however, that I advocate a different form of the old etymological view, which posits that a word has an original meaning to which all uses of the word can be traced. When it comes to ordinary words, I agree with Aitchison that "for the majority of words, meanings in the mind are

---

[11] J. Aitchison, *Words in the Mind* (Oxford: Blackwell, 1993), p. 9. When people slip with the tongue, the wrong word they choose is almost always of the same word class as the right word, a fact suggesting that words are stored in the mind by their word classes. There is also much evidence suggesting that words are stored according to semantic fields. In particular, co-ordintion (salt, pepper and mustard together) and collocation (salt and water together and butterfly and net together) seem to be strongly linked (see Aitchison, pages 74-75, 100-101). This also suggests that words have individual existence and individual meaning. The phrase "mental lexicon" is just a metaphor and is not used in a technical sense.

fuzzy, not fixed."[12] But as she further shows, the fuzziness does not prevent the mind from distinguishing between words, and, in a fraction of a second, choosing the right words in a complicated discussion. Therefore, let us look at *words* from another point of view.

THE TRIANGLE(S) OF SIGNIFICATION

The father of modern linguistics, Ferdinand de Saussure,[13] was the first to differentiate between the word as a *signifier* (as a mere sign inside a linguistic system) and that which it *signifies* (the mental image created in the minds of persons). A few years after the death of Saussure, C. K. Ogden[14] added another term, namely, "significatum" which we may call "reference," because it refers to the thing in the world denoted by the word. This is how we obtained the so-called "triangle of signification."

---

[12] Aitchison, *Words in the Mind*, p. 49. As explained in note 7 on page 10, the fuzziness only relates to the edges or the borders of the concepts in our mind. If the meaning of each concept could be limited and fixed with ease, the use of each word as a semantic signal would also be greatly limited. It is an advantage to see the core of the concept as quite clear, but getting more dim as we approach its edges, because the same word can be used with different senses in different contexts. Viewed in this light we can even understand a clause when a familiar word is used with a completely new sense.

[13] F. de Saussure, *Course in General Linguistics* (London: Duckworth, 1983), pp. 66-67. The French edition was published in 1915.

[14] C. K. Ogden, *The Meaning of Meaning* (International Library of Psychology, Philosophy and Scientific Method; London: Kegan Paul, Trench, Trubner & Co., 1930).

Figure 1.3
Triangle of Signification

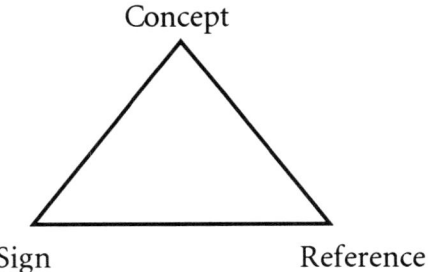

Concept

Sign   Reference

HEBREW EXAMPLE

Sign: *geber*
Concept: Young, vigorous man[15]
Reference: One or more living persons

Because we are discussing *meaning* in the context of translation, we should at this point introduce the concept[16] of a "presupposition pool," and stress that those who transfer meaning through translation between languages as far apart as Greek and English and Hebrew and English, must constantly keep in mind that they are dealing with two different situations of communication and two different presupposition pools. To act as if there was just one situation of communication will in many instances distort the message.

---

[15] The claim that "a young vigorous man" *is* the concept, is only partly true. A concept cannot be completely defined, so it is better to say that "a young vigorous man" is the nucleus of the concept.

[16] The observant reader will have realized that "concept" in this clause is used in a sense different from "concept" as used in the triangle. There is one semantic signal c-o-n-c-e-p-t, and the context helps us decide whether the reference is to the concept in the mind with fuzzy edges or to the more technical sense of an external idea.

> **PRESUPPOSITION POOl:** The common knowledge and understanding of the world upon which a particular group has built their language, their culture, their religion and their everyday life.

Generally speaking, a word uttered in Hebrew by Jesus would activate the same *concept* in the minds of the listeners whose native language was Hebrew. By help of the context they would instantly understand which side of the concept, represented by the word, Jesus was stressing. They also did not need any other linguistic tools, as we do, to get the same understanding. The triangle above, therefore, represents the situation in the real world, and it illustrates that *meaning* (in the general sense) is not tied up with words in a book or the sounds coming from a speaker; rather, meaning is connected with the minds of living people, of those having the same presupposition pool.

We can illustrate the nature of the situation by help of the painting on the cover of this book, which can be compared to a word/concept. If you look at it closely for at least 10 seconds, you will become familiar with all the different details and images. But after a while you will probably not be able to describe all of its details from memory, since you may not have caught all the little details (or even some of the more obvious ones!) when you analyzed it.

For example, do you recognize what the boy is doing? You might think he has lit a fire, but actually the light represents the reflection of the sun in a small brook coming from the glacier. This reflection has been a part of the picture all along, but it is easy to misinterpret what it represents. In bringing this to your attention, I have revealed the true import of the picture, specifically in regards to the boy and the light, allowing you to discard the alternative "fire" interpretation, which is a very good guess!

In a similar way, meaning has been present in each word/concept all the time, but all the details have not been equally visible or equally stressed. The context does not generate new meaning(s), but it serves as a forefinger, pointing to the side of the word/concept that the author wants to make visible.

Because we have a different presupposition pool than that of the Greeks or Hebrews of old, we have a considerable problem when trying to understand the *concepts* signaled by various Greek and Hebrew words. While an ancient Hebrew person would get an instant, but different understanding of the same word used in different contexts, we need to read entries in lexicons and look for explanations given elsewhere. And even then we would not get as clear an understanding of the word(s) as an ancient Hebrew- or Greek-speaking person. Additionally, their understanding was instantaneous. Therefore, to have a model by which we can illustrate the transmission of meaning through the two different systems of communication, and at the same time assess the quality of this transmission, we should use the model of two triangles rather than one.

Figure 1.4
Two Triangles of Signification

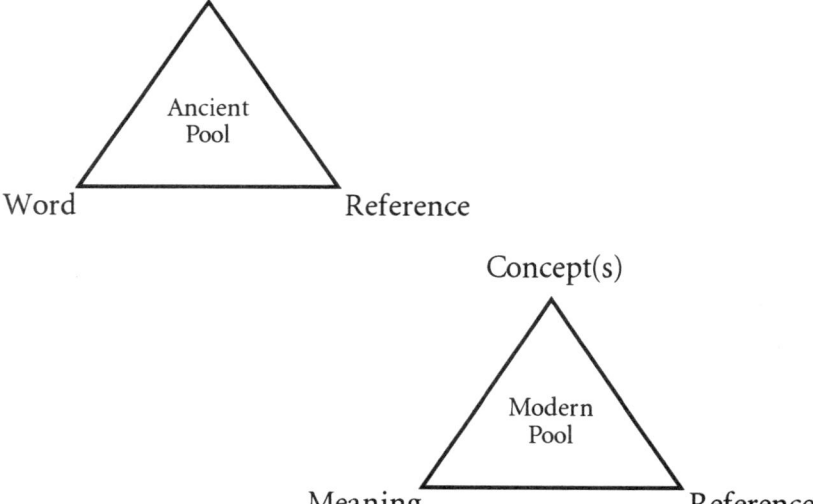

THE SENSE OF "REFERENCE" IN THE TRIANGLES

Looking at the two triangles representing an ancient and a modern presupposition pool respectively, we see there are both similarities and differences. One similarity is that, in the right corner of each triangle, we find "reference." The thing in the world denoted by a Greek or Hebrew word is the same as the thing denoted by the English term(s) used to translate the original word. The identity of Jesus is not, for instance, changed regardless of whether we call him "Christ" or use the Greek word *christos* or the Hebrew word *mashiah*. So "reference" in the right corner of both triangles has exactly the same meaning.

THE SENSE OF "MEANING" IN THE MODERN TRIANGLE

The real difference between the triangles is the left corner where we find "word" and "meaning" respectively. What does "meaning" actually signify when it is used in this technical way?[17] For the Greeks and Hebrews of old, a word such as "meaning" was unneccessary because they understood the concepts signaled by the words and thereby understood the text. So "meaning" is exclusively connected with the triangle representing our modern presupposition pool. This does not mean that "meaning" in the modern presupposition pool is equivalent with "concept" in the old one. The concept signaled by *kosmos* ("world"), for instance, includes much more than the "meaning" of this word as we construe it on the basis of its use in the Bible. Therefore, "meaning" is not identical with the sum total of all the glosses given in a lexicon in a particular entry.[18]

---

[17] The word "meaning" is a relative word, the "understanding" of which depends on the target group and the situation of translation. The setting of the technical use illustrated above is literal translation, where the target group gets a "minimum" definition, by help of which they themselves can work out the finer nuances.

[18] Some of these glosses are only used in classical Greek and must therefore be excluded as far as the NT "meaning" is concerned. Further, we find several

> **MEANING:** The sum of all the impressions *a native Greek or Hebrew* would get from the same word being used in different biblical contexts, and the minimum number of English words *we* need to signal these impressions.

But why is "meaning" found in the left corner of the triangle representing the modern presupposition pool, when "word," which is void of meaning, is found in the same corner in the triangle representing the ancient presupposition pool? The reason is that the two triangles represent two different situations of communication, and these situations are connected only by the act of translation. In the first situation the *author* chooses the word, which signals a concept, and in the second situation the *translator* chooses a word from the target language which he or she believes can serve as a similar signal in that language. This target language word is the "meaning," as described above, but it serves as a semantic signal (just as the source word did) of a concept in the minds of those speaking the target language. But once it is chosen, it serves as a signal for a concept[19] in the minds of those having the modern presupposition pool, just as the word in the source language did for those having the ancient presupposition pool.

THE SENSE OF "CONCEPT" IN THE TRIANGLES

The word "concept" is exclusively connected with the particular presupposition pool, and, therefore, the word "concept" on the top of both triangles is not completely identical in both pools; there may be some differences. This is also the

---

glosses which are either wholly or in part theological rather than philological, and these also must be excluded.

[19] When a Bible translation is the principle factor used in forming a new written language, as has been the case with Luther's translation and many missionary translations, the presupposition pool of the people lacks a clear understanding of many of the biblical concepts, so these must be taught to the Bible readers.

reason why a plural "s" is added in the modern triangle. In some instances one concept in Greek or Hebrew will represent more than one concept in English. The challenge for one reading a literal translation is to come to know the concept signaled by a Greek or Hebrew word so completely that the English "meaning" of this original word signals the same concept in his or her English mind as it did in the minds of the original readers.

PROTECTION AGAINST ANACHRONISMS

To understand the use of the two triangles of signification can be a good help for the translator who is concerned with the interests of the readers, and who wants to translate as literally as possible. Because of the clear differentiation between the two situations of communication, the triangles can also be helpful in avoiding certain kinds of translation errors, one example being anachronistic renditions. This is an important point, and the following illustration may help.

If we were to translate an English book written in 1930 into Norwegian and we found the words "the great war," we could not translate them by "den første verdenskrig" ("the first world war"). The sense or the lexical meaning of "the first world war" is appropriate, and today we apply the words to the war between 1914 and 1918, but in 1930 both the *concept* and *reference* were lacking. To speak of "the *first* world war" before the second had occurred would be an anachronism.

With respect to Bible translation, de Waard and Nida also warn about theological anachronisms: "Not only must one avoid going behind the text, but it is also important not to read into the New Testament doctrinal positions which developed in later times."[20] The first one to direct the attention of the scholarly world towards this problem in word studies was James Barr. In 1961 he published the book *The Semantics of Biblical Language*, where he militated strongly against this tendency. According to

---

[20] de Waard and Nida, *From One Language to Another*, p. 177.

the lexicographer Moises Silva, Barr's book "was a trumpet blast against the monstrous regiment of shoddy linguistics."[21]

Barr criticized the tendency to build on preconceived ideas when discussing the meaning of Greek and Hebrew words. He criticized the Norwegian scholar Thorleif Boman because he started with a definite idea of the difference between Hebrew and Greek thought and selectively tried to find evidence for this in the vocabularies of the Greeks and the Hebrews.

He also criticized G. Kittel's *Theological Dictionary of the New Testament*, particularly the first part of it because it tended to use *Wort* ("word") and *Begriff* ("concept") without any clear difference in meaning, and because he and his co-workers took theological ideas as a point of departure in their discussion of the different entries instead of building solely on linguistic evidence.

At the same time he criticized those who made too much out of the etymology of a word, arguing that the sense at speech time or at the time of writing was the only thing that counted. Barr's criticisms are basically sound and are viewed favorably by almost all scholars.[22] All translators should therefore make sure that they are using sound methods which prevent anachronisms and other errors from entering into their work.

All the different points in relation to the triangles may not be easy to grasp. But the central point is that there are two different presupposition pools and two different situations of communication, and these four factors must be accounted for in any theory of translation. A key point that we have alluded to in this chapter is that the single *words* of a text are more important in connection with *meaning* than what is commonly believed. This will be elucidated in greater detail in the next chapter.

---

[21] Moisés Silva, *Biblical Words and Their Meaning: An Introduction to Lexical Semantics* (Grand Rapids: Zondervan, 1994), p. 18.

[22] Silva, *Biblical Words and Their Meaning*, pp. 18-22.

EXCURSUS ON MEANING
USING THE GREEK WORD *AIŌN*[23]

To define *aiōn*, BAGD lists four principal senses of this word:

1) "very long time," "eternity";

2) "a segment of time, age";

3) "the world as a spatial concept," and;

4) "the Aeon as a person."

Right away we can see that the sum total of these four senses is not identical with "meaning," because 4) is not found in the Bible at all. But what about the three others? Do they together constitute the "meaning"?

I venture to say that only two English words are needed to convey the impression that a native Greek would get from all the uses of *aiōn* in the NT, and none of these correspond exactly to any of the four senses given in BAGD (although one is quite close to 1]).

Which two words am I speaking about? The Hebrew word which in the Septuagint is translated by *aiōn* is ʿōlām. The concept signaled by this Hebrew word relates to something that is concealed or hidden. The noun therefore indicates a time period with an undefined length, and this period may or may not be eternal. While the word in the OT usually only signals the time *period*, in time it also came to include the *quality* of a particular time period, and this duality is also found in the NT. So the two English words representing the "meaning" of *aiōn* must express both of these two thoughts. Let us consider the renditions of *aiōn* in the NWT.

---

[23] The Greek words *kosmos* and *aiōn* are the first entries in the *Greek-English Lexicon of the New Testament Based on Semantic Domains*, vol. 1, 2d ed. (New York: United Bible Societies, 1989), edited by Johannes P. Louw and Eugene A. Nida. Because I am somewhat critical toward their approach, it is fitting that we discuss these two words at length. The word *kosmos* will be discussed in the next chapter.

In the NWT the Hebrew word ʿōlām, in all instances where it stands without an intensifying element, is translated by "time indefinite," except in one instance.[24] This is a good choice because it allows the reader to find out when the concealed time is eternal and when it is not. On the other hand, the Greek word aiōn is translated by the words "eternal," "everlasting," or other, similar words, in 83 instances. In only 5 instances is it rendered by "from of old"[25] or "from the indefinite past."[26] Also, in the cases where aiōn is rendered "eternal" the meaning is "time indefinite," because "eternal" or "everlasting" can be subsumed under "time indefinite." The difference between the OT use, however, is that eternality is more frequently made visible by the use of aiōn than it is by the use of ʿōlām, and in the NT the NWT translators chose to make this explicit through translation.[27] The translators can hardly be criticised for this, but it shows that even in a literal translation there is a measure of interpretation.

In addition to "time indefinite," what is the second word or phrase expressing the "meaning" of aiōn? When the *quality* of a particular time period is sought, the English word used to convey this in many modern translations is "age." This rendition seems to be fitting in many instances, but this is not always the case. For example, in Galatians 1:4 (TEV) we read, "In order to set us free from this present evil age, Christ gave himself for our sins, in obedience to the will of our God and Father." But could someone be "delivered from the present age" when they are still living in what was at that time the present age? In this verse "age" is hardly fitting,[28] because this word almost exclusively focuses on time. To express the quality or

---

[24] The only exception is 1 Kings 2:45. Also, when ʿōlām occurs together with ʿad it is translated by "forever" or other, similar words.

[25] Luke 1:70; John 9:32; Acts 3:21; 15:18.

[26] Ephesians 3:9.

[27] In many instances "eternal" or "everlasting" is clearly made visible by the context. The creator cannot be anything else but "the eternal God," and "real life" is not "life to time indefinite," but "eternal life."

[28] This is also true in Hebrews 1:2 and 11:3.

characteristics of this time period we need a word or phrase with a wider meaning.

The NWT renders *aiōn* in this verse and in 33 other verses as "system of things." The word "thing" is something a translator will avoid because it is vague. And "system of things" is a really unidiomatic phrase which deserves the designation "wooden." But as a way of expressing the "meaning" of *aiōn* it has certain advantages because it, in contrast with "age," both implies an arrangement or order and gives the time element a prominent place, particularly when the phrase is qualified (as in "the wicked system of things," "the present system of things" and "the coming system of things").

Thus the "meaning" of *aiōn* is the sum of the two uses we have described (a time period of undefined length including eternity, and a time period characterised by a certain order), and the one concept in the minds of those sharing the same presupposition pool would help give the reader/listener the right understanding.

With this in mind, let us then look at one example where many translators have overstepped the borders of "meaning" as it is illustrated by the left corner of the modern triangle. Consider Matthew 13:38-39, which in the ASV reads: "The field is the world; and the good seed, these are the sons of the kingdom; and the tares are the sons of the evil one; and the enemy that sowed them is the devil; and the harvest is the end of the world; and the reapers are angels." This translation definitely gives the reader the wrong meaning. It is said that "the field is the *world* [*kosmos*]," at the same time as it is said that "the harvest is the end of the *world* [*aiōn*]." The only logical conclusion that can be drawn from this is that the harvest is the end of the *field*. But this is clearly not what the author intended.

The concept behind *kosmos* ("world") has certain similarities with the concept behind *aiōn*, but there is also a clear difference, because *aiōn* centers around time while *kosmos* centers around order and beauty. It is true that the side of *aiōn* which is made visible in Matthew 13:39 primarily centers around the characteristics (order) of a time period, but this order is clearly different from that which is signified by *kosmos*. Contrary to Louw and Nida, I claim that the rendition "world" is outside the "meaning" of *aiōn*, and the use of such a rendition can cause a contradiction in the text, as in the case of Matthew 13:38-39 (ASV).[29]

---

[29] According to the NT a new order (*aiōn*) will come, but not a new world (*kosmos*), so there is a clear difference between these two words.

CHAPTER 2

WORDS AS TRANSLATION UNITS

In his comparison of the vocabularies of the NT and the Septuagint, H. A. A. Kennedy divided his material into 6 groups of words:

1) theological and religious terms;
2) Hebrew and Aramaic loan words;
3) technical terms for Jewish customs and ideas;
4) everyday words;
5) Alexandrian words; and
6) new compounds.[1]

There can be no doubt that meaning is attached to the words in the 6 groups in different ways, and that some words will be rendered non-uniformly by idiomatic translations. To penetrate deeper into the meaning of words, let us do some word studies.

THE RENDERING OF THREE GREEK WORDS

AGAPĒ

We will first consider the Greek word for "love," namely, *agapē*. This word occurs 116 times in the NT, and TEV translates it as the noun (or verb) "love" in 114 cases.[2] However, the translators of the TEV subscribed to the idea that words only get meaning by help from the context, and, thus, they usually

---

[1] H. A. A. Kennedy, *Sources of New Testament Greek* (Edinburgh: T & T Clark, 1895).

[2] In Colossians 1:13 it is translated as "dear" in the phrase "his dear son." In Jude 1:12 the plural word is translated as "fellowship meals." NWT reads "love feasts."

translated words quite differently. But, why, then, is it that *agapē* is rendered uniformly in almost all its occurrences?

The *meaning* of *agapē* is easy to determine, but that is not the case when it comes to understanding its *concept* nor with its *reference.*[3] This is clearly seen if we try to define the word, for that is virtually impossible! We cannot with one or a few short sentences account for the contents of *agapē*, so the word cannot be defined, it must be described. Paul uses one whole chapter (1 Cor 13) to describe love, and still there is much to be said. The Greek writers used *a-g-a-p-ē* as a sign or symbol for this elevated attribute or state, and *the readers* had to assign meaning to the symbol. Because of the nature of this word, the translators of TEV similarly used *l-o-v-e* as a sign or symbol, and the modern English readers must themselves interpret its contents.

KOSMOS

Another word used in "everyday" speech and where even idiomatic translations let the reader do the interpreting, is the Greek word *kosmos* ("world"). In the NT it occurs 186 times. From the etymology of this word we find the notions of "order" and "beauty." In classical Greek it often denoted "the whole universe," but in the NT it refers to "the whole human family," "the human family outside the Christian congregation" and "the environment in which the human family lives."[4] How is the word to be translated? The NWT renders it as "world" in all instances save one,[5] and TEV uses "world" in 175 instances,[6]

---

[3] Not all words have definite references. Moisés Silva, *Biblical Words and Their Meaning: An Introduction to Lexical Semantics* (Grand Rapids: Zondervan, 1994), p. 107, compares four words which are different as to reference: 1) Plato (fully referential), 2) law (mostly referential), 3) cold (partly referential) and 4) beautiful (non-referential).

[4] It seems that in only one instance, in Paul's speech to the philosophers on Mars hill, is it used in the classical Greek sense of "the universe" (Acts 17:24).

[5] The one instance where it is translated differently is 1 Peter 3:3, where it refers to gold ornaments and beautiful clothes. Because the *reference* in this case is completely different from the other instances, it is translated "adornment."

even though different sides of the word or different senses are stressed in the different passages.

If we look at Kennedy's word groups, we should probably classify both *agapē* and *kosmos* as "ordinary words," the difference being that the first one consists of a whole bundle of meanings with edges that are difficult to pinpoint, while the last one has a few specific senses or uses. As to communication, the translators have not conveyed any interpretation of the words to the readers; they simply give them the bare "sign" (*w-o-r-l-d*), allowing the readers to find the fullness of meaning in each case by help of the context. This illustrates that, even though the old etymological approach no longer can be upheld, in many instances is it both possible and necessary to render certain words uniformly, even though it is done on a non-etymological foundation.

SARX

Let us now direct our attention towards a third word, one that is translated in many different ways in the idiomatic translations, namely, the Greek word *sarx* ("flesh"). There are several reasons for choosing this word, one of which is because it is an "everyday" word rather than a technical one. It occurs 133 times in the NT, a number that is easy to handle but large enough to illustrate the point. And the most important reason is because it is used by Nida and Taber as an outstanding example of how contextual consistency must overrule verbal consistency in translation,[7] and by P. Cotterell and M. Turner as an argument against literal translation.[8]

---

[6] The word *kosmos* is deleted in 3 instances (1 Cor 8:4; 2 Cor 5:19; 1 Joh 3:17); it is translated as "everyone" (Joh 18:20; 1 Joh 2:2), as "people" (1 Cor 1:21), as "everywhere" (1 Joh 4:1), and in a combination with *stoikheia* ("what is elementary") it is given the idiosyncratic translation "ruling spirits of the universe" (Gal 4:3; Col 2:8, 20). In 1 Peter 3:3 it is translated "make . . . beautiful."

[7] Nida and Taber, *Theory and Practice*, p. 16.

[8] P. Cotterell and M. Turner, *Linguistics and Biblical Interpretation* (Downers Grove: InterVarsity Press, 1989), p. 169.

The NWT translates *sarx* in every occurrence with its literal meaning, *flesh*. The TEV uses this lexical sense in only 18 instances. If we compare the entries on *sarx* and suggested senses in two lexicons, it might look something like figure 2.1 below.

Figure 2.1

Different Definitions for the Greek Word Sarx

Liddell and Scott	BAGD
flesh	lit., of the material that covers the bones
the *inner* or *fleshside* of leather	*the body* itself viewed as substance
fleshy pulpy substance of fruit	*a man of flesh and blood*
the *flesh* as the seat of affections and lusts, *fleshly nature*	*human* or *mortal nature, earthly descent*
In the NT also, *the body*	*corporeality, physical limitations, life here on earth*
the *physical* or *natural order* of things	*the external* or *outward side of life,* as it appears to the eye of an unregenerate person
	In Paul's thought esp., the *flesh* is the willing instrument of sin
	the *sarx* ("flesh") is the source of the sexual urge

The work of Liddell and Scott which covers both classical and NT use is the more sober source, while BAGD, in this instance, uses not only linguistic evidence but also leans heavily on theology. Taking the triangles into account, what do we find concerning the meaning of *sarx*? We find the following basic senses: 1) the material that covers the bones, 2) the fleshside of leather, and 3) the pulpy substance of fruit. These three senses do not represent the "meaning" in the left corner of the triangle, illustrating the modern pool, because 2) and 3) are not found in the NT, so only 1) represents the "meaning. "

But what about the other glosses? Where do they fit in? We find, for instance, "the body" and "a man of flesh and blood." How should we classify these words? Relative to the triangles they can be viewed as *references* because they denote the things in the world referred to by the word.[9] As for the other suggestions, these represent neither *concept*, nor *meaning* nor *reference*, but they seem to fall outside of the triangles.

There are at least three problems with the suggestions, "human and mortal nature," "earthly descent," "corporeality," "physical limitations," "life here on earth," "outward side of life," "willing instrument of sin" and "sexual urge." Here are the problems: 1) All of these senses, except "earthly descent," are vague and ambiguous and will mean different things to different people. 2) All of them, except "corporeality," are expressed by two or more words, and each of these words are themselves signaling different *concepts* in the minds of people with our modern presupposition pool. 3) None of them, save "human nature," are normally used to translate *sarx*; they are simply thought to be approximate representations of *sarx*. Therefore, other words that represent these glosses must be used in translating *sarx* in different contexts. In a way we have a situation where a host of different words signaling as many different concepts in English are the basis for the translation of one Greek word signaling one concept. No wonder such free translations introduce into the biblical text nuances that are not found in the Hebrew and Greek text! Let us now take a closer look at some different renderings of *sarx*.

---

[9] Another way of looking at these two senses, is to view them as idiomatic expressions that are parts making up the whole. We find an example of this in Genesis 42:38, where it is said that Jacob's "gray hairs" went down into the grave. This does not give "gray hairs" the sense of "body," even though the phrase in this case represents the whole body.

SOME PROBLEMATIC RENDERINGS OF SARX IN TODAY'S ENGLISH VERSION OF THE BIBLE

Figure 2.2

Problematic Translations of Sarx in TEV

VERSE	PROBLEM
In 14 instances *sarx* is not translated; five of these are quotes from Genesis 2:24, as we find in Matthew 19:5: "For this reason a man will leave his father and mother and unite with his wife and the two will become one."	The strong union resulting from two bodies being united or "glued" together is lost by rendering, "become one" rather than "become one flesh."
1 Corinthians 10:18: "Consider the Hebrew people of Israel." (NWT: "Look at that which is Israel in a fleshly way."	The implication that "Israel" can refer to something other than the ethnic group "Israel" is lost.
1 Corinthians 7:1: "Purify yourselves from everything that makes body and soul unclean."	"Body" (*sarx*) is used instead of "flesh" and "soul" instead of "spirit" (*pneuma*). Idiosyncratic substitution of words is confusing. The purification seems to be restricted to the literal body.
Romans 7:18: "I know that good does not live in me—that is, in my human nature."[10]	The rendition, "human nature" falls outside of the triangles and may mislead the reader. The possibility that Paul believed in *inherited sin* literally dwelling in his flesh is difficult to reconcile with this translation.[11] The use of *nature* could suggest to some readers that imperfection is a part of God's creation.[12]

---

[10] The word *sarx* is also translated "human nature" in Romans 7:5; 8:3 (twice), 4, 5 (twice), 6, 7, 8, 9, 12, 13; Galatians 5:17 (twice), 19, 24. It is translated as "natural selves" in Romans 6:19, as "sinful nature" in 8:3 and 13:14, as "physical desires" Galatians 5:13, as "natural desires" in Galatians 6:8 and Ephesians 2:3, as "perversion" in Jude 1:7 and as "sinful lusts" in Jude 1:23.

The 17 literal renderings of *sarx* in the TEV serve the readers' interests.[13] Several idiomatic renditions such, as "human being," "human race," and "birth," are relatively free of problems.[14] Other idiomatic renditions, such as "everyday troubles," "material benefits," "the world," "selfish motives" and "physical ailment"[15] represent choices where connotations and nuances are added or subtracted; thus, the interpreting is done for the reader, when it should be done by the reader.

The first box above contains three examples where *sarx* is not translated, and meaning is surely lost in these translations. However, all the renditions in the first three boxes can be said to be inside the triangles because they are, in some way, related to *reference* or *concept*.

This is not the case with "human nature" in the fourth box. It is not the *meaning* of *sarx*. But neither does it constitute a *concept* or a *reference*. So the phrase has nothing to do with the triangles. In fact, it is a general and indistinct phrase with no clear-cut lexical or semantic links to "flesh." It is true that different combinations of words in a particular context may give a word a sense that is far from its lexical sense, as will be shown in the next chapter. But the phrase "human nature" is not demanded by the context; it is an expression of the translators' views. In the TEV it occurs 15 times in Romans chapters 7 and 8, and 4 times in Galatians chapter 4 in connection with "sin," and is an *interpretation* or *paraphrase* of *sarx*.

---

[11] This view can be seen in Romans 5:12-19; 7:14, 17. In any case, it should be the reader who makes this decision, not the translator.

[12] In Romans 11:24 TEV uses the expression "contrary to nature [*phusis*]." The same Greek word is rendered "natural" in Romans 1:27 and 11:22. Each instance represents an order instituted from creation onward, and this is the natural way to construe "nature. "

[13] In 13 of these the reference is to "the flesh of the body" (see Luke 24:39; Joh 3:6; 6:51, 52, 53, 54, 56). In Romans 14:21 *sarx* is translated as "meat." Twice there is a contrast between "flesh and spirit" (Matt 26:41; Mark 14:38). In two other instances *sarx* occurs together with "blood" (1 Cor 15:50; Heb 2:14).

[14] Matthew 16:17; Luke 3:6; Ephesians 2:11.

[15] 1 Corinthians 7:28; 9:11; 2 Corinthians 1:17; 10:3; 12:7.

UNIFORM RENDERINGS BASED ON COMMUNICATION AND NOT ON ETYMOLOGY

Let us now compare the material we have gathered so far regarding the three words *agapē*, *kosmos* and *sarx* and use it as a basis for the evaluation of the communicative value of literal versus idiomatic translation. Looking at the TEV renderings of the three words, we find that *agapē* is rendered by "love" in 99% of its occurrences, *kosmos* is rendered by "world" in 94% of its occurrences, while *sarx* is rendered by "flesh" in only 13% of its occurrences. We may ask, "Why the difference?" and "Would the reader be confused if *sarx* was also rendered uniformly, as in the NWT?"

Louw, one of the chief proponents of the "semantic-domain" approach writes regarding the different meanings of *sarx* in different contexts:

> Even worse is the assumption that "flesh" adequately expresses these divergent meanings in English—which, of course, is not the case. It is, therefore, unwise to ask what the meaning of "flesh" is in the NT, and by this question suppose that there is *one* word in Greek which always means "flesh."[16]

Cotterell and Turner, who give valuable insights into linguistics, comment on a uniform translation of each Greek word, stating, "No doubt the desire for such a translation is fueled by the belief that somehow all the senses of *sarx must* belong mysteriously together."[17]

Both sources stress that there must be *semantic* motives behind literal translations, that is to say, a driving force behind a literal translation is the "etymological fallacy."

THE ETYMOLOGICAL FALLACY: The belief that a common, original meaning exists in all uses of the same word.

---

[16] Louw, *Semantics of New Testament Greek*, p. 39.

[17] Cotterell and Turner, *Lingusitics and Biblical Interpretation*, p. 169.

28

But this is not necessarily correct. This book was written in English and translated into Norwegian, and the translation method used was the *idiomatic* one. But if I were to translate the Bible for an audience eager to understand its details, I would have used the literal method. This difference in choice of method is not one of semantics but one of communication. And here is the crux of the matter: A literal translation need not be built on the "etymological fallacy"; it may simply be based on the principle that for particular target groups literalness is the best way to *communicate* the original message!

Let us expand on the theme of communication by the help of semantic signals (words signaling concepts), keeping in mind what was discussed in relation to the triangles: Just as there is an "etymological fallacy" is there also a "contextual fallacy." Consider:

THE CONTEXTUAL FALLACY: The view that *words do not have a meaning without a context* and its application to two different situations of communication (the original situation and the modern one) as if they were just one situation of communication.

Figure 2.3
Two Different Situations of Communication

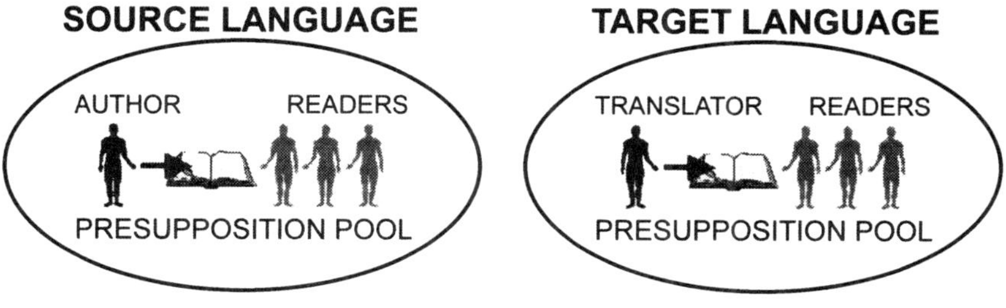

Because New Testament Greek and Biblical Hebrew are dead languages, people today who want to understand and translate the Bible must rely heavily upon the context. They have to look up Greek and Hebrew words in lexicons, which list English glosses representing the most common English words used to translate a given word in the source text.

The context is the principal factor to consider in order to find out which gloss is best in a particular clause. In this situation—when choosing between English glosses believed to be equivalent to Greek and Hebrew words—it seems logical that words do not have meaning apart from a context. But we should keep in mind that it is *a situation of translation* (the right part of figure 2.3) when some persons try to find the meaning of old texts and convey this meaning to modern men. The *original* situation of communication (the left part of figure 2.3) was completely different!

The authors of the Bible had the same presupposition pool as their audience.[18] Words were used to communicate, but these words served as semantic signals of particular concepts that were understood quite similarly by the author and his audience. Each concept signaled by a word had fuzzy edges and its contents and range of meaning was not necessarily always clearly defined in the minds of people at that time. But because our brain has a marvelous imaginative capability and is equipped to acquire meaning by the help of signs and symbols, the *combination* of words (semantic signals) would help the receptor to know which side of each concept the author wanted to make visible. In this original situation of communication, therefore, each word (or, rather, the concept signaled by the word) had an independent meaning, and the context simply revealed which side of the concept was being stressed. Because of this, the Hebrews needed, for instance, just one word, *nephesh* ("soul"), to communicate that which modern idiomatic translations use 30 or more glosses to communicate.

An idiomatic translation, therefore, builds on glosses, while a literal translation builds on concepts. This helps us to realize that to explain meaning as if there was just one context or one presupposition pool certainly is a fallacy just as great as the "etymological fallacy."

---

[18] This is broadly speaking. See note 38 on page 67.

> Idiomatic translations convey words that represent the interpretations of the translators. Literal translations convey concepts that the readers can interpret.

EXCURSUS ON CONCEPTS AND THEIR EDGES

The existence of words and concepts with independent meaning can be illuminated by the theory that human beings tend to group things together in their minds around some prototype.[19] An experiment by psychologist Eleanor Rosch showed, for instance, as respects birds, that the robin was viewed as "birdier" than the ostrich and the penguin. Aitchison concluded:

> To summarize, Rosch's work suggests that when people categorize common objects, they do not expect them all to be on an equal footing. They seem to have some idea of the characteristics of an ideal exemplar, in Rosch's words, a 'prototype.' And they probably decide on the extent to which something else is a member of the same category by matching it against the features of the prototype. It does not have to match exactly, it just has to be sufficiently similar, though not necessarily visually similar.[20]

The prototype theory may also, to a certain extent, explain why words are stored in the mind with fuzzy edges and not as

---

[19] J. Aitchison, *Words in the Mind: An Introduction to the Mental Lexicon* (Oxford: Blackwell, 1993), pp. 52-56.

[20] Aitchison, *Words in the Mind*, p. 55, 64. Similar theories include the "atomic globule" theory, indicating that words are built from a common pool of "meaning atoms" and the "cobweb" theory indicating that words are recognized as related because of the links which speakers have built around them. The common denominator between these and the prototype theory is that all theories express an ordered and systematic relationship between word meanings in the mind.

clear-cut identifiable entities, and why imagination and fantasy are so much needed.

We do not know exactly how the mind works, but there can be no doubt that it works in a systematic way, and that the brain has the ability to compare things with a synchronic[21] prototype. Therefore, to render words uniformly, we do not need a theory presuming that there must be some common etymological meaning to all occurrences of the same word. What we need is to point out that all occurrences of some words and some, or most, occurrences of other words have a common *concept* or *element of meaning* that unites them and ties them to some "prototype"; therefore, it is possible to use the same *sign* to represent *all* the occurrences even though they have different senses.

The word *kosmos* is a good example of the ability of the mind to see connections when the same symbol (word) is used for different meanings, and at the same time it also gives some clues as to the range of *concepts*. As we have seen, in the NT this word refers to the universe, the human family and the environment of the human family. But in 1 Peter 3:3 it is used for "adornment." The fact that the verb *kosmeō* has the senses "set in order" and "adorn" shows that some of the original elements of meaning (such as "order" and "beauty") were still attached to *kosmos* in the first century CE. It is possible that these meanings were the link (prototype) that served to combine all the senses of the word. However, it is not necessary for the mind to comprehend something that is a *clear-cut* link between the different meanings of a word. This "something" seen by the brain may be quite fuzzy. What counts, however, is that the link is of one kind and not of different kinds, so the brain is able to register a clear pattern. It would, of course, be confusing if *any* symbol (word) could be used for any meaning. People in the days of Peter who recognized the different uses of *kosmos*, would have no problem with the clause, "And do not let your *kosmos* be that of external braiding of the hair and the putting on of gold ornaments." However, they would have problems with the words, "And do not let your *sarx* ('flesh') be that of . .

---

[21] Etymology is diachronic, and involves the study of a word through time. That which is synchronic exists at the time of speech/writing.

." or "And do not let your *agapē* ('love') be that of . . ." These two clauses are perhaps meaningful in another context, but not in 1 Peter 3.

The use of *world* in English as a semantic signal equivalent to *kosmos* in Greek helps us to better understand the term *concept*. A person having the modern English presupposition pool has little problem in using *world* for the universe, the environment in which the human family lives and the human family itself, although the last mentioned may have been added to the presupposition pool by help of the Bible. However, to use "world" to denote *adornment* is not possible. There is no English verb from the same root as *world* with the meaning "to set in order" or "to adorn," as is the case with the Greek noun and verb *kosmos/kosmeō*. We, therefore, have an example where the two notions "world" and "adornment" are signaled by one word and represent one concept in Greek, while the English "world" and "adornment" signal two different concepts.[22]

Regarding the different occurrences of *sarx*, people in the first century CE could clearly see definite links, though TEV translates this word as "flesh" in only 13% of its occurrences. The detailed discussion above has shown that several of the TEV glosses are related to the right and upper corners of the modern triangle, thus being close to a "prototype concept." Some of these, such as "meat," "living beings," "man," and "body" are even closely connected with the literal meaning "flesh (covering the bones)," and that is also to a certain extent the case with several of the more figurative renderings. However, whether the "prototype concept" is "flesh (covering the bones)" or "that which is pertaining to man," or something else, is not necessary to establish. Suffice it to say that in all uses of the word there must be elements which are similar to the prototype; thus giving the word a kind of signaling power; that is, showing the readers that one side of a single concept is being made visible in each case.[23] The translation of *sarx*, therefore, is either consistently

---

[22] We have a similar example with *aiōn*, the meaning of which, as we have seen, can be expressed in English by two different phrases, each signaling a different concept.

[23] There may even be instances where the *literal* sense of a word is not found at all in the Bible. Commenting on the BDB Hebrew dictionary, using its

rendered "flesh," as in the NWT, or idiomatically, with a host of different words, as does TEV. This is not a question of semantics but a question of communication.

TECHNICAL WORDS

So far we have discussed words in just one of Kennedy's groups, namely, the one consisting of "everyday words." We will not discuss each group in turn, but direct our attention toward a special group of words which are of particular interest in a discussion of literal versus idiomatic translation, namely, the group of "technical" words.

J. Beekman and J. Callow devote an entire chapter to the subject of "Fidelity in translation."[24] They suggest that items from biblical time, such as wineskins and leaven, be retained in translation, and not substituted with some modern equivalents. Similarly, they recommend that references to historical events should not be substituted. Historical events and particular items may serve as points of reference, helping the readers to imagine the cultural context in which the text was written, thus making their mental images more colorful and accurate.

The same reasoning may also be used regarding words that are "technical" and/or have theological significance. In his book on lexical semantics, Moisés Silva rightly observes "that certain biblical terms denote *theological* entities," and that "technical or semi-technical terms *refer to* or *stand for* defined concepts or ideas."[25] He gives *nomos*, "a body of commands"

---

entry on *leb/lēbāb* ("heart") as an example, Barr says, "One of the amusing things, incidentally, is that although these words are usually glossed as 'heart' and commonly so translated, they never seem to mean the physical organ 'heart' at all, and this is no doubt why BDB begins with glosses such as 'inner man,' 'mind,' 'will,' before adding 'heart'" ("Hebrew Lexicography: Informal thoughts," in *Linguistics and Biblical Hebrew*, ed. W. R. Bodine [Winona Lake, Indiana: Eisenbrauns (1992)], p. 143).

[24] John Beekman and John Callow, *Translating the Word of God* (Grand Rapids: Zondervan, 1975).

[25] Silva, *Biblical Words and their Meaning*, p. 107.

and *hamartia*, "a violation of those commands" as examples.[26] However, he adds, "relatively few words in the Biblical vocabulary can be understood as in some way technical."

The word "concept" in the quote from Silva is used in the more general sense of "idea" as opposed to the way it is used in the triangles. The difference is that a concept in the mind, signaled by a word, is difficult to define because of its fuzziness, but the concept/idea denoted by the technical word is definite and clearly identifiable. A word becomes technical when it is commonly agreed that it refers to a definite idea.

Let us take a look at just such a technical word that also has theological significance, namely, the Hebrew word *nephesh* (Greek equivalent: *psukhē*). In the NWT the 754 occurrences in the OT and the 102 occurrences in the NT are consistently translated as "soul," but in other versions more than 30 different words are used. Some of these include, *animal, everyone, means of preparing food to stay alive, corpse, creatures, life, (they) wanted; appetite; mercy; people; breath, person, you, are willing, mind, soul.*[27] In addition to increasing the readers' dependence on the translators, an inconsistent rendering creates two problems for them.

First, there is the problem of *reference.* The words *nephesh/psukhē* are words of reference containing elements of meaning and connotations related to Jewish and Christian culture and beliefs. In different situations, different sides of the words/concepts are stressed, such as "life (as a soul)" or "the right to live (as a soul)." However, to translate the words in these situations as simply "life" or some similar word, strips them of

---

[26] Other technical words mentioned by Silva (*Biblical Words and their Meaning*, p. 79) are *sunagōgē* ("place of meeting"), *ekklēsia* ("assembly," "church"), *angelos* ("messenger," "angel"), *euangelion* ("good news," "gospel"), and *charisma* ("gift," "spiritual gift").

[27] Leviticus 24:18; Romans 13:1; Deuteronomy 24:6; Numbers 6:6; Genesis 1:21; Matthew 10:39; Psalm 78:18; Proverbs 23:2: Jeremiah 15:1; 1 Peter 3:20; Job 41:21; Joshua 10:30; 2 Samuel 3:21; Genesis 23:8; 1 Chronicles 28:9; James 5:20. R. W. F. Wootton, writing in *The Bible Translator* 26.2 (1975), p. 239, defends the use of different words for the same Greek word on semantic grounds. About *psukhē* and *pneuma* he writes:, "But it is practically impossible that a single word in another language should cover just the same very complex area of meaning as either of these Greek words."

their reference. Because there are other Hebrew and Greek words meaning "life,"[28] to translate *nephesh/psukhē* by "life" would be similar to translating "den første verdenskrig" ("the first world war") into English in a *recently* written book by "the Great War." It is not wrong to use "the Great War" for the war between 1914 and 1918, but the *reference* is lacking.[29] Both for a Jew and a Christian of the first century CE to hear the words, "you will lose your life" and "you will lose your soul" were completely different things.[30]

Second, we have the theological problem of the nature of the soul. James Barr states that an immortal soul is a Greek thought which is not found in the Hebrew Scriptures[31]; and Silva states that *psukhē* is "the immaterial aspect of man" and in some contexts may be used interchangeably with *pneuma* ("spirit").[32] How shall the reader come to know the real nature of *nephesh/psukhē* when they are translated with so many different words?[33] In the following passages different sides of the words are stressed. It is obvious from the comparison between the TEV and the NWT that the reader needs a uniform rendering to grasp the full meaning of *nephesh/psukhē*.

---

[28] Hebrew: *hayim*, Greek: *zōē, bios*.

[29] It is similar with *appetite, beast, breath* and the other words used to translate *nephesh/psukhē*. Other Greek and Hebrew words have these meanings, also.

[30] This can be seen in Matthew 10:28. The words "kill the body" are equivalent to "lose the life," but according to the verse that is not the same as "losing the soul." The Greek word translated "detroy" can mean "destroy," "kill," or "lose."

[31] James Barr, *Semantics of Biblical Language* (Oxford: Oxford University Press, 1975), p. 13.

[32] Silva, *Biblical Words amd their Meaning*, p. 122.

[33] Some will say that there has been a change in the view of the nature of the soul between the OT and the NT, indicating that Barr's view is correct as far as the OT is concerned and Silva's view is correct as regards NT. Because the first Christians were believing Jews, this is quite unlikely, and there is absolutely no evidence for such a view.

Figure 2.4

Translations of Nephesh and Psukhē

VERSE	TEV	NWT
GEN 2:7	"and the man began to live."	"and the man came to be a living soul."
EZE 18:4	"the person who sins is the one who will die."	"the soul that is sinning—it itself will die."
1KI 19:3	"and fled for his life."	"he rose up and began to go for his soul."
1KI 17:22	"the child started breathing again and revived."	"so that the soul of the child came back within him."
LEV 21:1	"No priest is to make himself ritually unclean by taking part in the funeral ceremonies when a relative dies."	"For a deceased soul no one may defile himself among his people."
MATT 10:28	"Do not be afraid of those who kill the body but cannot kill the soul; rather be afraid of God, who can destroy both body and soul in hell."	"and do not become fearful of those who kill the body but cannot kill the soul, but rather be in fear of him that can destroy both soul and body in Ge-hen'na."
MARK 8:35	"For if you want to save your own life, you will lose it; but if you lose your life for me and for the gospel, you will save it."	"For whoever wants to save his soul will lose it, but whoever loses his soul for the sake of me and the good news will save it."

Genesis 2:7 shows that man *is* a soul; Ezekiel 18:4 shows that the soul can die; 1 Kings 17:22 and 19:3 stress the meaning "to have life as a soul"; Leviticus 21:1 refers to persons who have ceased to be living souls; Matthew 10:28 evidently uses the word with the meaning "the right of continuing life as a soul" and Mark 8:35 uses the word with two different meanings: "to have life as a soul," and "the right of continuing life as a soul." If "soul" is lacking in these passages, the reader will lose important nuances of meaning. Just as the one English word "world" may be used to render 185 examples of *kosmos* where different sides

of the word are stressed in different contexts, so the one English word "soul" may be used for the 856 occurrences of *nephesh/psukhē*. In no way should this be a cause for confusion to the reader.

WORDS AND TRANSLATION

We have discussed the meaning, the concept and reference of the words, and we have shown that a literal or uniform translation of words may be the best way to convey the message in particular situations. Let us now return to the question we asked in the introduction about the basic translation unit and the role words may play in relation to such a unit.

"KERNELS" AS TRANSLATION UNITS

Originally the *word* was viewed as the basic translation unit. But in time the views of Saussure, Barr, Chomsky and others lead Bible translators to abandon it and look in another direction. The one who took the lead, and who undoubtedly has exerted the greatest influence on modern Bible translation, is Eugene Nida.[34] Nida is a brilliant theorist and is to be commended for his excellent work through more than four decades.

Nida acknowledged the works of Barr and Saussure,[35] but the one whose theories he took as his starting point was Noam Chomsky.[36] The generative grammar of Chomsky[37] presumes

---

[34] For many years Nida has traveled around the word in cooperation with the United Bible Societies. He has arranged seminars for translators, and has authored and co-authored scores of books about Bible translation. No person has more greatly impacted the making of Bible translation into a modern scientific discipline than Nida.

[35] E. A. Nida, *Toward a Science of Translating* (Leiden: Brill, 1964), pp. 5, 6.

[36] Nida, *Toward a Science of Translating*, p. 60.

[37] One important work expressing these ideas is Noam Chomsky, *Aspects of the Theory of Syntax* (Cambridge, Mass.: M. I. T. Press, 1965).

that sentences have what he called "deep structures." The active and passive sentences "The cat ate the mouse" and "The mouse was eaten by the cat" must, according to him, have a common deep structure from which both spring. However, what this "deep structure" was like, how it should be defined or found, is answered neither by Chomsky nor by Nida. After 30 years of study Chomsky has retracted many of his earlier ideas; and psycholinguist Jean Aitchison says that "Chomsky's latest ideas are mostly too imprecise and abstract to test."[38]

The "deep structures" only play an indirect part in the theoretical framework and procedures proposed by Nida. However, entities believed to occur on a level between the deep structures and the surface structures (the words as we see them), namely, the so-called "kernels," do play an important role. In the minds of Nida and Taber these are the basic translation units. To find the kernels in a sentence one has to find how the words fit four basic *semantic* categories,[39] which according to the authors are common to all languages, and on this basis restructure the expression. This means reducing long and complex sentences to short clauses by removing modifiers, eliminating the results of subordinating and co-ordinating processes, and change passives to actives and negatives to positives. The kernel of the phrase "the will of God" is "God wills"; of "the Holy Spirit of promise" is "God promised the Holy Spirit," and of "the day of the preparation" is "the day when (people) prepare (for the sabbath)."[40]

In the translation process the restructured phrases are used as translation units, and the words of the kernel are rendered into the receptor language rather than the Greek and Hebrew words of the original text.[41] Nida and Taber[42] compared the

---

[38] J. Aitchison, *The Articulate Mammal: An Introduction to Psycholinguistics*, 3d ed. (London: Routledge, 1989), p. 201.

[39] The four semantic categories are: *Object*, often nouns; *Event* (actions, processes, happenings), often verbs; *Abstract* (qualities, quantities, degrees), often adjectives and adverbs; and *Relations*, often prepositions and conjunctions (Nida and Taber, *The Theory and Practice of Translation*, p. 37).

[40] Nida and Taber, *The Theory and Practice of Translation*, pp. 36, 37.

[41] Not all translation committees working with idiomatic translations use this "kernel" approach method. Those working with the Norwegian Bible

words of Romans 1:5 in the literal RSV, the idiomatic NEB and TEV. Let us compare NWT and the TEV:

Figure 2.5
Romans 1:5 Comparison

NWT	"Through whom we[43] received undeserved kindness and an apostleship in order that there might be obedience of faith among all the nations respecting his name."
TEV	"Through him God gave me the privilege of being an apostle, for the sake of Christ, in order to lead people of all nations to believe and obey."

The NWT is strictly literal; in the TEV the following restructuring is evident:

1) "whom" is changed to "him";
2) "we" is changed to "me";
3) "God" is added as subject to "undeserved kindness";
4) "undeserved kindness [grace] and an apostleship" is restructured into "the privilege of being an apostle";
5) "Christ" is introduced instead of "his name";
6) The genitive "obedience of faith" is changed to "believe and obey";
7) The word order is changed.

There can be no doubt that the TEV rendering is easier to understand than the NWT, both for the ear and for the eye, but Nida and Taber's claim that the TEV does not introduce any features not *implicit* in the Greek text is not accurate. The words "grace" and "apostleship" (see number 4) seem to represent two distinct ideas rather than one, as the TEV interprets it. Such a

translation of 1978/84 did not (information obtained through personal communication). However, *the principles* behind the "kernel approach" are more or less followed by all.

[42] Nida and Taber, *The Theory and Practice of Translation*, pp. 8, 9.

[43] The footnote in NWT says:: "'We' used editorially. Or, 'I.'"

merging of two ideas is a typical trait of idiomatic translations. This illuminates the basic weakness of using "kernels" rather than words as basic translation units.

Restructuring the words into "kernels" represents an extra step of interpretation where synonyms are often used. But, as is often said, synonyms do not have exactly the same meaning and do not carry the same connotations,[44] and therefore there is a danger of adding conceptual or referential meanings to the text, thus falling into a trap similar to that of Kittel and his co-workers, as respects lexical semantics.

Let us illustrate this with an example from Nida and Taber: The expression "the foundation of the world" in Ephesians 1:4 is transformed into "(God) creates the world."[45] But this is misleading. How will a receptor understand the words "God creates the world"? Probably as a *reference* to Genesis 1 and the creation account, and the *mental image* the reader (with our modern presupposition pool) gets from "world" in this context is "the universe" or "the earth with everything in it." But this is evidently a wrong image and a wrong reference, because, as we have seen, it does not represent the usual way the Greek word *kosmos* is used in the NT. This word is normally used of the human family or of something related to the human family.

Looking at the ten instances of the expression "foundation of the world," we do not find any reference to the earth or the universe, but in Luke 11:50-51 the expression is connected with Abel, the son of Adam. This could suggest that the foundation of the world of *mankind* was meant, and the reference is to Adam and Eve begetting children. The word "foundation" used in the sense of founding a family is also found in Hebrews 11:11, where it is said that Sarah *conceived* (*katabolē*) a seed,[46] and the

---

[44] Says Louw, *Semantics of New Testament Greek*, p. 62: "Synonyms are not words that *have* the same meaning, but words that sometimes, or probably quite often, *can be* used for the same meaning."

[45] Nida and Taber, *The Theory and Practice of Translation*, p. 36.

[46] The rendering "foundation of the world" versus "creation of the world" may also have serious doctrinal implications. According to Ephesians 1:4 the Christians were "chosen" before the foundation of the world, and 1 Peter 1:20 seems to imply that Christ was known as redeemer before this point of time. If the point of reference is the creation of the earth, it is difficult to escape the conclusion that God knew about and had predestined the fall of man into

verb *kataballō* is used in the Septuagint with the meaning "to bear."

The view presented here, that "the foundation of the world" refers to the foundation of the human family, is a theological interpretation, as is the view of Nida and Taber, which refers to the creation of the universe. At the outset, therefore, we cannot deem one as better than the other. The point, however, is that one particular interpretation should not be forced upon the reader through translation, as is done by Nida and Taber in this instance.[47] Therefore, to give the reader the possibility of an "informed choice," I suggest that the *word* as a semantic signal for a concept be used as basic translation unit rather than the kernels. The use of kernels can do much good, particularly when we work with long and complicated sentences, but as shown, those using them also run the risk of adding concepts and references which are foreign to the biblical words.

WORDS AS TRANSLATION UNITS

The question of choosing the right kind of translation unit is closely connected with the purpose of the translation and with the interests of the target group. If the translators want the readers to have a part in the translation process, the translation unit cannot be anything but the word itself. This does not mean, as I already have shown, that I defend the etymological approach. Neither does it mean that I have overlooked the fact that the context contributes to communication by making visible certain sides of the concepts represented by the words, although I claim that the role of the context has often been exaggerated. I do believe, however, that just as words/concepts are stored in the mind as meaningful entities, words also occur in the text as meaningful entities, and therefore exist individually apart from the context. To justify the viewpoint

---

sin. If the point of reference is Eve's conceiving of children then there is no such meaning.

[47] The literal rendering, "the foundation of the world" is theologically neutral, because it can be interpreted either ways.

that the word may serve as the basic translation unit, two arguments will be used.

First, I point to the fact that literal translation outside the Bible is by no means dead. Peter Newmark, who has many years of experience in different kinds of translation, save Bible translation, took three French sentences consisting of 75 words and did his best to translate them into idiomatic, easy-to-understand English. The English version had 68 words. Comparing the words with the original, he found that "about 90% of the three sentences were literally translated." Newmark concluded regarding literal translation:

> By rule of thumb you know literal translation is likely to work best and most with written, prosy, semi-formal, non-literary language; worst and least with ordinary spoken idiomatic language. Further, it is more often effectively used than most writers on translation, from Cicero to Nida and Neubert (but not Wilss) lead you to believe.[48]

Second, consider the words of Jesus in Matthew 11:19 (TEV), "God's wisdom, however, is shown to be true by its results." And the results, as far as Bible translation is concerned, is that translators of the 19th and first half of the 20th century produced a great number of literal Bible translations which were understandable for the readers—yet even they were based on the "etymological fallacy" as regards the understanding of the words. It is similar today: to read the NWT and other literal translations, which follow the Greek and Hebrew sentence structure, demands more effort on the part of the readers. But as a reward, they may apprehend details and nuances of the text, which are lacking in many idiomatic translations.

We have now looked at the *word* from different angles. To get a better view of the role played by theology and bias in translation, we will now discuss how translators work with words, ascertaining at which stages the translators must choose (and thus exercise interpretation) in behalf of the receptors, and how the receptors can have a part in the this process.

---

[48] Newmark, *A Textbook of Translation*, pp. 31, 68.

CHAPTER 3

THE PROCESS OF BIBLE TRANSLATION

Do you remember the last time you spoke with a person with a speech impediment? As he or she pronounces a few words, perhaps stuttering along the way, you may have already guessed what the next word will be. You might even be tempted to complete the person's sentence before he does! The discipline of psycholinguistics has revealed that even in ordinary verbal communication in our own language, we guess substantially more of what the other person is saying than we realize, because neither our ears nor our brain are able to take notice of everything.[1] Thus, even when communicating in our mother tongue there is an element of interpretation, and sometimes we also misunderstand the message.

In the translation of a message from one language to another, the element of interpretation is much greater; and when languages are far apart in time and represent different cultures, as in the case of Greek, Hebrew, and Aramaic, the interpretative element is substantial. There is no question about it: Bible translation *is* interpretation! Our interest, however, is to ascertain the nature of the translation process and understand how the translators work. The process of translation has three principal stages: 1) understanding the sender's message, 2) transmission, and 3) formulation. Let us consider these three stages as we discuss the role played by theology and bias in Bible translation.

---

[1] Says Aitchison, *Words in the Mind* (Oxford: Blackwell, 1993), p. 178: "One of the best known facts about word recognition is that a lot of it is guesswork. People recognize words by choosing the 'best fit'; they match the portion they have heard with the word in their mental lexicon that appears to be the most likely candidate, and they fill in gaps, often without noticing they do so." Also, when we read we make a lot of guesses because we do not look at each word, one at a time, but we rhythmically move our eyes from one group of words to another.

UNDERSTANDING THE MESSAGE

Obviously we cannot translate a message that we ourselves do not understand. Therefore, the translator must work with the text to make sure that important semantic details have not escaped his or her notice. He must be thorough and consider all relevant details.

LINGUISTIC ANALYSIS

The translator knows the sender's language and the first step should be to analyze what the sender has written. Regardless of whether a literal or an idiomatic translation is planned, he or she must start with an examination of the lexical meaning of the words. After the translator has established word meaning, and thereby a rough understanding of a part of the text, the translator of the idiomatic translation will proceed to find the kernels of the text.

The one working on the literal translation will, at this point, probably use the model of the triangles, and in addition to finding the *meaning*, the translator will also find the *reference*, and try to find some clues as to the *concept*. This will help him to handle those words which cannot be translated uniformly in a correct way. The triangles, together with the context, will help the translator to differentiate between different *senses*. For example, in John 3:6, 8 the Greek word *pneuma* ("spirit," "wind") is used four times. In verse 8 *pneuma* is the subject of the verb "to blow" and naturally has the *sense* "wind"; in the other three instances it is best translated "spirit,"[2] a word with a wider range of meaning.

Next the translator will perform a syntactic analysis and determine the relationships between the words in each clause, and at the same time he or she should keep in mind the whole discourse. At this point, the literal translator may also perform a semantic analysis, perhaps even structuring the text into kernels; but this is simply a check on the syntactic analysis and

---

[2] The word *pneuma* may evidently represent more than one concept in Greek.

46

not the translational basis, as it is for the one making an idiomatic translation.

This syntactic analysis is important because the meaning can be different if the word is an object or an adverb or is a part of the predicate. For example, TEV translates Hebrews 1:8 as, "'Your throne, O God, will last for ever and ever!'" But NWT translates this same passage as, "But with reference to the Son: 'God is your throne for ever and ever.'" TEV takes "God" as a vocative (the Greek case for addressing a person) and the Son is therefore called "God." NWT takes "God" as a nominative (the Greek case for the subject of the clause), and the Son therefore is not referred to as "God." If we could establish without doubt whether "God" was nominative or vocative, we could also decide which of the translations is the correct one. However, neither in Hebrews 1:8 nor in our quotation of Psalm 45:7 is there a verb that can help us—and the morphology of the Greek word *theos* ("God") does not help us here because the same form is used both for the nominative and for the vocative (with a few exceptions). Thus, in this passage the theology of the translator is the decisive factor in the translation.[3]

Before completing the work, the translator must make a stylistic and connotative analysis: Is the text written as prose or poetry? Is there some kind of word play? Which connotations are connected with different words? The meaning of the text is of primary importance, but the translator should also give attention to style. Different words have different connotations, and even where the lexical meaning is similar, different words appeal to different feelings and have particular associations. For example, consider the words "denomination," "sect," and "cult." The first word is the more neutral one, even having a positive value. The word "sect" gives negative connotations, implying something deviant and narrow-minded. The word "cult" is even more negative, and would hardly be used of a religious group that is considered Christian. Translators, therefore, will strive to

---

[3] In Psalm 45 the words are directed toward a human king, and it can be argued that the one who did the anointing is "God" (*theos*) and not the one being anointed. This speaks in favor of understanding the construction in Hebrews 1:8 as nominative rather than vocative. But from a strictly linguistic point of view, both alternatives are possible.

find the connotations used by an author in a bygone era in order to convey them in a vernacular they will use in their translation.

SITUATION ANALYSIS

When someone speaks to an audience, he or she does not start from scratch; rather, the knowledge common to the speaker and the audience is used, and from there the speaker presents the argument until he or she is reasonably sure those listening have understood the message. Such a common "platform," shared by the speaker and his audience, is, as we have seen, a "presupposition pool."[4] When Peter, for instance, on the day of Pentecost addressed Jews and proselytes (Acts 2:14-40), the common platform was the law of Moses and the Hebrew Scriptures. But when Paul addressed the philosophers on Mars Hill (Acts 17:22-34), he took as his point of departure Greek poets and Greek culture. He even used the more philosophically oriented word *theios* ("divine") in verse 29 rather than *theos* ("god").

A translator should therefore ask: Who was the writer? For whom did he write? What was the purpose of writing? Where and when was it written? What is the message? The letters to the congregation in Corinth, for instance, answer several questions which are not stated, and they address certain situations known to Paul and to his audience. The more the translator knows about the situation in and around Corinth, the more he or she will be able to convey in his translation of the letters.

Therefore, a Bible translator must also have, in addition to a knowledge of the text and the author of the text, a thorough knowledge of the religion and culture of the Jews and other nations mentioned in the Bible, and of the Christian faith. And

---

[4] A discussion of this concept is found in P. Cotterell & M. Turner, *Linguistics and Biblical Interpretation* (Downers Grove: Intervarsity Press, 1989), pp. 90-97. While the concept of a "presupposition pool" refers to the knowledge common to a *group* of persons, the phrase "horizon of understanding" refers to the knowledge, motives and viewpoints of one *single* person.

here we have a problem! Because the translators have their own set of values and beliefs, they will not be indifferent toward their task. It is very difficult to detach themselves from the text and look at their translation in a balanced, scientific way, because their personal interests in the work and their *horizon of understanding* will inevitably influence them much more than if they were translating a non-biblical piece of literature.

When it comes to the presupposition pools, the literal and idiomatic translations part company. Also, the literal translation contains a great degree of interpretation, but it handles the presupposition pools of the different participants differently from the idiomatic translation. Those who work with idiomatic translations "translate" both the text and the presupposition pool from the source language to the target language, that is, they use the sentence structure of the target language, and process the text to the extent that the reader may understand the text by the help of a *modern* presupposition pool. The translators who work literally only translate the text, that is, they use the sentence structure of the source language and the presupposition pool of the author, and only when the readers will completely misunderstand the text will they deviate from literal renderings and use elements from the presupposition pool of the readers.

The last clause of Romans 12:20 well illustrates the problem of different presupposition pools. It reads: "But 'If your enemy is hungry, feed him; if he is thirsty, give him something to drink; for by doing this you will heap fiery coals upon his head.'" de Ward and Nida state: "The idiom 'heap coals of fire on his head' (Prov. 25:22 and Rom. 12:20) has often been seriously misunderstood as a means of torturing people to death."[5] However, in their comments on the letter to the Romans in the series "Helps for Translators" Newman and Nida state, "The imagery of the last clause in this verse is difficult, though all translations seem to prefer to retain the imagery rather than change the metaphor into a non-metaphor."[6]

---

[5] de Ward and Nida, *From One Language to Another*, p. 38.

[6] *A Translator's Handbook on Paul's Letter to the Romans*, Helps for Translators 14 (Stuttgart: United Bible Societies, 1973), pp. 242-243.

They conclude that the clause "is perhaps best taken in the sense of 'for by doing this you will make him ashamed.'" In addition to illustrating the problem of different backgrounds, the above example also shows that sometimes it is difficult to "translate" the presupposition pool of the author. Even though it is practically impossible to avoid misunderstanding this particular clause without an explanation, all translations, including TEV, translate the text literally. The reason for this may be becaue of the difficulty in finding a non-literal rendering which conveys the correct message. Newman and Nida's suggestion is probably correct in terms of capturing the author's meaning, but to use it in translation would take away important aspects of the metaphor's imagery. Thus, literal renderings may be preferred by idiomatic translations even when they require explanation.

TRANSMISSION

The transmission, or the change from the code represented by the source language to the code of the receptor language, occurs in the mind of the translator. No one knows exactly how this occurs, but if the translator's knowledge of both languages, the results of his or her different analyses of the text and other relationships, and their knowledge of history and culture as it relates to the source text, are compared to data programs and data files, it seems that the translator's brain works somewhat like a computer does, for in a very short time both can process great quantities of information. In their mind the relevant information is coupled with the translator's creative thinking ability, and the way the words should be rendered in the receptor language begins to take shape.

According to the theory of information,[7] the transmission of messages will always cause some "noise": some of the message

---

[7] Says the *Encyclopedia Britannica*, vol. 9, 1979, p. 574: "The chief concern of information theory is to discover mathematical laws governing systems designed to communicate or manipulate information. It sets up quantitative measures of information and of the capacity of various systems to transmit, store, and otherwise process information."

will be distorted or lost. This is so even in related languages, as the figure from Hjelmslev[8] illustrated. We can appreciate how this is true, to an even greater extent, when translating from Greek, Hebrew and Aramaic, which are much different from our modern languages. But translators, who must use approximately the same number of words as the source text, have to choose what they believe is the best way to convey the sender's thoughts, and, in choosing one thing, they must omit something else. In view of this we can appreciate the benefit that comes from considering a variety of Bible translations. Let us consider two examples.

Acts 17:18 illustrates how a single word may cause more than a little difficulty. The philosophers said about Paul: "What is it this chatterer would like to tell?" The Greek word translated "chatterer" is *spermologos,* which earlier[9] referred to a bird picking up one piece of grain here and another there. Kenneth Wuest,[10] who produced an expanded paraphrase, renders the sentence: "What would he desire to be saying, granted he was able to say anything, this ignorant plagiarist, picking up scraps of information here and there, unrelated in his own thinking and passing them off as the result of his own mature thought?" Wuest's paraphrase gives many of the naunces of the word; a literal and an idiomatic translation must choose the principal one.

Joshua 7:6 well illustrates a grammatical problem. In this past context we find the verb *wayyippol,* which means "to fall," and in the Germanic languages it is a momentary act without an inner constituency. Here the adverbial "until the evening" follows, so the situation expressed by the verb must have a

---

[8] Louis Hjelmslev, *Omkring sprogteoriens, grundlæggelse,* København (1966), p. 11. We have an example of where the word's etymology may be important.

[9] Here, however, we should be careful not to put too much stress on the etymological arguments. On the other hand there are situations where the etymology can be illuminating. In this case it seems that the word *spermologos* still had some of its original connotations when the philosophers used it in Acts 17:18.

[10] *The New Testament: An Expanded Translation* (Grand Rapids: Eerdmans, 1970).

duration of several hours. The verb is imperfective[11] and it indicates an act (falling upon one's face) resulting in a state (laying prostrate) which continues. It is impossible to express this in idiomatic English without circumlocution. NAB stresses the state and omits the act, "lay prostrate before the ark of the LORD until evening." The Berkeley version, by adding an extra clause, stresses both the act and the state, "fell on his face before the ark of the LORD, and remained there until evening." NWT stresses the act and implies the state by using an inelegant expression, "fell upon his face to the earth before the ark of Jehovah until the evening." The NWT rendering is "wooden," but its advantage is that in addition to conveying the full force of the Hebrew verb into English,[12] it also suggests to the observant reader that verbs which in the Indo-European languages are punctual and momentary, may be viewed as durative in Hebrew.[13] This is frequently unappreciated by many translators.

Because we already have some "noise" owing to the difference of languages, translators should try hard to avoid creating more "noise" in the process of transmission. Particularly care should be taken when translators are working their way through kernels, because the transmission occurs in the mind of the translator, and an extra interpretative element may in some instances complicate an already delicate process.

---

[11] See *Excursus on Greek and Hebrew Verbs*, pp. 79-89.

[12] Even the ambiguousness of the Hebrew text is conveyed by the NWT in its English translation. A possible but less likely interpretation is that Joshua and the elders fell down and rose, fell down and rose all day long. The more likely explanation is that they fell on their faces and remained in this position until the evening. The English text of the NWT can be interpreted both ways.

[13] A host of "punctual" verbs in Hebrew are realized in past contexts as participles and imperfects (suggesting non-punctual action) without any apparent frequentative or habitual force. This indicates that we cannot take for granted that *any* Hebrew verb has an inherent punctuality.

THE "PLANES" OF TRANSMISSION

Without taking Chomsky's "deep structures" into account, still we see that the translation or transmission of meaning may be said to occur on different levels. This means that in some instances there are similar expressions in the source language and in the receptor language, but in other instances phrases or sentences must be completely restructured.[14] Let us look at some examples.[15]

First we have the simple *word* level. In John 12:30 we find the Greek words *kai eipen Iesous*, which are translated, "And Jesus said." In both languages we find three words with the same meaning; the only difference is that in Greek the verb precedes "Jesus," but in English this word order is reversed.

Next we have the *syntactic* level where word order or word classes (for example, verbs and adjectives) may be changed. In NWT Exodus 20:5 reads, "because I Jehovah your God am a God exacting exclusive devotion." The expression "a God exacting exclusive devotion" is a translation of the two Hebrew nouns "jealous" and "god." The translators evidently reasoned that to translate the words literally (that is, as "a jealous God"), would give the wrong impression,[16] and they

---

[14] Our use of "restructuring" here has nothing to do with "kernels." To find the "kernel" of a sentence refers to the source language and the phase of understanding; to restructure a phrase because of the difference between the languages relates to the receptor language and the phase of transmission.

[15] Newmark, *A Textbook of Translation*, p. 47, uses a slightly different approach. With an emphasis on the source language structure he lists "Word-for-Word translation," "Literal translation," "Faithful translation" and "Semantic translation." With an emphasis on the target language he lists: "Adaptation," "Free translation," "Idiomatic translation" and "Communicative translation."

[16] Nida and Taber, *Theory and Practice*, p. 167, agree: "For example, 'I am a jealous God' (Exod 20:5) can be badly misunderstood if translated literally, for it may only suggest that God acts more like some jilted lover or that he has a mean, possessive disposition. More often than not, a literal rendering introduces quite unwarranted sexual connotations. Accordingly, in some languages this sentence must be semantically restructured by expansion to read, 'I am a God who demands that my people love no one else other than me.'"

chose to transform the adjective "jealous" into a participle, an adjective and a noun.

Then we have the *semantic* level. In Genesis 4:1 we find the words *wehā'ādām yāda' 'et-hawwa 'ishto* which are translated, "And Adam had intercourse with his wife—and she became pregnant." The words "had intercourse with" are translated from the Hebrew verb *yāda'*, meaning "to know." In English "to know one's wife" is not used as a euphemism for sexual relations, therefore a translation at the word-plane will provide little meaning.

Finally, we have the *situative* or *pragmatic* level. Matthew 5:3 says, "Happy are those conscious of their spiritual need." The Greek words translated are *hoi ptōkhoi tō pneumati*. The first two words mean "the poor" or "the beggars," and the last two mean "the spirit." The last words are in the dative case, suggesting an adverbial relation between "the spirit" and "the poor," such as "the poor in the spirit," or "the poor as to the spirit." To translate, "Blessed are the poor in spirit," as does RSV, may mislead the reader,[17] and that is why NWT has deviated from its typically literal renderings and made an extensive restructuring.

The element of interpretation on the part of the translator is increasing proportionally with the distance from the word level. And in pragmatic renderings the receptor is almost completely dependent upon the translator. In an effort to look after the interests of the receptor when a literal translation uses such renderings, footnotes should be used whenever possible. In Matthew 5:3 NWT has a footnote saying, "or, 'those who are beggars for the spirit,'" which is quite illuminating and helpful to the reader.

THE FORMULATION

Why is it that an artist's painting of a beautiful scencery is much more appealing than a photo of the same scenery? A

---

[17] Nida and Taber, *Theory and Practice*, p. 8, suggest a rendering similar to NWT, "[Happy are] those who recognize their spiritual poverty."

photo is a true representation of something in a fraction of a second, while the painting is a "distortion" of reality. Because we do not experience situations in fractions of seconds, but as something continuing and changing, the artist tries to communicate this by letting several details blend with each other, appealing to our fantasy. To apply the illustration, an interlinear translation is like a photo, an idiomatic translation is like a painting with a tendency for non-figurative expression, and a literal translation is like the "New Romanticism" painting.

Idiomatic translations should not be set up against literal ones, just as one form of painting should not be set up against another form, or against a photo. But this is often done. Regarding idiomatic translations, there is no doubt that they are unsurpassed when it comes to giving the receptor an *immediate* understanding of the text, provided that their interpretations are correct. However, this is not always the case, and the more a particular word is rendered by different words in the receptor language it is more likely that inaccurate interpretations are introduced, and which are in turn forced upon the reader.

In this discussion of the phase of formulation, let us return to Barr's critique of the confusion of sense and concept (or theological use) in word studies. Can we also apply this criticism to the translation of *combinations* of words, that is, to clauses? To put it differently, should we, when translating sentences, avoid using concepts and references and only use the lexical senses of the words? If so, we would get something like an interlinear translation without much communicative power. As shown in the previous discussion of the different planes of transmission, even a literal translation will to some extent use the concepts and references of words.

However, there is one area where Barr's critique can legitimately be applied to Bible translation, namely, when theological concepts are unnecessarily introduced. Barr criticized the use of theological applications of particular words in lexica, and similarly translations can be criticized if theological views are read into the text at the expense of linguistic evidence. Let us consider one example, namely, the rendering of the Greek word *stauros* ("stake"). Almost all Bible translations translate the word as "cross," but NWT uses "torture stake." The cross is a modern Christian symbol and has particular connotations, and the use of this word in the NT seems to be an anachronism.

EXCURSUS ON *STAUROS*
"CROSS," "TORTURE STAKE" OR "POLE"?

From the point of view of lexical semantics it is clear that *stauros* means "pole" or "stake." With reference to classical Greek we read: "The exact technical form and significance of execution are not conveyed by the words *stauros* and *(ana)stauroō* without further definition."[18] Is the same true regarding the use of *stauros* in the NT? A translator has two ways to find the answer: 1) He or she can look for clues in the NT itself regarding the shape of *stauros*, and 2) archaeological and historical evidence can be considered.

Regarding the NT, there is no hint that *stauros* had changed from being a generic word that could refer to pieces of wood in any shape to become a technical word denoting a pole with a crossbeam. To the contrary, there are five examples where the instrument on which Jesus died is referred to as *xulon*, which is also a generic word for tree.[19]

One Bible dictionary defines "crucifixion" as "the act of nailing or binding a living victim or sometimes a dead person to a cross or stake (*stauros* or *skolops*) or a tree (*xulon*)."[20] Seneca (c. 4 BC—65 CE) wrote:

> I see crosses there, not just of one kind, but made in many different ways; some have their victims with head down to the ground; some impale their private parts; others stretch out their arms on the gibbet.[21]

---

[18] E. Brandenburger, "σταυρός," NIDNTT 1 (Grand Rapids: Zondervan, 1979), p. 391.

[19] Acts 5:30; 10:39; 13:29; Galatians 3:13; 1 Peter 2:24.

[20] Gerald O'Collins, "Crucifixion," in *The Anchor Bible Dictionary*, vol. 1, ed. David Noel Freedman (New York: Doubleday, 1992), p. 1207.

[21] Dialogue 6 (*De consolatione ad Marciam*) 20, 3.

Commenting on what happened at the time Jerusalem fell in 70 CE, Josephus wrote:

> The soldiers out of rage and hatred amused themselves by nailing their prisoners in different postures; and so great was their number that space could not be found for the crosses [plural of *stauros*] nor crosses for the bodies.[22]

Because of the huge numbers of bodies it is likely that for economical reasons they used one piece of timber for each victim rather than two pieces.

We should also take note of the fact that while the instrument on which Haman was hanged is called '*ēts* ("tree") in the Hebrew text, the Septuagint uses the verb *stauroō* ("hang on a stake") and the latin Vulgate uses *crux* ("stake" or "cross"). To the best of my knowledge the first one to mention the shape of the instrument on which Jesus was hanged is the author of the Letter to Barnabas from the first part of the second century CE. He says that the shape was that of a T.[23] As a matter of fact, there is absolutely no evidence from the first century showing the shape of the instrument on which Jesus died!

How, then, should *stauros* be translated? Using the triangles, we find that neither "cross" nor "torture stake" represent the *meaning* of *stauros*, but both are more like *references*; the first describes the form of the "thing in the world" and the second describes the effect of the use of this "thing." There can be little doubt that the rendering "cross" is a theological anachronism. It is a word with one of the heaviest bundles of theological and Christian connotations in our vocabulary, and most, if not all, of these connotations were completely lacking when the NT was written. Consequently, a modern reader of the NT will get images in his mind which are foreign to the NT when he reads the word "cross."

---

[22] *The War of the Jews*, 5.11.1.

[23] *The Epistle of Barnabas* 9, 8. However, we may note that the author says that the 318 servants of Abraham that were circumcised foreshadow Jesus and the cross (*stauros*). This is because 18 is in Greek expressed by IH, the first two letters of *Iēsous* ("Jesus"), and 300 is expressed by the letter T. The author of the letter to Barnabas, therefore, was not a mere neutral reporter.

Something to an even greater extent than that just discussed above prevents the reader from having a part in the translation process, and it is this: some proponents of the "semantic domain" approach suggest that yet another Greek word used for the instrument of Jesus' execution (*xulon*) should also be translated "cross." Louw[24] suggests for instance that *xulon* ("a piece of wood") in Acts 5:30 and the four other instances it is used should be translated as "cross." But if *xulon* is translated literally, the alert reader may learn that all is not well with the rendering "cross." This would at least encourage the reader to look deeper into the subject. If *xulon* is translated as "cross" the reader is at the mercy of the translators.

The "torture stake" of NWT is neither anachronistic nor does it have theological overtones; it is neutral as to the shape of *stauros*. But some readers might criticize it. There is no problem using the reference of a word in translation, but when a neutral expression of that reference (the thing in the world) exists, as well as several words stressing different sides of the reference, the interests of the readers are best served by using the neutral alternative. Thus, by using the epithet "torture" the reader may get the impression that pain or suffering is a part of the lexical meaning of *stauros*, while it is just *one important consequence* of being fastened to the instrument denoted by the word. The neutral terms "stake" or "pole" would have better served the interests of the readers in this instance.[25]

---

[24] Louw, *The Semantics of New Testament Greek*, p. 59.

[25] Another point is the NWT rendition of the verb *stauroō* as "impale." This is criticized by Countess (*The Jehovah's Witnesses' New Testament*, [Phillipsburg, New Jersey: Presbyterian and Reformed, 1982], p. 87) because the word has the meaning "to pierce through with a pole or a stick," and Jesus was not pierced through. However, Countess errs in this claim. One way to define "impale" is "to fix in an inescapable and helpless position" (*Encyclopedic Unabridged Dictionary of the English Language*, 1989).

IS IT POSSIBLE TO AVOID BIASED RENDERINGS?

Countess' conclusion regarding NWT is as follows: *"The New World Translation of the Christian Greek Scriptures* must be viewed as a radically biased piece of work. At some points it is actually dishonest."[26]

What, then, is bias? *Webster's New Twentieth Century Dictionary* defines it as "a mental leaning or inclination; prepossession; propensity toward an object, not leaving the mind indifferent; as, a bias resulting from misinformation." According to this definition *all* Bible translators are biased, so it is meaningless to use the term in the first place. However, Countess and the other critics who never actually define the word, evidently use it in a more specific way.

An important word of caution is given by de Waard and Nida, when they encourage translators to exercise intellectual honesty and integrity and be unbiased in all their work. This means that the translator should not "promote by means of Bible translating the cause of a particular theological viewpoint, whether deistic, rationalistic, immersionist, millenarian, or charismatic." Also, in this same vein, translators should not "introduce idiosyncratic interpretations." They also say that "it takes a special brand of intellectual honesty to let the Bible say things which seemingly contradict one's own theology."[27]

Everyone agrees that a translator should not be allowed to manipulate the text of the Bible according to his own good pleasure. However, the above quotes from de Waard and Nida are not entirely unproblematic, because they imply that the theology of the majority be the criterion for what should be termed biased.[28] It is obvious that if research inside a particular scientific discipline was branded as biased because it presented ideas contrary to the majority opinion, and subsequently was neglected, there would not be much development and

---

[26] Countess, *The Jehovah's Witnesses' New Testament*, p. 93.

[27] de Waard and Nida, *From One Language to Another*, pp. 32-33, 59.

[28] For example, Bowman, *Jehovah's Witnesses*, p. 82 speaks with contempt of those who are "prejudiced against the doctrine of Christ's diety," which seems to imply that those who do not accept the trinity doctrine are biased.

progression. Indeed, it is due to the fact that Nida and others did *not* follow the majority, but went their own way, that paved the way for idiomatic translations in the first place!

Earlier we discussed how theology *must* play a part in the translation process, and to *a priori* exclude certain kinds of theology would be methodologically unsound. What counts is not the *kind* of theology used, but if it is well founded and used in a strictly scientific way.

This means that the criterion of bias should be *language* rather than theology. I therefore propose the following definition:

> *Bias in Bible translation is characterized by renderings that either 1) contradict lexicon, grammar or syntax; or 2) definitely weaken or distort the meaning by addition or subtraction of unwarranted semantic elements in order to promote the translator's own theology.*

This means that when Countess says concerning NWT's rendering of John 1:1, "It is the contention of the present writer that the translation 'and the Word was God' is justifiable because the New Testament teaches the deity of Christ,"[29] this is not bias, because grammar and syntax are not decisive in this passage and theology must play an important role. But it also means that when the NWT renders the phrase "and the word was a god," this cannot be branded as biased either.

On the other hand, there are many examples of biased renderings also in what are generally considered respected Bible translations. One outstanding example is the widespread rendering of "hell" for the Greek word *geenna*. This must be termed biased because it represents a violation of normal translation procedures in order to promote a religious doctrine. Regardless of our conception as to the religious meaning of

---

[29] Countess, *The Jehovah's Witnesses' New Testament*, p. 70.

geenna, it cannot be disputed that it was a geographical place and that the word is a proper name.[30] Normal translation procedures require that proper names are not substituted by other words. The form of the name in the original language may be a little different from the form in the receptor language, because the stock of phonemes are different,[31] but it is still the same name and not a completely different word. When the chosen word also has particular connotations, as in the case of "hell," the distance to the original word becomes even greater. The fact that the word "hell" occurs in most Bible translations[32] supports my claim that the theology of the majority cannot serve as the criterion for what should be termed bias.

THE LEGITIMATE ROLE OF THEOLOGY IN BIBLE TRANSLATION

The definition of bias, proposed above, does not, however, sanction *any* theological coloring of the Bible, because the role of theology must be curtailed by grammatical and syntactical rules, when possible. We have already seen that theology plays an important role in understanding the text, in addition to doing linguistic analysis. This is also true in the phase of formulation. There are even instances where theology is the *only* deciding factor.

Let us look at one example, related to the Trinity doctrine. Greek Bible manuscripts consist of either capital letters (uncials) or small letters (minuscules), so when we use a capital letter in

---

[30] According to Matthew 5:22 *the body* can be thrown into *geenna*, indicating that it is a physical place. In the OT the name occurs in its Hebrew form *gei hinnom*, and the inconsistency of the translations is seen in the fact that it is always translated as "the valley of Hinnom" (2 Chr 33:6) and never as "hell."

[31] For instance, *Wien* in German and *Vienna* in English.

[32] Of the 15 modern translations found on the Gramcord CD ROM (1996) the following 12 have "hell": NRSV, DRBY, ASV, NASB, NIV, NJB, NKJV, RSV, TEV, KJV, RVB el infierno ("hell"), LUTH Hölle ("hell"). Only 3 use Gehenna: NAB, YNG, SEGR la géhenne.

the first position of a word in the English text, this is done according to the judgment of the translators. There is no disagreement in using a capital letter in first position in proper names or in the word "God," when it refers to the eternal creator, but what about the Spirit[33] of God? Should we translate "The Holy Spirit" as most translators do, or "the holy spirit" and "holy spirit" as does NWT? The choice of using capital letters or not is based *completely* on theology. Whether or not a translator uses the article in this situation is only partly based on theology.

A computer search of the Greek NT yielded the following statistics: The words "holy spirit" were found in 49 instances without the article and in 39 instances with the article. Thus, there can be no doubt that those rendering the words without the article, as "holy spirit," linguistically have a stronger case than those using the article in all 88 instances. Further, we may note that in 23 instances the anarthrous (= without the article) expression is preceded by a preposition, which may (or may not) imply definiteness. In any case there are 26 instances where there is no grammatical reason to imply the article.[34] More than 150 years ago Thomas F. Middleton wrote a treatise on the Greek article. He said quite logically, "For there being but one Holy Spirit, he could not be spoken of indefinitely." How then would he explain all the instances without the article? Consider:

> The fifth sense of πνεῦμα ["spirit"] is easily deducible from the fourth [referring to "the Third Person of the Trinity"]; being not here the Person of the Holy Spirit, but his *influence* or *operation*: the addition of ἅγιον ["holy"] is explicable as before. And in this meaning a remarkable difference may be observed with respect to the article. Though the Holy Spirit himself be but one, his influences and operations may be many; hence πνεῦμα

---

[33] I use capital letters in the "Spirit of God," "the Son" and "the Father," and other words, not as a token of reverence, but simply because these are definite objects which are time and again referred to.

[34] D. Pitt Francis, *The Holy Spirit: A Statistical Inquiry*, in *The Expository Times* (1989), pp. 136-137, tried, by means of a statistical analysis, to show that the article indicated personality on the part of The holy spirit. This view was refuted by A. Byatt, *The Holy Spirit: A Further Examination*, also in *The Expository Times* (1989), pp. 215-216.

and πνεῦμα ἅγιον are, in this sense, always *anarthrous,* the case of *renewed mention,* or other references being of course excepted. The expressions of being "filled with the Holy Ghost," "receiving the Holy ghost," "the Holy Ghost being upon one," &c. justify this observation.[35]

Middleton draws the conclusion that because the third Person of the Trinity cannot be indefinite, the cases without the article refer to an impersonal force, His influence or operation. He even suggests that some of the references *with* the article may refer to this impersonal force because they are anaphoric. In fact, because the *first* occurrence of *pneuma hagion* in any New Testament book is anarthrous, except in two instances where the article may be required for other reasons, none of the 39 instances with the article are conclusive as evidence for its use in translation.[36]

The importance of these examples in our context is seen in the fact that translators must choose between just *two* possibilities, either to use capital letters or not, and, where the Greek article is lacking, either to supply the English definite article or not. A neutral alternative is lacking. So, ultimately, the choice will be governed by one's theology: If the translators believe in the trinity, they will translate "The Holy Spirit," but if they do not, they will translate "holy spirit." And neither alternative indicates bias, for when there are but two choices,

---

[35] T. F. Middleton, *The Doctrine of the Greek Article Applied to the Criticism and Illustration of the Greek New Testament,* A New Edition with Prefatory Observations and Notes by Hugh James Rose (Cambridge: J. & J. J. Deighton, 1833), p. 126.

[36] The two instances where the first occurrence has the article (1 Cor 6:19; Eph 1:13) are clearly anaphoric. In the first case this is indicated by the attributive position of the following preprositional phrase, and in the second by the epithet "promised." In three books, Luke (1:15), Titus (3:5) and Hebrews (2:4) the first occurrence neither is preceded by an article nor a preposition. In eleven books, Matthew (1:18), Mark (1:8); John 1:33; Acts (1:2), Romans (5:5), 2 Corinthians (6:6), 1 Thessalonians (1:5), 2 Timothy (1:14), 1 Peter (1:12), 2 Peter (1:21) and Jude (1:20), the first occurrence lacks article but is preceded by a preposition. In the following books the words *pneuma hagion* are not found: Galatians, Philippians, Colossians, 2 Thessalonians, 1 Timothy, Philemon, James, 1 John, 2 John, 3 John and Revelation.

and grammar is not decisive, theology plays a legitimate role even as the sole authority. We will return to similar examples later.

In addition to stressing the legitimate role of theology in Bible translation, the above example also stresses the importance that the translator have an accurate knowledge of the relationship between Jesus and his Father (and The holy spirit), because more controversy is stirred up about the correct translation of particular passages concerning Jesus than any other topic, perhaps even all other topics combined. Therefore, an entire chapter is devoted to this topic.

Having related bias to language rather than to theology, and concluded that when there are but two possible choices of translation, when the grammar is not decisive, theology *must* be used, we will take a look at one particular use of theology. This example is not entirely indicative of bias, but all the same it may deserve criticism. What I have in mind are renderings which accord with grammar and syntax, and where foreign semantic elements neither are subtracted nor added, but where the reader is *unnecessarily* influenced by theological doctrine, without having the matter brought to his or her attention. In this light, the following rule is put forth:

> *A word, phrase or sentence of doctrinal importance, where there are more than two translation choices, and where there are no compelling linguistic reasons to choose one over the others, is liable to criticism if the chosen rendition represents a particular theological view, which is not brought to the reader's attention, together with the alternatives.*

Let us use the "realm of the dead" as a translation of the Hebrew *she'ōl* and the Greek *hadēs* as an example of a rendering deserving criticism. This rendering cannot be said to be biased as is the rendering "hell," because we cannot with certainty know whether the words *she'ōl* and *hadēs* are common nouns or proper names. The connotation of "realm," however, is life and activity, and the same is the case with the "realm of the dead." It is true that most evangelical Christians, together with most other religions of the world, believe in life after death, but there is nothing in the words *she'ōl* and *hadēs* that suggests this. To introduce elements into a translation in order to promote such a view, when this is not brought to the attention of the reader, is open to criticism. It is interesting to note that a number of newer translations[37] have transcribed the words *she'ōl* and *hadēs,* thus choosing a neutral rendition.

Because translation is interpretation and the translators' total understanding of the Bible must be taken into account, we must accept that the theology of the translators influences the translation, even though it is a theology different from our own —and we must even accept such a rendition as the "realm of the dead." Looking at the situation from the readers' viewpoint, however, it would be helpful in such situations to have footnotes or other explanations helping the readers to work with the text on their own.

HOW CAN THE READER HAVE A PART IN THE TRANSLATION PROCESS?

The translation process starts with the thoughts of the author and ends when the mind of the receptor grasps these thoughts and understands them correctly. The translator is the liaison between the Bible writers and the modern readers, and when discussing the reader's part in the process, we may profit from a schematic figure illustrating the parts of the translation process.

---

[37] Of the fifteen modern versions found on the Gramcord CD ROM (1996) eight transcribe *hades/she'ōl*: NRSV, Darby, ASV, NASB, YOUNG, NIV, NKJV, RVB; three have neutral renderings: RSV ("death"), TEV ("death"), SEGR du séjour des morts ("the place of the dead"); four have renderings which are open to criticism: NAB ("netherworld"), NJB ("underworld"), LUTH hölle ("hell"), KJV ("hell").

Figure 3.1

The Process of Idiomatic Translation

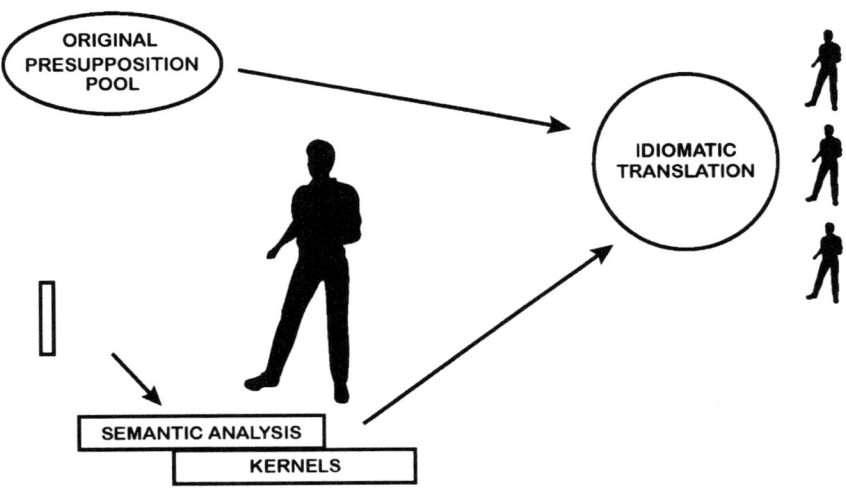

Figure 3.2

The Process of Literal Translation

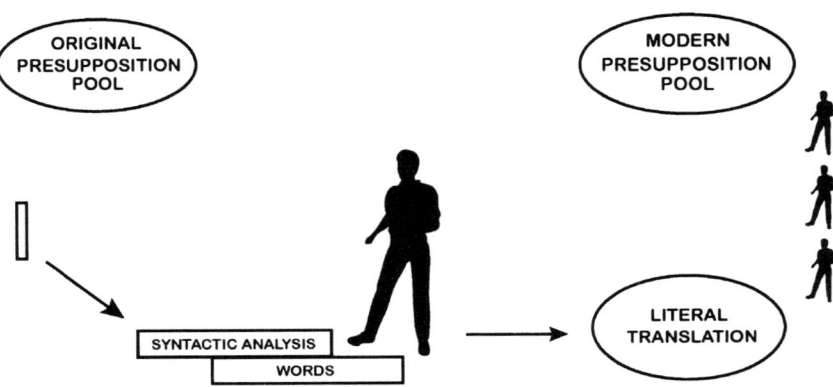

The medium is the written word, found in ancient manuscripts and translated into English, and there are two audiences that we have to take into consideration: the original readers[38] and the modern readers.

The original readers shared two things with those who wrote the Bible: 1) their presupposition pool and 2) their language. Because of this, they would get an instant understanding of the author's words, though they might not in all situations completely understand the application of the words or their meaning in the greater context.

The modern readers do not share the same presupposition pool or the same language with those who wrote the Bible. Rather, they have their own modern presupposition pool and their own language.

The translator knows both the presupposition pools and language of those who wrote the Bible, and the presuppositions and language of the modern readers, thus he or she fills the same position in relation to the modern audience as those who wrote the Bible filled in relation to the ancient audience.

The translator has two options, and his or her choice depends upon the interests of the target group. He or she may work with the goal of giving the modern readers the same impression as the ancient readers received, and to achieve this would be to make an idiomatic translation. Or the translator may work with the goal of giving the modern readers all the necessary linguistic tools to determine for themselves what the

---

[38] When I say "original readers" I mean the Christian communities to which the different parts of the NT were adressed and the Hebrew population who used the OT. It is somewhat simplified to say that they had a common "presupposition pool," or that the Hebrews had one in common and the Greeks had another. Language changes through time, and Greek words may have had different meanings in different areas. However, the language of the OT from its oldest to its youngest part is much more uniform than should be expected, and the Jews' presupposition pools in OT times were relatively similar, something which was also the case with the Christians in the first century. So, *broadly speaking*, these two groups each had a common presupposition pool which is completely different from the modern one(s). A third group would be non-Christian readers of the NT. Their presupposition pool would be somewhat different from that of the Christians, and they had to do some "translation" inside their own language, because the NT concepts signaled by such words as *psukhē* ("soul"), *pneuma* ("spirit"), *hadēs* (connected with death), and *theos* ("god") are completely different from what the same words signaled in classical Greek.

Bible writers meant. To achieve this would be to make a literal translation.

The literal translation is based on linguistics, the idiomatic translation on semantics. This is seen in the fact that kernels are the fundamental translation units for the idiomatic translation, and they are found by a *semantic* analysis, while a syntactic analysis plays a secondary role. In the literal translation, however, the word is the fundamental translation unit, a *syntactical and grammatical* analysis are the principal tools, and a semantic analysis plays a secondary role.

The idiomatic translation uses the presupposition pool of the modern readers; thus in addition to translating the text, it also "translates" the ancient presupposition pool, as it were. The literal translation translates only text; so the reader must become absorbed in the ancient presupposition pool.

The readers have no part in the idiomatic translation but everything is made ready for them, so they simply receive the translated text. The literal translation is much less concerned with the semantics of the text, which makes it possible for the readers to have a share in the translation process.

The points discussed above argue that the readers may have a share in the translation process if they acquaint themselves with the presupposition pool of those who wrote the Bible, and if the translator consciously works with the readers in mind and arranges the text in such a way that the readers may make informed choices. The last point has been the focus of this chapter, and we may sum up our conclusions as follows:

- The readers can have no direct share in the phase of understanding; the analysis of the source text and its situation is something the translators must do alone. But by using the word as translation unit, the translators have an objective guide for their understanding, and it is much easier for them to take a fresh look at the text, and thus not be inclined to automatically adopt familiar readings found in earlier translations.

- The transmission of the text basically occurs in the mind of the translators; naturally, this, too, is a phase in the translation process in which readers cannot directly participate. But, again, those translators whose minds are lexically and philologically programmed—not theologically and doctrinally programmed—will better serve the interests of the readers.

- It is in the formulation phase where the translators more directly can arrange the text to help the readers have a share in the translation process. Missionaries often test the quality of the Bible translation on which they are working by reading the text aloud, and at important junctures they have the auditors guess what the next word will be. Because a language is an ordered system, which means it is predictable, and the human mind works systematically, such a procedure may expose those words in the draft which do not give the right connotations. In a similar way it is obvious that when there is an increase in the number of English words used to render one Greek or Hebrew word—or when there is an increase in the number of Greek and Hebrew words rendered by the same English word— then the less ordered is the translation, and the more removed from the original text are the readers.

- In the formulation phase the translator therefore may render all technical words with the same English word, and do the same with other words when the meaning will not be distorted by this procedure. Theology should not be at work on this "word-plane" level.

- Translators will oftentimes be making choices for the reader, but they should strive to restrict this as much as possible. When they make choices regarding passages of doctrinal importance or if they make decisions regarding other important questions, they should let the readers know the different possibilities.

- In important passages, when there are but two choices and grammar and syntax are not decisive, the translators must make their choice on the basis of their theology, but where there are several choices, they should strive not to be unduly influenced by their own beliefs.

- An extensive use of footnotes and appendices with data about particular passages will be of immense help to the reader.

Now that we have sketched vital translation principles and have illustrated them, there is a critically important matter that we need to examine before we study the NWT and the criticisms levied against it, and that is the relationship between Jesus Christ, his Father, and The holy spirit.

EXCURSUS ON GREEK AND HEBREW VERBS

To begin with, a native English speaker has difficulty understanding all the nuances expressed by Greek and Hebrew verbs, because both verbal systems are so different from English. Let us make a comparison (NB: do not be misled by similar names in the different systems.)

Figure E.1
English Tenses

English	
Present	writes
Future	will write
Future Perfect	will have written
Past	wrote
Perfect	have written
Pluperfect	had written

Figure E.2
Greek Tense Forms

Greek	
Present	imperfective aspect, time indifferent
Future	future tense
Imperfect	imperfective aspect, past time
Aorist	perfective aspect
Pluperfect	prepast time resulting in a subsequent state

Figure E.3
Hebrew Tense Forms

Hebrew	
Imperfect	imperfective aspect, time indifferent
Perfect	perfective aspect, time indifferent

The basic difference between the verbal systems is that, in Greek, *aspect* is grammaticalized[1] and this is also true in Hebrew, but not in English. This means that while English is capable of expressing any aspectual nuance found in Hebrew and Greek, it must do so by circumlocution, because there are no grammatical forms in English with inherent aspectual meaning.[2]

In the Hebrew verbal system there is nothing similar to the English tense system. In Greek we find a similarity in the future, perfect and pluperfect for these have almost the same meaning as the English conjugations with the same names. But the central place of aspect in the Greek system, which has one perfective conjugation (aorist) as well as two imperfective conjugations (present and imperfect), also makes the Greek system very different from the English verbal system. It is important to realize that the term "perfect," both in English and Greek, is applied to verbal conjugations, thus being labels of groups of verbs with similar morphological characteristics, while the term "perfective" is used for one of the two aspects, thus being an abstract expression which is not tied up with grammatical form.

---

[1] Grammaticalization means that a particular grammatical characteristic is connected with the verb form and is not dependent upon the context.

[2] Most linguistic works on English say that English has aspects, but this is because *aspect* is used in a sense different from how it is used in this study (See J. Hewson and V. Bubenik, *Tense and Aspect in Indo-European Languages*, Current Issues in Linguistic Theory [Amsterdam: J. Benamins, 1997], p. 145). If "aspects" are defined as "viewpoints," the perfective one being a focus encompassing both the beginning and the end of an event or state, and the imperfective one being a focus on a small sequence after the beginning and before the end, then English is capable of expressing aspects. But there is no English form, the purpose of which is exclusively to express aspect. Both in Hebrew and Greek, the fundamental parts of the verbal system are exclusively aspectual and their area of use are much broader than that of simple past and past continuous, which in English are used to express viewpoint. So, while both English and Hebrew/Greek are capable of expressing durative and punctual viewpoints, their fundamental role in the verbal system and their completely different areas of use, make Hebrew and Greek aspects qualitatively different from what is called "aspect" in English.

ILLUSTRATING THE CHARACTERISTICS OF VERBS

Events and states can be viewed and described in the same way that *things* are viewed and described, and therefore I will use a bar of silver and a casted lion as illustrations. The difference between the two objects well illustrates the difference between *events* and *states*.

Figure E.4

A Bar of Silver and a Casted Lion

A state is a static situation that continues without any input of energy, and each moment of the state is similar to every other moment or to the whole state. Similarly with the silver bar, regardless of which part of it you inspect, it is similar to any other part. This is not the case with the casted lion which is not homogenous. It can represent an event which is not homogenous. A close-up view of one part of an event may be very different from a close-up view of another part,[3] and therefore its description may be different when we focus on the beginning, the middle, the end, or on the event as a whole.

Regarding our silver bar and the casted lion, they may exist at present, or perhaps they only existed in the past, or their production may yet be reserved for a future time. We can

---

[3] Remember the proverbial five blind men who described an elephant by touching it. One felt the trunk, another the tail and another the belly. Each description was true but only regarding a part of the elephant.

express this when we speak about the object, and, similarly, people of all times have been interested in the time of events and states, and have used different speech and writing markers to signal past, present or future time. No group of people who speak a language have done so without also being conscious of time.

So far we have spoken of objects in the real world, but our marvelous mind may also speak of objects that exist only in our imagination. Regarding the future, this is quite natural, for we cannot look into the future, and it remains to be seen what will happen. If we were to speak about a silver bar or a casted lion it might be done in the form of a wish: we want or hope to get hold of such objects. In reference to the past, we may express uncertainty about whether or not such objects ever existed, and therefore our reference to them is not a reference to something which *certainly* was a part of the real world.

There is also a real and an imagined world in the description of states and events, expressed by a difference in mood. When we speak of the real world we normally use the indicative mood, but when we express a command, a wish, or uncertainty about the reality of something, we have stepped into a world of imagination. In such situations the Greeks used the imperative, the subjunctive, or the optative moods and the Hebrews used the imperative, the jussive, and the cohortative.

In addition to placing things in a timeframe and expressing whether they are real or imagined, the perspective or distance from which things are seen is important. We may look at a thing from some distance, thus seeing and describing it as a whole, or we may take a closer look and inspect a small part of it. Similarly, it is possible to describe an event as a whole without attention to details, or describe a small part of it where the details are focused upon. This is my explanation of aspect and it is a completely new way of viewing Greek and Hebrew aspects.[4] In some languages, such as Hebrew and Greek, aspects

---

[4] It draws heavily on the modern linguistic definition of aspect, and has many similarities both with Fanning's definition of Greek aspect and Waltke/O'Connor's definition of Hebrew aspect. However, it adjusts their definition in order to explain the examples which are not accounted for by their definitions.

are grammaticalized, which means that there are different morphosyntactic forms to indicate the aspects. In English, tense is grammaticalized, but not aspect. In Hebrew, aspect is grammaticalized and not tense, and in Greek aspect is grammaticalized and so is time, to certain extent.

THE SEMANTIC PLANES OF A VERB PHRASE

Speaking and writing, as well as translating what is spoken and written, means communication. The verb is central when communicating with others, but when we are in a quest for the meaning of the verbal system of an ancient language, when we do not have informants, we should keep in mind that there are several factors contributing to verbal meaning, and that it is not always easy to isolate which factors contribute to the meaning of a particular verb phrase or clause. Let us now discuss the different semantic planes with a stress on aspect.

TENSE. The concept of "tense" is defined as "the grammaticalization of location in time."[5] This means that whether the time of the verbal action is past, present or future, related to speech time or to some other time, it is seen by the verb form itself and not by the context alone. Thus, the words "went" and "taught," in English, are past tense. Given Comrie's definition of "tense," neither Hebrew nor Greek have tenses, save possibly Greek future, which is viewed by most researchers as a tense.[6] The word "tense," for Hebrew perfect and imperfect, or Greek present, aorist or imperfect really is a misnomer, though it still is used in most studies on the Greek verb and in some studies on the Hebrew verb.[7] In this book we call the

---

[5] B. Comrie, *Tense* (Cambridge: Cambridge University Press, 1985), p. vii.

[6] See S. Porter, *Verbal Aspect in the Greek of the New Testament, with Reference to Tense and Mood* (New York: Peter Lang, 1993), pp 76-83. Porter denies that tense is grammaticalized at all in New Testament Greek.

[7] All the three recent dissertations on the Greek verb (Porter, Fanning and Olsen [Mari Broman Olsen, *A Semantic and Pragmatic Model of Lexical and Grammatical Aspect* (New York and London: Garland Publishing, 1997)] differentiate between tense and time in a fine way. D. B. Wallace has a very

mentioned groups "conjugations" and speak of Greek present and Greek imperfect without adding the word "tense." It is difficult enough to compare Hebrew and Greek conjugations with English tenses, so we should not set traps for the readers by using confusing terminology.

AKTIONSART. This is a German word that means "kind of action." The *Aktionsart* of a word is related to its lexical meaning, and therefore it is an objective entity in that its contents cannot be altered by parsing or by anything else.[8] The word "sing," for instance, means that words accompanied by a melody come out of someone's mouth. Regardless of the tense used, or whether a participle, an infinitive or a finite verb is chosen, the contents or *Aktionsart* of the word remains unaltered. It is important to note that expressions such as "durative" and "punctiliar," which have been wrongly ascribed to aspect, rightly belong to *Aktionsart*.

The verb "sing" is by nature (or objectively speaking) durative. The action is not less durative in the clause "he sang" than in "he was singing," though the stress may be different. On the other hand, the verb "knock" has a punctiliar *Aktionsart*. The clause "he knocked at the door" is either punctiliar (one knock) or frequentative (a series of knocks). But the clause "he was knocking at the door" can only be frequentative. What is frequentative can either be viewed as a series of punctiliar

---

fine discussion of this subject in his *Greek Grammar Beyond the Basics: An Exegetical Syntax of the New Testament* (Grand Rapids: Zondervan, 1996), pp. 504-510. The valuable Hebrew syntax written by Waltke and O'Connor (*An Introduction to Biblical Hebrw Syntax* [Winona Lake, Indiana: Eisenbrauns, 1990]) also distinguishes between time and tense. However, the recent comparative grammar of the Semitic languages written by E. Lipinski, (*Semitic Languages: Outline of a Comparative Grammar* [Orientalia Lovaniensia Analecta 80; Leuven: Uitgiveij Peeters en Departement Oosterse Studies, 1997]), while generally having a high quality, takes for granted that verbs in Hebrew having past meaning also have past tense. It is methodologically unsound to draw such a conclusion, since the past time can be a function of the context (thus being pragmatic) just as well as being a function of the verb (thus being semantic).

[8] Some verbs can have different meanings and others can have one kind of *Aktionsart* in one context and another kind of *Aktionsart* in another context. So, strictly speaking, *Aktionsart* is not completely objective, but as a rule it is.

actions or as one durative action. In this light we might also consider the verb "love," which is a state. English participles are not normally used with such verbs, because they are durative.[9] What we learn from this is that the "kind of action" of the verb should not be applied to aspect, but to *Aktionsart*.[10]

PROCEDURAL TRAITS. In most languages we find verbs which consist of two elements, the so-called phrasal verbs such as "pass over," "eat up," "break into," and "cut off." In such verbs the *Aktionsart* is, in a way, extended. The first two examples have a durative *Aktionsart*, but one other element is added, namely, the end of the action is included in the verb. We say that the verbs are both durative and *telic*. The third example can also be durative and telic, or it can be punctiliar; the fourth is punctiliar. This shows that elements can be added to the lexical *Aktionsart* in order to communicate different nuances.

The additional element in the phrasal verb is a preposition or an adverb, but there are other constructions which can extend, modify or specify the *Aktionsart* of a verb in a similar way, namely, the verbal arguments, that is, the subject and the object. Whether the subject and/or object is a count noun or a non-count noun, is singular or plural, is definite or indefinite will also affect the meaning or nature of the whole event described. Based on the nature of the verb in combination with the parameters mentioned earlier, we get 5 different situation types:

---

[9] We can hardly speak of durative *Aktionsart* in connection with states, because there is no action.

[10] Bowman's explanation of Greek aorist (*Jehovah's Witnesses, Jesus Christ, and the Gospel of John* [Grand Rapids: Baker, 1989], p. 23) contains the usual confusion, "An *aorist* is a past tense verb that denotes a single event or an act at a single point of time, as opposed to an ongoing process or state or condition."

Figure E.5

Verbs in Five Situation Types

STATES	static	durative	non-telic	"love God"
ACTIVITY	non-static	durative	non-telic	"walk in the garden"
ACCOMPLISHMENT	non-static	durative	telic	"build a house"
SEMELFACTIVE[11]	non-static	non-durative	non-telic	"knock at the door"
ACHIEVEMENT	non-static	non-durative	telic	"reach the top"

The crucial characteristic of the situation types is telicity. It has nothing to do with tense, or whether the end of a state or event was reached before speech time or another point of time. But telicity has to do with whether or not the end is *conceptually* included. Thus, telicity is an objective characteristic which shows whether or not the event or state is viewed as a complete(d) whole or not. It is important to keep this in mind when we later come to aspect and reject the traditional explanation that the perfective aspect views the event or state as a *completed* whole, and the imperfective aspect as *incomplete*. The "slot" where "complete" belongs is already occupied by telicity.

VOICE. The subject and object are not only important for the extended *Aktionsart* (the procedural traits) of a verb but also for the voice of the clause, because voice has to do with the relationship between the action, the agent and the patient.[12] We offer the following scheme for the Hebrew voice based on the different relationships between the agent, patient and the action[13]:

---

[11] The word "semelfactive" means "to do something once."

[12] The word "agent" refers to the one doing the action, from a semantic point of view, while "patient" refers to the one whom the action affects.

[13] Because voice has a bearing on the understanding of aspect, and aspect is what really distinguishes Hebrew and Greek from English and other Germanic languages, we cannot discuss voice and aspect generally; rather, we must do so in a language-specific way. I therefore use Hebrew examples in this scheme.

Figure E.6
Scheme for Voice in Hebrew

ACTIVE (QAL)	The agent (subject) acts on the patient (object)	"God created the earth"
PASSIVE (NIPHAL)	The patient (subject) is acted upon by an agent (mentioned or not)	"The earth was created by God"
REFLEXIVE (HITHPAEL)	The agent (subject) acts upon her- or himself	"The woman beat herself"
RECIPROCAL (HITHPAEL)	Two agents act upon one another	"The man and the woman beat one another"
CAUSATIVE (HIPHIL)	The agent (subject) lets the object have a share in the action	"God let a wind blow over the earth"
RESULTATIVE (PIEL)	The agent (subject) leads the patient (object) through an action into a state	"The woman completely broke the vase"[14]
FACTITIVE (PIEL)[15]	An agent leads a patient (object) into a state which in the Qal is expressed by a intransitive verb.	Active: "She is righteous" Factitive: "She is justified"

ASPECT. The principal difference between the perfective and imperfective aspect, as it is described in all (or almost all) studies, is that the perfective aspect includes the *beginning* and the *end* of a state or an event, but the imperfective does not include them. The imperfective aspect is portrayed as a viewpoint from the inside, as linear action, as something which is not bounded, but open, because neither beginning nor end is

---

[14] The force of the Piel is difficult to express explicitly in English. In the Qal the verb *shābār* means "to break," in the Piel it means "to lead an object into a condition of complete brokenness." A good English example where the resultant state is clearly stressed is the command, "Sit down!" Formally we ask for an action, namely, to seat one's self in a chair. But what is stressed is, "Take your seat and continue to be seated."

[15] Hebrew also has passive counterparts to the Piel and Hiphil stems, namely, Pual and Hophal, respectively.

included. The perfective aspect is portrayed as a viewpoint from the outside; it is punctiliar and closed because both the beginning and the end are included. While this definition accounts for many traits in both Greek and Hebrew, it does not account for everything. This is seen from the following observations regarding biblical Hebrew:

When discussing aspect, grammars and commentaries almost always use the deductive-nomologic model of the natural sciences, where a law of nature is used as the premise. In the discussions of aspect, the traditional definition is used as the premise, similar to using a law of nature, and the aspectual explanations themselves are never tested. The deductive-nomologic explanation goes like this:

Figure E.7

Deductive-nomologic Syllogisms

Water expands when freezing.
"A" is water and is freezing.
"A" expands.

Figure E.8

Deductive-nomologic Application of the Perfective Aspect

The perfective aspect (aorist) includes the beginning and end of an event.
"A" is perfective (aorist).
"A" includes the beginning and the end of the event.

Figure E.9

Deductive-nomologic Application of the Imperfective Aspect

The imperfective aspect (imperfect) focuses on a sequence between the beginning and the end of an event.
"A" is imperfective (imperfect).
"A" focuses on a sequence between the beginning and the end.

To find the true nature of the aspects we need a model which is not deductive-nomologic, but rather one that is hypothetic-deductive. This means that we use the traditional definitions of the aspects as hypotheses (not laws), and then test them against Biblical clauses. Using the hermeneutic circle, the Biblical clauses are interpreted in the light of the definition of the aspects and this definition is modified in the light of the Biblical clauses. Following this procedure we learn that the definitions of aspects must be modified both regarding the Greek and Hebrew verbs.

The similarities between the traditional definition of aspect, exemplified by English on the one hand and Hebrew and Greek aspects on the other, are:

1) In both cases aspect represents the subjective viewpoint of the reporter.

2) In both cases aspect represents a particular focus, either of a small part or of a larger part, of an event or state.

The differences are:

1) Aspects are not grammaticalized in English as they are in Greek and Hebrew, even where they represent the most fundamental characteristic of the verbal system.

2) In English, the relation of the viewpoints to the beginning and the end is what makes the aspects different. While the end is also important in Greek and Hebrew, the principal differentiating factor is the area of focus, that is, whether it is narrow or wide.

3) The use of the English aspects are basically restricted to just two situations: either one V-ed (for example, built a house [where V stands for "verb"])[16] or one was V-ing (for example, was building a house).

Greek and Hebrew aspects express a host of different situations; in fact, in Hebrew the areas of use are virtually unlimited. We can see from the above points that the nature of English, Greek, and Hebrew aspects are similar because they are all viewpoints. But their important role in the languages and their versatility makes the Hebrew and Greek aspects qualitatively different from those of English. Any comparison between them in order to understand the Greek and Hebrew aspects in the light of the English ones, should be executed with the utmost care. Let us, then, look at some observations outlining the nature of Greek and Hebrew aspects:

1) Almost any event can be portrayed by the imperfective or perfective aspect without any change in its objective nature.[17] There are, for instance, 470 OT verses that occur in more or less identical form twice or even three times. For example, "When your days are full" in 2 Samuel 7:12 is expressed by the

---

[16] There is a question as to whether or not we can, in this example, speak of aspect at all. We may simply view it as past tense without any particular viewpoint.

[17] A good example is Nehemiah 3:14, 15: "And the Gate of the Ash-heaps was what Malchijah . . . repaired [perfective]; he himself proceeded to build it [imperfective] and to roof it over [imperfective] . . . And the Fountain Gate was what Shallun . . . repaired [perfective]; he himself proceeded to build [imperfective] it and to roof it over [imperfective] and to set up [imperfective] its doors." In these two verses all nine verbs have a durative *Aktionsart*, but the perfective aspect is used in two cases and the imperfective aspect in seven. For all nine actions both aspects could have been used, without signaling any difference in the objective nature of the actions.

imperfective aspect, but in 1 Chronicles 17:11 it is expressed by the perfective aspect. In Isaiah 7:1, "The army of Aram came up" is described by the perfective aspect and in 2 Kings 16:5 it is described by the imperfective aspect. In 59 instances different verb forms are used in the parallel verses, without any change in the objective contents.[18]

The only instances where just one aspect is available, are those situations where the action is past, the subject and object are singular, definite and countable, or the verb is intransitive and the context explicitly shows that the action was not finished. In such situations only an imperfective aspect can be used. One example is Jeremiah 37:12: *wayyētsē* [and go out] *yirmeyāhû* [Jeremiah] *mîrûshālayim* [from Jerusalem]. Which we translate as, "And Jeremiah began [or: 'tried'] to go forth from Jerusalem." Jeremiah did not actually leave the city.

2) Both perfective and imperfective verbs can be factitive and resultative. A primary meaning of the Piel voice as described above is that its verbs are resultative. This means that the end of an action is reached and the object is lead into the resulting state. There are 2,216 occurrences of Piel perfect and 1,508 occurrences of Piel imperfect in the Hebrew text of the Bible. The end of the action is reached in all those that can be defined as resultative. This shows that the imperfective aspect cannot be a view from the inside of an event, before the end is reached, and that the end of an event cannot be the real distinguishing factor between the perfective and imperfective aspect. However, an endpoint may have some importance, because even though the end of the *event* is passed when the imperfective aspect is used in the Piel stem, it can still be defined as open, since the end of the resulting state is not yet reached.

3) The imperfective aspect can be ingressive (beginning of action included). The father of modern Hebrew aspectual theory, S. R. Driver, defined the imperfective aspect as "nascent" or "inceptive." Even though this characteristic is much less common than Driver thought, there are several hundred

---

[18] For a complete list of the differences see R. Furuli, "Imperfect Consecutive and the Verbal System of Biblical Hebrew" (Mag. Art thesis: University of Oslo, 1995), pp. 116-122.

imperfective verbs in the Hebrew text where the beginning of the action is included. This also argues against the view that the imperfective aspect is a view from the inside, without including the beginning.

4) The perfective aspect is often ingressive with stative verbs. In a good many instances where a stative verb is used in the perfective aspect, the meaning is ingressive (or inceptive), that is, the entrance into the state (and the first part of the state) is stressed. The clause "David became king" is ingressive; he entered the state of and continued to reign as king. The clause "David was king" only observes that the state of David's reigning held. When the beginning can be included both in an imperfective event (point 3) and in a perfective one, it cannot be the principal distinguishing factor, even though one situation is a state and the other an event.

Taking into consideration both how aspect is generally defined (with the end of an event as distinguishing points) and the special characteristics of Hebrew as shown above, I see no other possibility than to suggest a definition of Hebrew aspect centered around distance and scope:[19]

> *The imperfective aspect is a close-up view of a small part of an event or state where the details are in focus, and the perfective aspect is a broader view, from some distance, with the details not in focus.*

---

[19] I am not using "scope" in the technical sense of formal semantics but, rather, as indicating the part of the event on which the viewer directs his focus.

Figure E.10

The Imperfective Aspect Illustrated

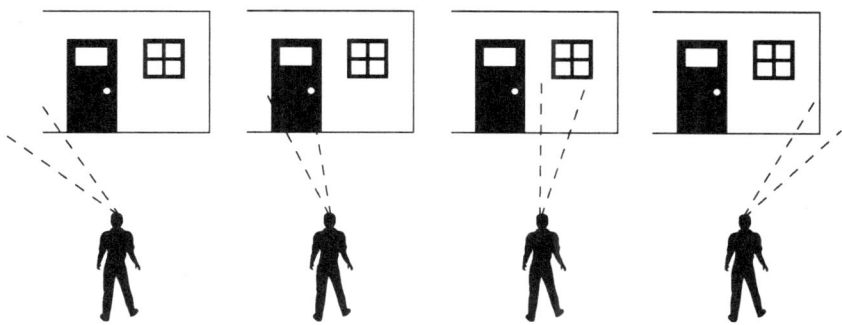

Let me explain this a bit more. We can illustrate the aspectual difference with the help of a camera with a zoom function. If we do not use the zoom we might focus on the whole object including its end-points, but its details are not visible. If we use the zoom we might focus on a small area of the object where the details can be clearly seen. The Hebrews did not have cameras with zoom functions, so while this modern invention may be used as an illustration, the Hebrew mind would define aspect in relation to distance and scope.

Through the perfective aspect we view the situation from a distance, with a wide focus, which normally, but not always, includes beginning and end. Through the imperfective aspect, we take a close-up view of a part of the situation with details made visible by zooming in on them, as it were. In terms of "boundedness," it means that the imperfective aspect is always unbounded and the perfective one is bounded in most instances, but not in all.[20]

---

[20] Strictly speaking both aspects are by nature unbounded because they represent the focus on a small area, or on a broader area of an event or state respectively. However, since the perfective aspect, in Greek, in most cases represents past meaning, and this is also often the case in Hebrew, and because the view is so broad that the end of the aspectual focus in most instances coincides with the end of the event or state, the perfective aspect appears as bounded.

Figure E.11

The Perfective Aspect Illustrated

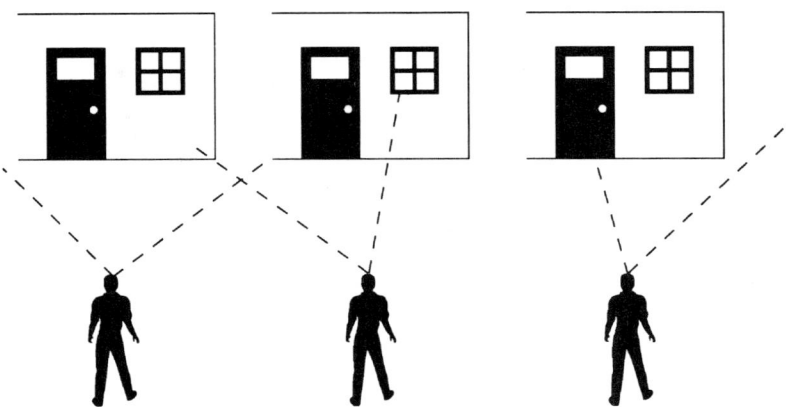

For instance, if our object is a house, we might, by using the zoom see many different things up close. One perspective may show the corner of the house and a small part of the wall, another may show a window and a part of the wall, still another might show the door, and so forth. If we do not use the zoom and if we look at the house from some distance, the perspective is wider and usually the whole house is visible. However, it is possible that just a part of the house will be visible if our focus is on the surroundings of one side. English, Hebrew, and Greek aspects have a narrow or a wide focus. The difference is that the English focus is a frontal, which cannot be directed to any one of the sides, but the Greek and Hebrew focus can be directed towards all sides; yes, they can even be directed towards an area before the beginning of an event or after its end.[21]

It is, however, important to remember that the aspects do not signal that events and states have a certain constituency

---

[21] We should not associate any quality with the concept "distance." What counts is the scope of the aspect, and distance is used because scope is a function of it, and to show that actions and states can be viewed in exactly the same way as things are viewed. Apart from this, "distance" has no meaning in aspectual discussions.

or show that the action of an event is/was ongoing or not;[22] this is what the Aktionsart does. The aspects are just peepholes through which we can view events and states.

> *The role of aspects in relation to verbs can be compared to the role of the article in relation to nouns. For instance, the Hebrew and Greek words for "all/every" (kol and pas) will, without the article, often focus on the individual members of the group, but with the article the focus is on the group as a whole. Similarly, the imperfective aspect will focus on a small part of the event and the perfective aspect will often focus on the event as a whole.*

I agrued in Chapter 2 that words/concepts have independent meaning, and the role of the context is only to make visible a particular part of this meaning. In a similar way, all the action of an event is tied up with the lexical meaning of the verb, its Aktionsart, and the procedural traits of the event, and the aspect is chosen simply to make visible a certain part of this action. But the combination of aspect with the other semantic planes is important, because by this, particular nuances of meaning can be conveyed.[23]

To emphasize that aspects are "nothing," just holes, we will also show that there is a similarlity between aspect and mood. There is some similarity between aspect and mood because both represent a strictly subjective viewpoint. The difference is that the subjective view of mood relates to an imagined, unreal world, while aspect relates to the real world. It is important to

---

[22] This would indicate that the aspects were objective, a view that is impossible to reconcile with the data in the Hebrew Bible.

[23] The combination of the imperfective aspect and a semelfactive or telic verb can, for instance, signal an iterative or habitual event ("She was knocking at the door," "Every year he went up to Jerusalem"). The combination of the perfective aspect and a stative verb often signals the beginning of the state ("He became king," rather than "He was king").

note that even though aspect is concerned with real events and states, they do not necessarily make visible the *whole* event or state. To put it differently, we cannot take for granted that situations where the perfective aspect is used have reached their end and that those where the imperfective aspect is used have not come to a close. This is so because reaching the end of an event or state is an objective feature, while aspect is just the subjective way the reporter wants to portray the situation.

Let us, then, look at some Greek and Hebrew examples to see if the portrayal of the aspectual differences, as they relate to distance and scope, can be upheld. Keep in mind that the following examples show where the focus is in each case, and do not describe the objective contents of these situations.

IMPERFECTIVE EVENTS
(B= beginning, E= end, xxx = focus)

EVENT

1) xxxB———E— = conative
   (an attempt)

2) —Bxxx———E— = inceptive
   (including the beginning)

3) —B—xxx———E— = progressive
   (neither beginning nor end is included)

4) —B———-xxxE— = egressive
   (before the end)

5) —B———xxxEx— = resultative
   (the end included)

EXAMPLES

1) Mark 15:23: "Here they tried to give him [imperfect] wine drugged with myrrh, but he would not take it."

2) Acts 11:2: "When Peter came up to [aorist] Jerusalem, those who were circumcised began to debate [imperfect] with him."

3) Mark 12:41: "and began observing how the crowd was dropping [imperfect] money into the treasury chest."

4) Mark 4:38: "Teacher, do you not care that we are about to perish [imperfect]?

5) Mark 2:5: "Your sins are forgiven [present]."[24]

IMPERFECTIVE STATES

STATE

6) —Bxxxxx——E—
(past state still in progress)

7) —B——xxx——E—
(present part of state stressed)

EXAMPLES

6) John 5:6: "he had already been sick [present] a long time."

7) Acts 9:26: "They were all afraid [imperfect] of him."

---

[24] B. M. Fanning, *Verbal Aspect in New Testament Greek* (Oxford: Clarendon Press, 1990), p. 202, calls phrases similar to this one "Instantaneous present." Wallace, *Greek Grammar Beyond the Basics*, p. 509, rightly criticizes this definition.

PERFECTIVE EVENTS

EVENT

8) —xBxxxxxxxxxxEx— = constative
   (beginning and end included)

9) —Bxxxxx——E— = ingressive
   (beginning included but not end)

10) —B———xxxExxx= egressive
    (end is stressed)

EXAMPLES

8) Acts 8:39: "Jehovah's spirit quickly led [aorist] Philip away."

9) Acts 16:10: "Now as soon as he had seen the vision, we sought [aorist] to go forth into Macedonia."

10) Acts 7:36: "This man led them out after doing portents and signs in Egypt."

PERFECTIVE STATES

STATE

11) —xBxxxxxxxxxxEx— = seen as a whole
    (beginning and end included)

12) —xBxx——E— = ingressive
    (beginning included)

13) —xxxBxxxxxx—E— = a part is viewed
    (beginning included)

14) —B——xxxxExx = egressive
(end is included)

EXAMPLES

11) Romans 5:14: "Nevertheless, death ruled as king
[aorist] from Adam down to Moses."

12) Matthew 2:16: "Then Herod, seeing that he had been
outwitted by the astrologers, fell into a great rage
[aorist]."

13) Hebrews 4:4 "'And God rested [aorist] on the seventh
day from all his work.'"[25]

14) 1 Thessalonians 2:18: "For this reason we wanted [aorist]
to come to you."

GREEK AND HEBREW ASPECTS

Based on the above discussion and examples, we can
conclude that Hebrew imperfect and imperfect consecutive
represent the imperfective aspect, and perfect and perfect
consecutive represent the perfective aspect.[26] Time is completely
absent from this system and must be construed entirely on the
basis of the context.

---

[25] The quote is from Genesis 2:2, so the state of rest began a long time before
Hebrews was written. The argument in Hebrews 4 is that the rest continued
into the future. This means that the beginning of the rest and a large part of
it (but not including its end) was the focus.

[26] Most Hebrew grammars view the four mentioned groups as four different
conjugations, where two and two pairs have basically the same meaning.
Imperfect consecutive and perfect have about the same meaning and that is
also the case with imperfect and perfect consecutive.

But what about Greek aspect? Hebrew and Greek belong to two different families of languages, and I have defined aspect primarily on the basis of the Hebrew verbal system. Is it sound to project the same aspectual definitions to Greek, also? The answer is yes, not because both languages are used in the Bible, but because the Greek aspects behave in exactly the same manner. Greek aspects relate to the beginning or end of an action as do their Hebrew counterparts, which is obvious from the examples given above.

Because there are six conjugations[27] in Greek compared to two in Hebrew, and because one of the six codes both for aspect and for time and another is a tense, the subjective choice is much more restricted in Greek than in Hebrew. But the *nature* of the aspects evidently is the same: subjective viewpoints indicating narrow or focus.[28]

Greek present and imperfect represent the imperfective aspect. Greek present is time indifferent, while the imperfect, in addition to the imperfective aspect, also includes past time. Greek aorist represents the perfective aspect, and is time indifferent.[29] Greek perfect is primarily resultative: an action is finished with a resulting state. The pluperfect is a prepast example of the perfect. Future is future tense.

---

[27] I speak from the point of view of the Greek text of the NT (synchronic) and not from a historical (diachronic) point of view.

[28] One advantage of viewing Greek aspects in the light of Hebrew ones, is that tense is completely absent from the Hebrew system. The only way to define aspects in dead languages is by help of induction, that is, generalizations are made on the basis of the use and meaning of the different conjugations. But this is certainly difficult when a morphosyntactic form codes both for aspect and time, as is the case with the aorist and the imperfect in Greek. The problem in such a situation involves knowing which nuances of the verb phrase's meaning are related to aspect and which are related to time. In Hebrew we have just aspect, not time, so it is easier to isolate aspectual meaning.

[29] Porter and Olsen argue that aorist is time indifferent, while Fanning claims that it includes past time.

ASPECT AND COMMUNICATION

Returning to aspects, we should keep in mind the consequences of defining aspects as *subjective* viewpoints. In Greek grammars we find that both the perfective and imperfective aspects are described with different subheadings, such as "durative present," "iterative present," "ingressive aorist" and "gnomic aorist." While such classifications are not wrong, they give the reader the impression that the present (=the imperfective aspect) and the aorist (= the perfective aspect) consist of groups with different semantic contents, and it conceals the fact that the meaning ascribed to the different groups is a function of the interplay of the different semantic planes and not just a property of aspect. Thus, the strictly subjective nature is lost.

Taking a look at figure E.12 we see that meaning, and the communication of meaning from the sender to the receiver, consists in the sender's choice of words and his or her combination of these in the different semantic planes. Each word or each semantic plane or the combination of these do not necessarily match the precise thoughts which the sender wants to convey, but they are the best means available. So the sender chooses the best fit, the combination which he or she believes will communicate his or her thoughts in the best way.

Figure E.12
Communication Between Sender and Receiver

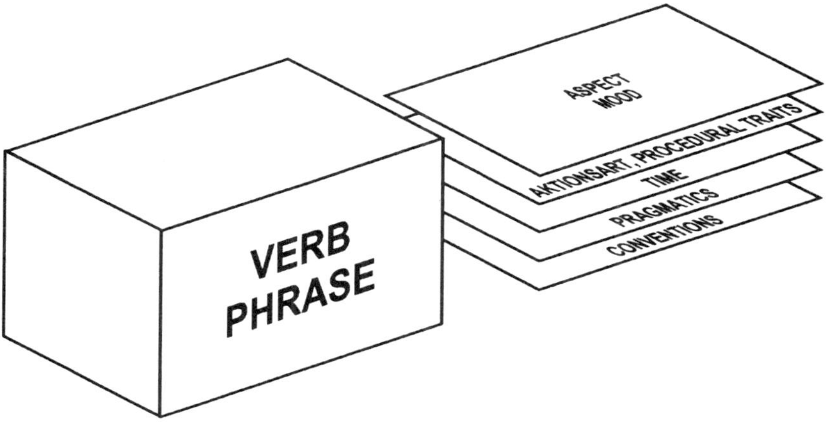

Let us use a conative event (= an attempt which is not fully executed) as an example. If the sender's language has a word for "try to," the author can express his or her thoughts lexically and choose words telling that the person tried to do this or that but did not succeed. But the author can also use grammatical means, that is, he or she can express the thought by the use of aspect. Because the situation is objectively open, (neither beginning nor end was reached) both a Hebrew and a Greek author would choose the imperfective aspect, which subjectively is/seems to be open.

However, the actual verb in the imperfective aspect and the *Aktionsart* of the verb are not enough to communicate that the situation is conative, because the focus of the imperfective aspect *can* also be on the beginning, the middle, the conclusion of an action, or even include the the end and a resulting state. So the interplay between aspect and the other semantic planes, together with linguistic convention,[30] is what will communicate that the action was only attempted. It is similar with all the other uses of the imperfective (or perfective) aspect. So there is no conative subgroup to the imperfective aspect, neither *is* the aspect conative, ingressive, durative or egressive, but situations fitting one of these descriptions can be communicated by the sender through help of a combination of the imperfective aspect and other semantic planes. One should always keep in mind that the aspects are just peepholes through which events and states are seen.

---

[30] The concept "linguistic convention" is important but it will not be elucidated here. As has already been discussed, the users of a language have a common presupposition pool. One side of this is that the native speakers know what is commonly accepted. English, where subject and object are not morphologically marked, has, for instance, the convention that the subject normally comes before the object. In the clause "John taught Paul" we know that "John" is the subject and "Paul" is the object. So Greek and Hebrew convention will, together with the aspect and the other semantic planes, contribute to the meaning.

THE TRANSLATION OF VERBS IN THE NWT

In the Introduction of NWTREF, page 7, we read, "Special care was taken in translating Hebrew and Greek verbs in order to capture the simplicity, warmth, character and forcefulness of the original expressions."

There is no doubt that the rendering of verbs in the NWT is quite different from most other translations, so the Bible reader may wonder if this has a solid foundation.

GREEK VERBS

The NWT follows the traditional approach that is outlined in such monumental works as Robertson's *A Grammar of the New Testament Greek*. Most translations follow the same principles, the difference being that the NWT has made the details and the dynamism of the system visible for the readers, while most others translations have not deemed this necessary or practical to do so.

The approach of the NWT means that a difference in rendition between the perfective and imperfective aspects is scrupulously sought. The result has been a very dynamic translation which has a great appeal to the readers, to their minds and their emotions.

The rendering of the present imperative (imperfective) in Matthew 7:7 as "keep on asking" is certainly better than the lame "Ask" of the RSV. And, similarly, the rendering of the aorist imperative (perfective) of Romans 12:2 as "quit being fashioned after this system of things" is better than, "Do not be conformed to this world," again found in the RSV.

A consistent distinction between the aspects may also clear up contradictions in the text which are found in some translations. The RSV contains the following contradiction in the book of 1 John:

> 3: 9: "No one born from God commits sin."

> 2:1: "but if any one [born from God] does sin."

Because the NWT scrupulously differentiates between the aspects, it has rendered these two texts so that there is no contradiction:

> 3:9: "Everyone that has been born from God does not carry on sin (present, imperfective)."

> 2:1: "And yet, if anyone [born from God] does commit a sin (aorist, imperfective)."

In the above examples it is important to indicate aspectual differences in translation, but it can be discussed whether the authors of the NT generally wanted to convey such fine nuances by their choice of aspect, as the various NWT renderings indicate. To use an English example, we could ask, Is there a difference in meaning between the clauses: "This morning John was singing in the bathroom" and "this morning John sang in the bathroom"?

Because the verb "sing" has a durative *Aktionsart*, the objective action is identical in both cases. Even if we ask for stress, it is not evident that there is a difference. So it can be argued that the two clauses are different ways to express exactly the same thought.

There is no method by means of which we definitely can know the precise nuance that should be made visible in a translation from a dead language. But because aspectual nuances evidently are important in some cases, the interests of the readers will best be served by making the nuances visible in all cases, wherever possible, as does the NWT. This translation is a study Bible, and it has certainly achieved its stated objective in relation to Greek verbs, with the result that the readers can make "informed choices."

HEBREW VERBS

The traditional approach is not followed in connection with Hebrew verbs. Says NWTREF, Appendix 3C, page 1573: "The *New World Translation* has not followed the unfounded theory of *Waw* Consecutive when translating Hebrew verbs. This age-old theory does not convey the power and forcefulness of the Hebrew verbs in their original states. Therefore, the *New World Translation* presents the Hebrew verbs with accurate meaning and dynamism by maintaining a distinction between the perfect and the imperfect states of the Hebrew verbs."

This is a radical view indeed, not foremost because the "waw consecutive" theory has been abandoned, but rather because the Hebrew verbal system is viewed as having just two components and not four, as is almost universally believed. Let us now consider this in more detail.

The principal spokesman for the modern aspectual theory of Hebrew verbs was S. R. Driver.[31] He entertained the four-component model of Hebrew verbs, but at the same time he indirectly outran this model by writing that the force of imperfect consecutive could be "nascent" or "incipient."[32]

Already in 1888 Benjamin Newton had discarded the "waw consecutive" theory and he produced a translation without using it.[33] But little happened in this field before the late 1930s. At this time, Alexander Sperber published articles which argued that the traditional view of Hebrew verbs was wrong, and that there was little consistency at all in the system.[34] His explanation for this involved dialectal differences in particular parts of the Bible. However, much of his data clearly militated against the "waw consecutive" theory.

In the 1940s, things started to happen at the Southern Baptist Theological Seminary in the US. Three theses, critical to the "waw consecutive" theory, were published in the course of 12 years.[35] In addition to these theses, James Washington Watts

---

[31] See S. R. Driver, *A Treatise on the Use of the Tenses in Hebrew*, 3d ed. (Oxford: Clarendon, 1892).

[32] According to him, the Hebrew *wayyōmer* could be translated "he proceeded to say" rather than the usual "he said."

[33] *The Altered Translation of Genesis ii,5*, (1888), pp. 49-51. See NWTREF, pp. 1472, 1473.

[34] See his "Hebrew Based upon Greek and Latin Transliterations," *Hebrew Union College Annual* (1937/38), pp. 103-274; and "Hebrew Based upon Biblical Passages in Parallel Transmission," *Hebrew Union College Annual* (1939), pp. 153-249.

[35] Leo Eddleman, "Waw Consecutive and the Consecution of Tenses as Reflected by Eight Century Hebrew" (Ph.D dissertation, Southern Baptist

published a grammar,[36] and also translations of portions of the Bible without using the "waw consecutive" theory. None of the aforementioned sources use a great deal of linguistics in their arguments, but they marshal much sound data against the theory.

The work with the Greek part of the NWT was started in the 1940s and the Hebrew part followed from 1950 onward. Given the above situation, with most experts seconding the "waw consecutive theory," it was a bold step for the NWT translators to abandon it. Evidently they made a thorough study of the Hebrew text of the Bible, and what they found, together with the accumulating evidence of the weaknesses of the theory, helped them take their stand, a stand which undoubtedly is correct!

In the years following the completion of the Hebrew portion of the NWT, which was finished in 1960, several studies have been published that endorse the view that the "waw consecutive" theory should be abandoned.[37] But, still, the almost universal view is that the Hebrew verbal system has four components and not two, as the NWT translators presumed. Three basic views can be observed:

1) *THE SYSTEM IS ONLY ASPECTUAL.* The perfect represents the perfective aspect and the imperfect represents all that is not perfective. Imperfect consecutive represents the perfective (the opposite of simple imperfect) and perfect consecutive represents the imperfective aspect (all of which is

---

Theological Seminary, 1943); J. J. Curtis, Jr., "An Application of the Syntax of Hebrew Verbs to the Writings of Amos" (Ph.D. dissertation, Southern Baptist Theological Seminary, 1943); and E. B. Scoggin, "Application of Hebrew Verb States to a Translation of Isaiah 40-55" (Ph.D. dissertation, Southern Baptist Theological Seminary, 1955).

[36] J. W. Watts, *A Survey of Syntax in the Hebrew Old Testament* (Grand Rapids: Eerdmans, 1964). It was first published in 1951.

[37] D. Michel, "Tempora und Satzstellung in den Psalmen," (Ph.D thesis; 1960); O. L. Barnes, "A New Approach to the Problem of the Hebrew Tenses and its Solution without the Recourse to Waw Consecutuve," (1965); P. Kustar, "Aspekt im Hebräischen, (Ph.D thesis, 1972); and L. McFall, "The Enigma of the Hebrew Verbal System," (1982).

not perfective). This is the view presented by Waltke and O'Connor.[38]

2) *THE SYSTEM IS BOTH ASPECTUAL AND TEMPORAL.* Imperfect represents the imperfective aspect and perfect represents the perfective aspect. The consecutive forms are roughly converted forms (imperfect consecutive = perfect and perfect consecutive = imperfect). Imperfect consecutive is both an instantaneous past tense and the perfective aspect. This is the view of Joüon and Muraoka.[39]

3) *THE SYSTEM IS BOTH ASPECTUAL AND TEMPORAL.* The "imperfect consecutive" is a past tense and not an aspect. The other three components are aspects. This is the view of E. Lipinski.[40]

Now let us take a look at the pros and cons for the view that imperfect consecutive (IC) is a separate conjugation with past meaning:

Figure E.13

The Pros and Cons for Viewing the Imperfect Consecutive as a Separate Conjugation with Past Meaning

PROS	CONS
IC is different from a simple imperfect because of prefixed *wa* and different stress. It should therefore have a separate meaning.	In unpointed texts there is no difference, so the difference might have been invented by the Masoretes.
	How the conjugation *waw*, together with a short "a" can transform a verb to the opposite aspect, has never been fully explained.

---

[38] *Biblical Hebrew Syntax*, pp. 477, 497, 525, 546.

[39] P. Joüon and T. Muraoka, *A Grammar of Biblical Hebrew* (Roma: Editrice Pontificio Istituto Biblico, 1991), pp. 386, 390.

[40] *Semitic Languages: Outline of a Comparative Grammar*, p. 341.

IC is the normal narrative verb form with past meaning.	There are at least 399 examples of ICs with definite, non-past meaning, and 46 examples of imperfects with prefixed *we* with past meaning.[41]
IC is a preterite because the short imperfect stem is used in most instances. A similar short stem serves as preterite in Accadian and Ugaritic.	The short imperfect stem is, in Hebrew, used for modality. A confusion between past time and past tense may be the cause for claims about an Accadian and Ugaritic preterite.[42]
IC is always sentence-initial; when an adverb or another element occurs first, the perfect is used. This suggests that IC is perfective because it plays the same role as the perfect.	This observation (on the Pro side) can simply be a matter of style, not of semantics. There are so many exceptions to the rule that the argument practically vanishes.

The conclusion regarding imperfect consecutive is that in the almost 50 years that have passed since the NWT translators discarded the theory, no strong evidence has been discovered to defend the theory. The traditional, four-component model of the Hebrew verbal system is even more enigmatic today than it was in 1950.

THE MEANING OF THE ASPECTS

The NWTREF (Appendix 3C, page 1572) gives the following definition of Hebrew aspects: "The Hebrew verb has two states, the perfect state and the imperfect state. The perfect state

---

[41] See Rolf Furuli, "Imperfect Consecutive," for the particular passages. Other pros and cons are also discussed.

[42] In Greek, there are not many clear examples of aorist being used for non-past time. Nevertheless, two recent dissertations (Porter and Olsen) conclude that aorist does not include past tense. To the best of my knowledge, there exist no studies of Semitic verbs which systematically have studied the difference between past time and past tense, in the Semitic languages.

indicates completed action. The imperfective aspect indicates incomplete or continuous action, or action in progress."

This definition of aspect evidently is viewed as valid for Greek verbs, also. However, the definition, particularly the part which says that the perfect state indicates completed action, is at odds with the model of Greek and Hebrew verbs presented in this book.

This model is completely new and is presented here for the first time, so it would not be right for me to evaluate the definition given by the NWT translators in the light of it. But to help the readers make "informed choices" we need to consider the situation in greater detail.

We may start by noting that a brand new grammar by the distinguished scholar E. Lipinski, comparing the different Semitic languages, uses the same words in its definition of aspects as did the NWT translators. But such an agreement is not normally found in linguistic works on aspect and in other modern treatments of Hebrew grammar.

The NWT translation comittee worked with the biblical text in the 1940s and 1950s, during a time when most grammatical works on the biblical languages endorsed the completed/incomplete distinction between the aspects. It was really only from 1970 onward that the linguistic study of aspect gained momentum, when theses and monographs on this subject began to appear with increasing frequency.

There was one problem with the old definition which soon became apparent, namely, that a definition of the perfective aspect as "completed" put undue stress on the termination of the action. In the definition "completed" a temporal element might also be included, because what is objectively completed must also be past in relation to the time of speech/writing, or to some other point of time. Thus, it is not possible to define a perfective aspect as "completed," when it is time indifferent.

The use of "complete/incomplete" by Waltke and O'Connor is better because it takes away the inherent time factor, but from the point of view of the model presented in this book it is still unsatisfactory. This is so because it might suggest an objective definition of aspect. A situation which is complete must contain beginning, middle and end, but as seen in figure E.12, in some cases a state will continue beyond the focus of the perfective verb, and when the focus in connection with the perfective aspect is ingressive, the end of the state is not included. So "complete" is not a fitting definition for these situations.

What about the definition "incomplete"? It also suggests that aspects are objective, because incompleteness must also be seen in relation to the beginning, middle and end. In addition, terms such as "continuous action" or "action in progress" which are terms of *Aktionsart* or procedural traits, will even more strongly stress the objective nature of aspects.

Therefore, I return to the definition of aspect as articulated on pages 79-92 of this book. The imperfective aspect is a close-up view of a small part of an event or state with details visible, and the perfective aspect is a broader view from some distance with details not visible.

ASPECTS AND TRANSLATION

To return to the question of translation, we may ask: To which extent will a different view of aspects affect translation? Will the rendition of particular passages be different if we believe that the aspectual opposition is completed/incomplete, compared with the view that sees the opposition as complete/incomplete, or as a close-up, narrow perspective/a broader perspective from some distance? How should the NWT be viewed in relation to these questions?

To find the meaning of a clause, it is mandatory that we scrutinize the interplay of all the relevant semantic planes. The NWT translators evidently were extremely careful in finding all the different nuances of each clause, and because *Aktionsart* and procedural characteristics are much more important factors than aspect, their translation of Greek clauses was relatively unaffected by a definition of aspect in *Aktionsart* terms. This conclusion is confirmed by the fact that the time indifferent aorist is more often used for completed events than is the case with the corresponding Hebrew perfect; therefore, it is often fitting to render Greek aorist with English past tense. However, one may wonder if a future tense would not have been a better choice for the aorist of *erchomai* in Jude 1:14. Still, the NWT's choice of past tense illustrates the extreme faithfulness of the NWT translators toward their own translation principles.

The situation is more complex for Hebrew than for Greek. The definition of the imperfective aspect as "incomplete," or as indicating "continuous action" would not greatly affect the translation of the Hebrew imperfect or imperfect consecutive, compared with what would be the case if we used the definitions given in this book. In fact, what is seen by a close-up view, through the aspect peephole, is "continuous action." Thus, confusion between a subjective aspect and an objective situation viewed through the peephole of the aspect has little consequence for translation.

The translation of the Hebrew perfective aspect may, however, be affected. A definition of Hebrew perfect as "completed" introduces an element of past time, and if this conjugation really is time indifferent, it is clear that such a definition will affect its translation. This will not so much influence the translation of prose texts, provided that the translators are sensitive to the different semantic planes, particularly the context. But in poetic and prophetic texts, where the context has less importance for the choice of time in translation, the problem will be more noticeable. A definition of perfect as "completed" will, in such texts, tend to give more renderings with past tense than what is warranted.

To give an example of the problems involved in translating the Hebrew verbs, and at the same time give a practical test of the quality of the NWT, I have chosen Psalm 107. From working with this Psalm in the classroom, I know it is difficult to translate, in terms of vocabulary, syntax and, not least, the verbs.

After working with it in connection with this book, and comparing the NWT with other translations, my judgement is that the NWT translation of it is a really beautiful piece of work which recommends the scholarship of its translators.

PSALM 107

The Psalm starts with the exhortation "give thanks to YHWH." A similar exhortation is found in verses 8, 15, 21(22), and 31(32). So the Psalm consists of five parts: verses 2-7, 9-14, 16-20, 23-30, and 33-43. The most important problem is the time perspective of each part, and to find that is not easy, a fact which is seen in the different choices of the following 10 translations:

Figure E.14

Tenses Chosen by Different Translations for Psalm 107

TRANSLATION	PAST	PRESENT	FUTURE
NWT	2-20	23-42	43
NRSV	2-30	33-42	—
NAB	1-42	—	43
ASV	1-16	17-42	43
NASB	1-30	33-43	—
NIV	1-41	42-43	—
NJB	1-36	37-43	—
NKJV	1-20	23-43	—
RSV	1-30	33-43	—
TEV	1-41	42-43	—

Why is it so difficult to fix the time of the different parts of this Psalm? Because the meaning given to the conjugations by the traditional four-component model is very difficult to reconcile with the actual occurrence of verbs in the Psalm. The problem is that perfect (P) and imperfect consecutive (IC) normally are used for past time and imperfect (I) and imperfect conjunctive (ICJ) normally are used for present or future time. But in the Psalm they occur together! Take a look at the following numbers:

Figure E.15

The "Chaotic" Occurrence of Verb Forms

PART	VERSES	P	IC	I	ICJ
1	2-7	4	2	3	—
2	9-14	5	2	3	—
3	16-20	2	2	4	2
4	23-30	1	7	8	1
5	33-43	1	12	4	3

The verbs of parts 1 and 2 create few problems. The 9 perfects and 4 imperfect consecutives suggest that the setting is past. At least the last five occurrences of the 6 imperfects are somewhat anomalous in a past context, but they do not constitute a great problem. All the versions use a past setting for these two parts.

When we consider part 3, the picture is more complicated. There are 2 perfects and 2 imperfect consecutives which clearly suggest past time, but at the same time there are 4 imperfects and 2 imperfect conjunctives, which just as strongly suggest present or future time. Of the translations listed above, 9 out of the 10 listed, including the NWT, use a past setting for this part. Regarding the two imperfect conjunctives of verse 20 ("heal" and "deliver/escape") all translations except the ASV use past tense.

In 3 of the translations part 4 is viewed as present (NWT, ASV, and the NKJV), while the rest continue with the past setting. The 1 perfect and 7 imperfect consecutives in this section would suggest past time, while the 8 imperfects and the one imperfect conjunctive suggest present or future time.

In 7 of the versions we find a present setting for part 5 (NWT, NRSV, ASV, NASB, NKJ, and RSV; one version, NJB, takes verses 37-43 as present), and two versions (NIV and TEV) take verses 42 and 43 as present, and only NAB views the whole Psalm as having a past setting. The 1 perfect and the 12 imperfect consecutives would suggest past time, and the 4 imperfects and the 3 imperfect conjunctives would suggest present or future time.

It is quite interesting that the imperfect consecutives "dwell" and "establish" of verse 36, "plant," "sow," and "make fruit" of verse 37, "bless" and "become many" of verse 38, "wander" of verse 40, and "set" and "place" of verse 41, by the 7 versions using a present setting, are translated by present tense.

This flies in the face of both of the leading views of the traditional model (which claims that imperfect consecutive is a preterite, and that it is the perfective aspect)! It is also strange that the same 7 versions, except the NWT, translate the two imperfect consecutives "become few" and "bring low" of verse 39 by past or perfect tense.

This enhances the problem with the belief that the imperfect consecutives are different from normal imperfects. So there can be no doubt that this Psalm is very difficult, if not impossible to reconcile with the traditional four-component model. Using a past tense setting for the whole Psalm, as does the NAB, implies that 22 imperfects and 6 imperfect conjunctives must be translated by past tense, and this is inconsistent, to say the least. Using the present tense setting for part 4 and 5, or just part 5, implies the translation of 19 and 12 imperfect consecutives, respectively, with present tense, and this is even more inconsistent.

But what about the NWT definition of perfect as "completed"? How does this affect its translation of the Psalm? The 11 perfects in the past setting of verses 2-20 evidently represent actions which had come to their end. In the present setting of verses 22-43 we find two perfects. The perfect "see" in verse 24 is translated by a present perfect, though all the other verbs in this part (4) are translated by present tense. It is likely that the choice of present perfect in this case rests primarily on the definition of perfect as "completed," because I can see no other reason why this verb should not also be translated by present tense, as does the NKJV (or as future, as does the ASV).

In verse 42, the clause with the perfect "shut" is translated as, "it has to shut its mouth." This makes the clause almost modal, because "have to" can in English be used instead of ordinary modals. This indicates a kind of stress, and the translators have chosen this construction because of the use of the perfect.

What is interesting with this example, is that the definition of Hebrew perfect as "completed" seems to have been transferred from the objective to the subjective sphere. To use "completed" in the objective sense means that the event is past in relation to some point of time. But this is not the case in verse 42. So, at most, the phrase "has to shut" can be viewed conceptually "completed," or, better, as conceptually completed in an imagined world. If this is the way the translators reasoned, it takes away some of the problems with the definition "completed," because then it is not strictly objective, but in no way does it make the definition acceptable.

By way of conclusion, from this Psalm we can learn that the Hebrew verbal system is quite enigmatic, and that the only way to come to grips with it and to explain it to others is to use definitions which can account for *all* the uses of the verbs in the Bible.

CHAPTER 4

THE TRINITY DOCTRINE
AS A TRANSLATION PROBLEM

The following discussion is neither meant to be apologetic nor theological but rather philological. I am not so much interested in the trinity doctrine as an expression of faith, as I am in its origin and in the possibility of using it as background information for Bible translation. The basic question is whether the doctrine can be traced back to the Bible. Do the words used to articulate the doctrine represent a concentrate of the biblical words about God? Or does the doctrine represent theological opinions invented *after* the Bible was completed? The trinity doctrine is a translation problem, because it, more than any other doctrine, has influenced the renditions of particular passages about Jesus and The holy spirit, and these very passages are at the heart of the discussion of the role of bias in Bible translation.

Our understanding of God cannot be based upon reason or logic alone[1]; we cannot figure out who God is. We are completely dependent upon his revelation. At the outset we do not know what God is like, and, therefore, there is no *a priori* reason why he could not be "one substance but three persons" as the trinity doctrine teaches. True, this teaching does represent a contradiction of terms, but this is not without parallel among the things created by God. The electron, for instance, may both be viewed as a particle and a beam, which is a mutually exclusive description. If we have a vessel with liquid helium and we lower the temperature to a point just above absolute zero, the liquid may, in a "violation" of the law of gravity, start to flow upwards and over the rim of the vessel. Einstein's theories of relativity also contain expressions that seem to contradict common sense. Therefore, to find out what God is

---

[1] We can, however, use our powers of reason to learn some things about God (Rom 1:19, 20; 12:1).

like we should start with an open mind, study his revelation of himself, as found in the Bible, and accept the results even though they might appear to be a contradiction of terms.

To pose the problem more explicitly, if it can definitely be shown by considering various passages in the Bible that there is just one God and at the same time that the Father is God, the Son is God and The holy spirit is God (and if the word "God" is used in exactly the same sense in reference to these three), then we can use the trinity doctrine as a translation principle, even though its words represent a contradiction of terms. In such a case, the doctrine cannot be attacked using the laws of philosophy and logic, because its different parts are expressed in simple unambiguous words, rooted in God's revelation. This would force us to accept something which, to our human mind, seems to be a contradiction. But it really would not be, given the above scenario, because human words, only by analogy, describe spiritual realities.

If, on the other hand, biblical passages which fulfill the requirements of the preceding paragraph cannot be found, then the trinity doctrine is the result of human reasoning and human viewpoints. In this case, it can be attacked because it is not found in the Bible, and thus not a part of God's revelation. In this case, too, its inherent contradictions can be attacked on the basis of the laws of philosophy and logic, because its words no longer have "diplomatic immunity," which they would have if they were rooted in God's revelation. What, then, can we learn about this subject?

The Old Testament stresses the unity of God. God is one! (Deut 6:39) The Spirit of God is also mentioned, but there is no description of any relationship between God and his Spirit, nor is any personality ascribed to the Spirit. One commenator writes, "In the Old Testament the spirit of Yahweh was a mysterious divine force that produced peculiar effects on or in men."[2]

In the New Testament there are some passages which mention the Father, the Son and The holy spirit together,[3] but

---

[2] E. J. Fortman, *The Triune God: A Historical Study of the Doctrine of the Trinity* (Grand Rapids: Baker, 1972), p. 14.

[3] For instance, Matthew 28:19; 2 Corinthians 13:13; Galatians 4:4-6.

there is no description of any relationship between the three. The fact, therefore, is that none of the writers of the biblical books saw the need for an ontological identification of the Father, the Son and The holy spirit, or a description of their relationship with each other. They certainly did not formulate a creedal confession expressing faith in an ontological realtionship between the three. The trinity, therefore, as a *fully* stated doctrine, is not found in the Bible! But do the tenets that make up the doctrine exist in the Bible?

SOME HISTORICAL THOUGHT LEADING UP TO THE DEVEOPMENT OF THE TRINITY DOCTRINE

The scriptural points with which the minds of the church Fathers wrestled can be stated as follows: The Word, whom they identified with Jesus Christ, is called *theos* ("god," Joh 1:1). The Word became flesh (Joh 1:14). Wisdom, whom they also identified with Jesus Christ, was produced as the beginning of God's ways (Prov 8:32). The Son, Jesus Christ, was generated (begotten) by God (Heb 1:2, 4). Christians should be baptized in the name of the Father, the Son, and The holy spirit (Matt 28:19). Jesus was the saviour of mankind (Joh 3:16) and he should be honored together with the Father (Rev 5:12).

Surrounded by unbiblical religions, different philosophical movements and heretical Christian groups, the Fathers saw the need to defend this biblical material, to explain and define it.[4] This they did in their writings, many of which we still have, and in their church councils, where they tried to make a synthesis of these explanations and definitions. Thus, the trinity doctrine gradually came into being, particularly as a result of the decisions made by the councils at Nicaea in 325 CE, at Constantinople in 381 CE, and at Chalcedon in 451 CE.

---

[4] I will not go into much detail here, but simply stress that the Fathers did zig-zag their way toward a fully expressed trinity doctrine. The viewpoints and decisions of different councils went back and forth and the fight against perceived heresies and political questions seems to have shaped the doctrine more than a genuine quest for biblical truth.

Before we start to review the material I should point out that I am neither an expert in patristic thought nor an expert in the different Greek philosophical systems, though I have undertaken an extensive reading of some of the original sources as well as many books that make use of the primary sources. Therefore, I am confident that I can present here excerpts from the Fathers and historians that will throw light on the origins of trinitarianism.

There are two important sources from which the Fathers drew, namely, the Bible and Greek philosophy. Nobody denies that the Fathers were influenced by both; the question is to what extent they were influenced by each source. Or to put it differently: Was it the Fathers' understanding that Jesus should be worshiped—that it was such an understanding that led them to view him as God, because only God should be worshiped? And was it their understanding that only God could save mankind which led them to believe that the saviour, Jesus, was God? Or was Plato's trinity an important basis for the Christian trinity doctrine? Or could it be that the trinity doctrine was a combination of Greek philosophy and the Fathers' understanding of the Bible?

The questions are very complicated, and different answers have been given. Most church historians give the Bible a more prominent place than Greek philosophy,[5] though nobody denies that the Fathers also were influenced by philosophy. There can be little doubt that a certain kind of religious faith (or lack of it) in the authors influenced the stress they placed either on the Bible or on philosophy as the most important source, as Hanson[6] also points out.

The first section below is about the subordinationist view of the Ante-Nicene Fathers, and there is little disagreement about this issue; what is said is generally accepted by most experts in patristic thought. The second section about the belief in the eternal generation of the Son, among the same Fathers, is

---

[5] An old but fine discussion is found in Edwin Hatch's *The Influence of Greek Ideas and Usages on the Christian Church*, ed. A. M. Fairbairn, 5th ed. (Peabody, Mass.: Hendrickson, 1995 [repr. of 1895 ed.]).

[6] R. P. C. Hanson, *The Search for the Christian Doctrine of God* (Edinburgh: T & T Clark, 1988), p. 824.

also generally not disputed. What may be challenged are the links I draw between the Fathers, Platonism, Middle-Platonism, Neo-Platonism and the thoughts of Philo. I believe my case is quite strong, but I freely admit that scholars disagree on some of these issues. So the reader must take it for what it is: an attempt to illuminate the sources of thought about Jesus, which do not have their origin in the Bible.

THE SUBORDINATIONIST VIEW OF THE ANTE-NICENE FATHERS

Going through the writings of the Ante-Nicene Fathers, we find that practically all of them entertained subordinationist views, that is, they believed that the Son was inferior to the Father; and these views were based upon their interpretation of biblical passages. This is seen by the scores upon scores of scripture quotations they used to prove their position. Following is a sketch of the views of the principal Ante-Nicene Fathers and Ante-Nicene literature.

When you consider what they wrote, we find that many of them viewed Jesus as both inferior to the Father and also one who is *theos* ("god"). What each one meant by applying *theos* to Jesus must be deteremined by considering the writings of the paricular Father whom we are studying. For now we should keep in mind that there is no evidence that any of the Fathers used *theos* in the later trinitarian sense of the word, nor in the modern sense.

Didakhe, or *Teaching of the Twelve Apostles,* which is an expression of Christian faith from around 100 CE, adds nothing to the biblical expressions regarding baptism, and it simply states that they should "baptize in the name of the Father the name of the Son and of the Holy spirit in living water" (7:1).[7]

Clement, bishop of Rome, wrote a letter around 100 CE wherein he said, "Let all nations know thee, that thou art God alone, and that Jesus Christ is thy child" (59:4).[8] Clement did not

---

[7] Kirsopp Lake, *The Apostolic Fathers,* vol. 1 (The Loeb Classical Library; Cambridge, Mass.: Harvard University Press, 1975), p. 321.

[8] Kirsopp Lake, *The Apostolic Fathers,* vol. 1, p. 113.

say that Jesus should be worshiped; rather, he said, "Let us reverence [*entrepō*] the Lord Jesus Christ" (21:6).[9]

Ignatius wrote an epistle at the beginning of the second century. In his letter to the Romans (Introduction), he twice refers to "Jesus Christ our God," but just before this he spoke of "the Most High Father, and of Jesus Christ his only Son." In 3:3 he again speaks of "our God Jesus Christ." In his letter to the Smyrnaeans (1:1), he said, "I glorify Jesus Christ, the God who made you so wise," and in his letter to Polycarp (8:3) he speaks of "our God Jesus Christ."

However, in his epistle to the Magnesians he differentiates between the Father and the Son "Before the ages he was with [*para*] the Father" (6:1). He also says that the Son "came forth from [*apo*] the one Father and is with [*eis*] one and departed to the one" (7:2) One church historian says about Ignatius that he "never held that the Father suffered, nor did he confuse the Son with the Father."[10]

Justin Martyr (110-165 CE) stated the following when discussing the importance of baptism: "For in the name of God, the Father and Lord of the universe, and of our Saviour Jesus Christ, and of the Holy Spirit, they then receive the washing with water."[11] About Jesus he further stated, "We reasonably worship Him, having learned that He is the Son of the true God Himself, and holding Him in the second place, and the prophetic Spirit in the third."[12] However, in the same book Justin said that good angels and the Spirit also are worshiped by the Christians.[13]

In chapter 128 in *Dialogue with the Jew Trypho,* Jesus is called both "God the son of God" and "Angel." In both chapters

---

[9] Kirsopp Lake, *The Apostolic Fathers*, vol. 1, p. 47.

[10] Robert M. Grant, *Gods and the One God* (Philadelphia: Westminster Press, 1986), p. 108.

[11] ANF 1, p. 183.

[12] ANF 1, p. 166.

[13] ANF 1, p. 164. A footnote says this about including the angels in worship: "This is the literal and obvious translation of Justin's words. But from c. 13, 16 and 61, it is evident that he did not desire to inculcate the worship of angels."

61 and 129 he quotes Proverbs 8:22, "The Lord created [or, 'made,' chapter 61] me the beginning of his ways for his works." The difference between Jesus Christ and God, in the eyes of Justin, as well as the subordination of Jesus, is clearly stated in the two following quotes:

> The Scripture has declared that this Offspring was begotten by the Father before all things created; and that that which is begotten is numerically distinct from that which begets, any one will admit.[14]

> I say that there is, and is said to be, another God and Lord, subject to [or, according to the footnote, 'going away, departed'] the Maker of all things; who is also called an Angel, because he announces to men whatsoever the Maker of all things—above whom there is no other God—wishes to announce to them. . . . He who is said to have appeared to Abraham, and to Jacob, and to Moses, and who is called God, is distinct from him who made all things,—numerically I mean, not [distinct] in will.[15]

Irenaeus (c. 130-200 CE) differentiated between Jesus as *theos*, and the Father: "No other is named as God, or is called Lord, except Him who is God and Lord of all, who also said to Moses, 'I am that I am' . . . and His Son Jesus Christ our Lord."[16] He also wrote, "There is one God, the Father over all, and one Word of God, who is through all."[17]

Theophilus (116-181 CE) also believed that the Logos, in a way, was produced:

> But when God wished to make all that he determined to do, He begot this Word, uttered, "the firstborn of all creation."[18]

---

[14] ANF 1, p. 264.

[15] ANF 1, p. 223.

[16] ANF 1, pp. 330, 419.

[17] ANF 1, p. 546.

[18] ANF 2, p. 103.

God, then, having his own Logos internal within His own bowels, begot Him, emitting Him along with His own wisdom before all things. He had this Word as a helper in the things that were created by Him.[19]

Clement of Alexandria (150-215 CE) called Jesus "God and creator."[20] However, in the same book he quotes Jesus' words from Matthew 19:17, that just one is good, namely, God. He then says that "the God and Father of our Lord Jesus is good."[21] He spoke about "the nature of the Son, which is nearest to Him who is alone the Almighty One." A few lines later he says about the Son, "To him is placed in subjection all the hosts of angels and gods; He, the paternal Word, exhibiting the holy administration for Him who put [all] in subjection to him."[22]

Tertullian (160-230 CE) was a philosopher, lawyer and theologian. He was the first to use the Latin word *trinitas*, but the meaning he ascribed to the word was completely different from the one it came to have in the last part of the fourth century. According to him the Word was a person in the sense of a being numerically different from the Father and subordinate to him:

> Thus the connection of the Father in the Son, and of the Son in the Paraclete, produces three coherent persons *who are yet distinct* One from Another. These Three are one *essence* not one *Person*, as it is said, "I and the Father are one" in respect of unity of substance, not singularity of number.[23]

In the rest of the chapter he quotes many passages from the Bible showing that the Father and the Son are two distinct beings, and that the Father is the God even of the Son.[24] In the

---

[19] ANF 2, p. 98.

[20] ANF 2, p. 234.

[21] ANF 2, p. 227.

[22] ANF 2, p. 524.

[23] ANF 3, p. 621.

[24] ANF 3, pp. 600, 602.

same book, at the end of chapter 4, the expression "two different Beings" is used, and at the end of chapter 7 he writes, "While I recognize the Son, I assert his distinction as second to the Father." In chapter 9 he states:

> For the Father is the entire substance, but the Son is a derivation and portion of the whole, as He Himself acknowledges: "My Father is greater than I." . . . Thus the Father is distinct from the Son, inasmuch as he who begets is One, and He who is begotten is another; He too, who sends is one, and He who is sent is another; and He, again, who makes is one, and He through whom the thing is made is another.[25]

Tertullian even said that "Father" was not an eternal designation of God:

> He [God the Father] has not always been Father and Judge, merely of the ground of His having always been God. For He could not have been the Father previous to the Son, nor a Judge previous to sin. There was, however, a time when neither sin existed with Him, nor the Son."[26]

Athenagoras (late second century CE) expressed that Logos was a work, but in accordance with more detail that we will see later, he also believed that the Logos was eternal: "I will state briefly that He is the first product of the Father, not as having been brought into existence (for from the beginning, God, who is the eternal mind [*nous*], had the Logos in Himself, being from eternity instinct with Logos [*logikos*])."[27] He calls Jesus "God" but he does not use this word of the Spirit: "The Holy Spirit Himself also, which operates in the prophets, we assert to be an effluence of God, flowing from Him, and returning back again like a beam of the sun."[28]

---

[25] ANF 3, p. 604.

[26] ANF 3, p. 478.

[27] ANF 2, p. 133.

[28] ANF 2, p. 133.

Hippolytus (170-236 CE) viewed the Logos as one who was brought forth by the Father, but who also was *theos*:

> Therefore this solitary and supreme Deity, by an exercise of reflection, brought forth the Logos first; not the word in the sense *of being articulated by* voice, but as a retinociation of the universe conceived and residing in the divine mind. Him alone He produced from existing things . . . The Logos alone of this *God* is from *God* himself; wherefore also *the Logos* is God, being *the* substance of God.[29]

Novatian (210-280 CE) composed a book on the trinity wherein he wrote, among other things, the following: "For Scripture as much announces Christ as also God, as it announces God Himself as man."[30] Jesus Christ, however, was not equal with the Father:

> Yet he obtained this from the Father that he should be both God of all and should be Lord, and be begotten and made known from Himself as God, in the form of God the Father. . . . Whence it is proved that *the claim of* a certain divinity would be robbery, to wit, that of equalling Himself with God the Father. . . . For who does not acknowledge that the person of the Son is second after the Father, when he reads that it was said by the Father, consequently to the Son, "Let us make man in our image and our likness."[31]

After this we find fifteen quotes from the Bible to prove that Jesus Christ is different from the Father. Later in the same book he points to the fact that Paul and Apollos are different "persons."[32] In a similar vein he says concerning Jesus: "In receiving, then, sanctification from the Father, He is inferior to

---

[29] ANF 5, pp. 150, 151.

[30] ANF 5, p. 620.

[31] ANF 5, pp. 633, 636.

[32] See ANF 5, pp. 637-638.

the Father. Now, consequently, who is inferior to the Father, is *not the Father*, but the Son."[33]

Origen (185-255 CE) probably was the most learned and influential of the Ante-Nicene Fathers. Prestige writes:

> Origen insisted most emphatically on the distinct and concrete individuality of the Son, and stressed no less emphatically the gulf which separates the triad of the godhead from all created beings. He nevertheless permitted himself to utter some extraordinarily strong statements of the subordination of the Spirit and the Logos.[34]

Origen's important writing *De Principiis* is extant for the most part in a Latin translation by Rufinus. Rufinus was against Arianism[35] and admits that he altered some passages from Origen's work. Emperor Justin, who wanted to prove that Origen was a heretic, quoted, in his letter to Menna, passages about Jesus Christ from the Greek version of *De Principiis*.[36] If these quotes are genuine, then they show that Origen held to a strong subordinationist view:

> Now this the Son is begotten of the will of the Father, who is the Image of the Invisible God, and the effluence of His glory, the representation of His substance (*hupostaseos*), the firstborn of all creation, a creature (*ktisma*), Wisdom. For Wisdom herself says: "God created (*ektise*) me as the beginning of his ways unto His works."[37]

---

[33] ANF 5, p. 638.

[34] G. L. Prestige, *God in Patristic Thought* (London: S. P. C. K., 1952), p. 132.

[35] Arius claimed that Jesus was created by God as his first creature and that there was a time when he did not exist. He became the symbol of those fighting against the belief that the Father and the Son were consubstantial, even though, as Hanson (*The Search for the Christian Doctrine of God*, p. xvii) shows, he probably played only a minor role.

[36] R. S. Franks, *The Doctrine of the Trinity* (London: Gerald Duckworth and Co., 1953), p. 89.

[37] Franks, *The Doctrine of the Trinity*, p. 92.

Jesus Christ is to be worshiped, but not in the same manner as the Father:

> Accordingly, we worship with all our power the one God, and His only Son, the Word and the Image of God, by prayers and supplications; and we offer our petitions to the God of the universe through his only-begotten Son.[38]

All the Fathers who are quoted in this section believed that Jesus was *theos*, and that he should be worshiped or shown honor, though they did not necessarily use the words "God" and "worship" with the same meaning as when they were applied to the Creator of the universe, the Father. Regarding the relation between the Father and the Son, we can summarize this section with a quote from Hanson:

> With the exception of Athanasius virtually every theologian, East and West, accepted some form of subordinationism at least up to the year 355; subordinationism might indeed, until the dénouement of the controversy, have been described as accepted orthodoxy.[39]

It is interesting that in the period before Nicaea a universal subordinationist view existed among the Fathers. At the same time many of them believed that only God could save mankind and that Jesus should, in some sense, be worshiped. What relieved any real tension was probably that "worship" had a scale from mere respect in one end, to real worship in the other. This means that while the Fathers in this period used the Bible extensively, they did not conclude that passages contained therein contradicted the view that Jesus was different from and inferior to God the Father.

---

[38] ANF 4, p. 644.

[39] Hanson, *The Search for the Christian Doctrine of God*, p. xix.

THE ANTE-NICENE FATHERS' VIEW OF THE ETERNAL GENERATION OF THE SON

From one point of view is it wrong to say that the Ante-Nicene Fathers believed in the Son's eternal generation. Strictly speaking, they did not believe that *the Son* was eternal, but *the reason* of God, from which the Son came forth (or was articulated), was eternal.[40] From another point of view, the Word, even before he came forth, was a part of God's reason; thus, the Son, in this sense, was eternal. In the writings of these Fathers we, for the first time, meet this self-contradictory dualism, where they refused to decide between the fighting parties' "either this or that" views, and instead said "both this and that"—a way of thinking which became so characteristic for the church councils that gave rise to the trinity doctrine.

Looking at the statements of the Fathers about the eternal generation of the Son, we are baffled by the lack of scriptural quotations. Instead of using phrases as "because it is written" and "as it is said," the language of many of them is more philosophical, and the author tries to reason with the readers, appealing to their intelligence. The reason for this might be twofold: 1) There are no passages in the Bible which say that the Word, Wisdom or Son is eternal.[41] 2) Greek philosophy had a profound influence on many of the Fathers, and the eternal and unchangeable existence of God and of his Ideas was fundamentally a philosophical thought.

The eternal existence of the Son is one of the most important aspects of the trinity doctrine, and it was definitely

---

[40] E. J. Fortman, *The Triune God*, p. 50, writes: "If God must have His Logos from eternity, must he also have His Son? Later theology and dogma will say yes unequivocally, but the apologists are not quite clear on this point and rather seem to say no. For them, if the origination of Logos from God is eternal, the generation of the Logos as Son seems rather to be pre-creational but not eternal, and it is affected by the will of the Father."

[41] The nearest we come is Hebrews 1:2, where the Son is said to have made the *aiōnas*, so he must necessarily have existed before them. However, while the word *aiōn* can be used for "eternity," it may, as in this verse, mean "the ages," "the system of things," that is, periods of time characterized by given circumstances.

the most important point at issue in Nicaea; therefore, as an aid in helping us understand the source and background of the trinity doctrine, it is important to discuss the origin of the belief in the Son's eternal generation. Below we will present evidence that three primary sources influenced the formation of this conviction, namely, Platonism, the combination of Middle Platonism and Jewish speculation found in Philo of Alexandria, and Neo Platonism.[42]

If we compare the account of Noah and the flood in the Bible with the account of the Babylonian "Noah" in the book *Atrahasis*, we find so many striking parallels that it is impossible that the two accounts have originated separately. Because the Babylonin cuneiform documents are older than any existing Bible manuscripts, many researchers have concluded that the Bible adopted material from a Babylonian original. However, no one can deny *the possibility* of the reverse, namely, that the Babylonian account was borrowed from a Hebrew original, or, more likely, that both have a common source.

This aptly illustrates the problem of pinpointing the source of the thoughts of particular church Fathers. It would therefore be methodologically wrong just to compare the thoughts of the Fathers with these philosophical systems and claim that a resemblance with one system proves that the origin of a particular Father's thought was from that very system. However, as to time, all the philosophical systems we are discussing existed prior to the Fathers, with the exception of Origen and Neo-Platonism. Thus, our problem may be reduced to this question: When the Fathers used the same words and expressions as were common in a particular philosophic system, did they also adopt the *references* behind the words, that is, the teachings of the system, or did they just use the words because these were the normal expressions of the day?

We cannot answer this with certainty. But because there are no passages in the Bible which clearly show that the Son is eternal, and becaue the Fathers' quotations from the Bible in

---

[42] There may also be other influences, such as those from the Stoic doctrine about the creating Logos who is God, but the three mentioned above seem to be the chief ones. Compare E. P. Meijering, *Orthodoxy or Platonism in Athanasius: Synthesis or Antithesis?* (Leiden: Brill, 1964), p. 54.

relation to this subject are sparse, and since they use philosophical language to articulate their thoughts on this matter, there is a strong probability that not only the words but also their thoughts about the Son's eternal existence were influenced by Greek philosophy.

Plato's trinity consisted of a nameless God, *Hen* ("the One"), *Nous* ("The Ideas") and *Pneuma* ("The Spirit" or "world-soul").[43] The interpretation that originated with Aristotle, described the Ideas as self-subsistent, real incorporeal beings, and one of them, the idea of the Good, was God.[44] Another interpretation that emerged was that the Ideas were not real beings but only the thoughts of God, thus existing inside God. This view was adopted by Neo-Platonism. A third view was voiced by Philo, a Jewish philosopher from Alexandria writing in the first part of the first century CE. He taught that the Ideas, which constitute the intelligible world and which are contained in the Logos, have two successive stages of existence, first as thoughts of God and later as real beings created by God.[45]

When Philo applied his view to "Wisdom" as spoken of in the book of Proverbs (particularly in chapter 8), which was identical with the Logos, wisdom was conceived of having three stages of existence. 1) Wisdom existed from eternity as a

---

[43] A. Grillmeyer, *Christ in Christian Tradition: Volume One From the Apostolic Age to Chalcedon (451)* (Atlanta: John Knox Press, 1975), p. 107.

[44] Compare Meijering, *Orthodoxy or Platonism in Athanasius*, pp. 11, 12.

[45] H. A. Wolfson, *The Philosophy of the Church Fathers* (Cambridge, Mass.: Harvard University Press, 1970), p. 258. Consider Hanson's observation on this matter: "Wolfson was obsessed to an excessive degree with the influence of Philo on the Fathers; Philo's *Logos*-doctrine is confused and obscure" (*The Search for the Christian Doctrine of God*, p. 60). Regarding other influences, he writes: "But in fact all Greek-speaking writers of the fourth century were to a lesser or greater degree indebted to Greek philosophy" (*The Search for the Christian Doctrine of God*, p. 858). However, Hanson seems to mean that the Bible can be interpreted to bolster almost any of the competing viewpoints regarding the Son and The holy spirit. Therefore, the Bible is the principal source of the Fathers, and they use philosophical language to explain their interpretations of it because of their familiarity with this language. Only specialists can throw light on the question about who gives a true representation. In any case, it is clear that Philo taught that the Logos existed from eternity.

thought of God; 2) Wisdom was created as a real incorporeal being and was used as God's instrument, or, rather, as a "plan," in the creation of the world; and 3) Wisdom was implanted within our world and acted as the instrument of divine providence in every part of it.[46] Many of the Fathers who held the subordinationist view of the Son, and at the same time held a two stage theory of the Son's generation, seem to have adopted it from Philo.[47]

Already *Ignatius*, writing in the middle of the second century, spoke of "Jesus Christ His Son, who is His eternal word (*logos aidos*)."[48] What he meant by this is not clear, but after him the Philonic influence seems to be at work, as noted by one source:

> Beginning with Justin Martyr, however, down to Clement of Alexandria among the Greek Fathers and to Lactantius among the Latin Fathers, the discussion of the preexistent Christ shows unmistakable evidence of the influence of the Philonic Logos. All these Fathers seem to have identified the Johannine Logos with the Philonic Logos, they also seem to have known of Philo's twofold stage theory of the preexistent Logos, and they seem to have consciously transferred this twofold stage theory from the Philonic Logos to the Johannine Logos.[49]

Justin Martyr implies the eternity of Logos by saying, "God begat before all creatures a Beginning, a certain rational power from himself, who is called . . . Logos."[50]

---

[46] Wolfson, *The Philosophy of the Church Fathers*, p. 177.

[47] Grillmeyer, *Christ in Christian Tradition*, p. 108, writes: "There are two sources of the Logos doctrine of the Apologists: Christian tradition (the prologue of the Gospel of John) and Hellenistic philosophy (of the Middle Platonic and Stoic types)."

[48] ANF 1, p. 62.

[49] Wolfson, *The Philosophy of the Church Fathers*, p. 192.

[50] ANF 1, p. 227. Compare Wolfson, *The Philosophy of the Church Fathers*, pp. 192, 193.

Tatian showed a similar viewpoint by saying that the Logos "was in him [God]," and "by His simple will the Logos springs forth," that is, the Father "begat him."[51]

Athenagoras wrote: "I will state briefly that He is the first product of the Father, not as having been brought into existence, for from the beginning, God, who is the eternal mind [*nous*], had the Logos within Himself, being from eternity instinct with Logos [*logikos*]. . . . He came forth to be the idea and energizing power of all material things."[52]

Theophilus wrote:

> The Word, that always exists, residing within the heart of God. For before anything came into being He had Him as a counselor, being His own mind and thought. But when God wished to make all that he determined on, He begot His Word, uttered, the firstborn of all creation, not Himself being emptied of the Word [Reason], but having begotten Reason, and always conversing with His Reason.[53]

Hippolytus believed that the Logos was eternal *theos* and of the same essence as the Father: "For He who was co-existent with His Father before all time, and before the foundation of the world, always had the glory proper to the Godhead."[54]

Novatian wrote:

> But He who is before all time must be said to have been always in the Father; for no time can be assigned to Him who is before all time. . . . he has a beginning in that He is born, inasmuch as He is born of the Father who alone has no beginning. He, then, when the Father willed it, proceeded from the Father, and He who was in the Father, came forth from the Father.[55]

---

[51] ANF 2, p. 67.

[52] ANF 2, p. 133.

[53] ANF 2, p. 103.

[54] ANF 5, p. 167.

[55] ANF 5, p. 643.

Tertullian also believed that the Son was eternal, and because he is the one who gave the most detailed description of this belief, we will provide a lengthy quote from him on this point:

> For before all things God was alone . . . yet even not then was He alone; for He had within Him that which he possessed in Himself, that is to say, His own Reason. . . . This Reason is His own thought (or Consciousness) which the Greeks call *logos*, by which term we also designate Word *or Discourse.* . . . For although God had not yet sent *out* His Word, He still had Him within Himself, both in company with and included within His very Reason, as He silently planned and arranged within Himself everything which He was afterwards about to utter through His Word. . . . Observe, then, that when you are silently conversing with yourself, this very process is carried on within you by your reason, which meets you with a word at every movement of your thought. . . . Thus, in a certain sense the word is a second *person* within you. . . . The word is itself a differing thing from yourself. . . . I may therefore without rashness first lay this down (as a fixed principle) that even then before the creation of the universe God was not alone, since He had within Himself both Reason, and, inherent in Reason, His Word, which He made second to Himself by agitating it within Himself.[56]

After highlighting the eternal stage, Tertullian explains what is involved in the second stage:

> Then, therefore, does the Word also Himself assume His own form and glorious garb, *His own* sound and vocal utterance, when God says, "Let there be light." This is the perfect nativity of the Word, when He proceeds forth from God— *formed* by Him first to devise and think out *all things* under the name of Wisdom—"The Lord created *or formed* me as the beginning of His Ways;" then afterward *begotten,* to carry all into effect.[57]

---

[56] ANF 3, pp. 600, 601.

[57] ANF 3, p. 601.

Side by side with the two stage theory used by Justin Martyr, a one stage theory of the eternal generation of the Son emerged. The first one to introduce the groundwork for this idea was *Irenaeus*: "But the Son, eternally coexisting [*semper . . . coexistens*] with the Father, from of old, yea, from the beginning."[58] The words "from of old, yea, from the beginning" may have been intended to qualify the length of time denoted by "always coexisting," or they may have a similar meaning.[59] But the one who really elucidated the one stage generation theory was Origen, and in addition to philosophical arguments he also tried to find support for this view in the Bible: "Because his generation is eternal and everlasting [*aeterna ad sempiterna generatio*] as the brilliancy which is produced from the sun."[60] Also, "The Father did not generate the Son and dismiss him after he was generated, but he is always generating him [*aei genna*]."[61]

Origen evidently alludes to Hebrews 1:3, "He is the reflection of his glory," and he quotes Proverbs 8:25 which reads, according to the Septuagint: "Before the hills he generates [*genna*] me." The Septuagint verb is imperfective, focusing on ongoing action, but the Hebrew verb is perfective and can only mean that the action "to generate/create" was finished in the past.[62] Hebrews 1:3 does not say anything about time or eternity.

Origen (185-255 CE) studied under Ammonius Saccas, the originator of Neoplatonism, from 208 CE, while Plotinus, who made Neoplatonism into a coherent system was taught by this teacher between 232 and 242 CE. Comparing the systems of

---

[58] ANF 1, p. 406. In the same book (p. 380) Ireneaeus shows his faith in the world of ideas: "He Himself [God] receiving from Himself the model [*exemplum*] and figure [*figurationem*] of those things which have been made."

[59] Wolfson, *The Philosophy of the Church Fathers*, p. 199.

[60] ANF 4, p. 247.

[61] In Jerem., Hom. IX 4 (PG 13, 357A); Wolfson, *The Philosophy of the Church Fathers*, p. 201, note 14.

[62] A Hebrew perfect may portray the action as complete, with its beginning and end included. If the context shows that the action occurred in the past, it is not only complete but also completed.

Philo and Plotinus we find some differences, of which we will take note of those relating to the realm of the Ideas. Both of them take Plato as a point of departure and start with "the One." The world of the Ideas is called Logos by Philo, while Plotinus restores the original Platonic and Aristotelian term Nous. In Philo, the Logos is created by the Demiurge (the One), while Plotinus claims that Nous is continuously being generated (*aei gennomenon*)[63] by God from eternity. Origen composed his writings before Plotinus; Wolfson rightly says that the "similarity between Origen and Plotinus is striking, and it certainly cannot be explained as a mere coincidence."[64]

But Wolfson traces it back to what both learned from Ammonius. It therefore seems that the two-stage view of the Son's eternal generation was influenced by Philo's thoughts whereas the one-stage view was influenced by Neo-Platonism.

Summing up the position of the Ante-Nicene Fathers we find that Ignatius, Justin Martyr, Irenaeus, Clement from Alexandria, Theophilus, Tertullian, Athenagoras, Hippolytus, Novatian and Origen accepted the biblical witness that the Son was different from the Father. But at the same time, based partly on Philonic and Neo-platonic thoughts, they believed in the Son's eternal generation. Let us now ascertain how this "both this and that" situation became formalized.

WORDS EXPRESSING SPIRITUAL CONCEPTS

The problem with the words of the trinity doctrine is that the words are meant to explain *concepts* of things that transcend the borders of our material worlds; we have no empirically based understanding of things in the spirit realm, though we attempt to use language to explain spiritual things. In such a situation, where the referents are qualitatively completely different from any referents existing in the natural world, then, when we are using words in reference to spiritual referents, it is

---

[63] See Wolfson, *The Philosophy of the Church Fathers*, p. 203, note 26.

[64] Wolfson, *The Philosophy of the Church Fathers*, p. 203.

important at the outset that we understand that we are making analogic use of words for the possibility of discourse respecting spiritual realities. Prestige, who criticizes the Arians extensively, says that "the supreme scandal of Arian theology was its misuse of biological language to express the act of creation."[65]

The Arians asked, for instance, how a son could be as old as his father, and because this is biologically impossible, they concluded that the Son was created. What Prestige calls "a scandal" is due to his starting and ending with the ordinary meaning of the words in question. But we can safely say that certain Bible writers, in their anthropomorphic descriptions of God's features (for example, God's hair, nostrils, breath, etc.) deviate from any intent that their words should apply to God in a manner literally descriptive of God; thus, they write descriptions as analogies: they write about God in his wisdom as though he were an aged man having white hair; they write about God's fury as though he were a man breathing furiously, etc. Let us illustrate how we use words for making sense of spiritual things.

Have you ever tried to explain colors to a person born blind? In such a situation, what would you say? It would of course be extremely difficult. One solution could possibly be to let him smell the odour of different flowers and say that just as there are differences in scent among different kinds of flowers, which only can be detected by the nose, there also may be different colors for different objects, which can be detected only by the eyes. To use words normally applicable in a certain kind of context (for example, as description of the sense of smell) for use in another biological context may be done for purpose of analogy; however, this analogical way admittedly is not of much help to the blind person, but it or something like it is the best we can do.

It is similar with God, who is a spirit (Joh 4:24), and with his Son and his angels, who are spirits as well. Heaven, or the spiritual world, is not visible to humans, and therefore we are "blind" as to its nature. To make the best of the situation and to give humans a vague impression of what God and his world are

---

[65] Prestige, *God in Patristic Thought*, p. 151.

like, the Bible uses descriptions from our biological world, and they ascribe to God human-like attributes. Nothing of this is literal; God does not literally consist of gems and gold, and angels do not have wings. But Bible writers, in order to help us apprehend certain spiritual majesties, employed analogical references to things in the world of mankind as signals or symbols for the greater realities.[66]

I, therefore, will go in the opposite direction of Prestige and claim that it is the "biological" language that counts; and that the way Athanasius and other defenders of the consubstantiality of the Father and the Son used the language, is similar to discussing the color and size of the wings of angels. They took as their point of departure the spiritual *concepts* which the biblical words refer to, made up their mind respecting the meaning of these concepts, and discussed them as if they were part of a material world. But this is to start in the wrong end. Human reason and logic cannot be used to understand God's spiritual substance informing His existence; we are, however, dependent upon his revelation of himself, his Son and his Spirit. We therefore have no other choice but to start with the *words* in their normal or "biological" sense. They are the building blocks, and from these we may get an analogical concept in the references being made.

Nothing illustrates better the difference described than a comparison between the interpretative methodology of Arius and Athanasius, for Arius starts with the words and uses them analogically for presenting certain concepts in the relationship between God and His Son; however, Athanasius starts with illogical concepts and then tries interpeting the words of Scripture in light of his idiosyncratic (or, special) understanding of these concepts. The fact that Athanasius' concepts are illogical to our human mind is not the key issue; rather, it is the fact that such concepts are decided upon and accepted apart from Scripture, and then used as a basis to define scriptural words and concepts that, taken in their natural sense, would clearly

---

[66] Examples of this are Paul's words in 1 Corinthians 15:35-57, where he uses a grain that is sown and the fact that animals and men have different "flesh," and that the sun, the moon and the stars differ in glory, to give the Corinthians an idea of what the resurrection body will be like.

contradict the illogical concepts of Athanasius, as we will now illustrate.

THOUGHTS AND CONCEPTIONS OF ATHANASIUS

Athanasius was present at the council of Nicaea, and some time afterwards he became the chief proponent for the creed that eventually became the trinity doctrine. Let us look at some of his principal opinions.

1) *He would not accept the biblical words as absolute proofs because words had no definite meaning in themselves.*

He wrote:

> For terms do not disparage His Nature; rather the Nature draws to Itself those terms and changes them. For terms are not prior to essences, but essences are first, and terms second. Wherefore also when the essence is a work or creature, then the words "He made" and "He became," and "He created" are used of it properly, and designate the work. But when the Essence is an Offspring and Son, then "He made" and "He became" and "He created" no longer properly belong to it, nor designate a work; but "He made" we use without question for "He begat."[67]

After these words Athanasius gives examples of how sons may be called servants and servants may be called children without changing their nature as sons and servants.

Athanasius' reference to the importance of the context as a means for the apprehension of words is sound.[68] While there are

---

[67] NPNF 1, p. 349; compare Meijering, *Orthodoxy and Platonism in Athanasius*, p. 92.

[68] His application of the principle, however, is tantamount to being guilty of "the contextual fallacy." To fail to differentiate between the two different "presupposition pools" and the two different situations of communication in the natural and spiritual worlds creates even more problems than when modern people fail to distinguish between the presupposition pools and situations of communicatoin in Greek and Hebrew, and those of today.

hardly situations where "the essence" may "change" the meaning of a word, there may be contexts where different sides of the word/concept are being made visible. The Hebrew word *hāwā*[69] and the Greek *proskuneō* basically mean "to fall down." If a person in biblical times fell down before a king it was usually an act of obeisance and not of worship, though worship could also be implied. However, when God is the object the only possible sense is "worship," because there can be no other intention by falling down before God than that of worshiping him.[70] A translator, therefore, can translate the words by "worship" with God as object, but use "do obeisance" or similar words when a creature is object—or the translator can use "do obeisance" or something similar wherever *proskuneō* occurs and let the reader decide what is meant by the action.[71]

The example above cannot, however, be compared with the create/beget-example of Athanasius, because worship/do obeisance are normal lexical meanings of the Greek and Hebrew words (or different sides of the concept behind the word), and all agree that God should be worshiped. What Athanasius does is first decide that the Son, who is called "Wisdom" and the "Word," is eternal and uncreated, and based on this premise, any biblical passage saying that he is created or made cannot be taken at face value. Armed with such an interpretative model, any biblical argument was neutralized, because he arbitrarily assigned meanings to certain words.

---

[69] The verb occurs in the causative-reflexsive *st-* form. Earlier it was analyzed as *Hithpael* of the root *shāhā*. Compare Murray J. Harris, *Jesus as God: The New Testament Use of* Theos *in Reference to Jesus* (Grand Rapids: Baker, 1992), p. 267.

[70] 1 Chronicles 29:20 is a case where different sides of the concept are made visible, because of the nature of the object or the adverb. The people bowed down (*qādād*, "to bow down"), and made *hāwā* ("worship," "fall down," "do obeisance") to YHWH and to the king. There can be little doubt that the people worshiped God but showed honor to David.

[71] Matthew 28:17 and other instances where *proskuneō* is used with Jesus as the object also illustrate how the doctrine of the trinity has influenced Bible translation. In Matthew 28:17 NWT uses "did obeisance" while TEV has "worshiped." In Revelation 3:9 we find an example where, without question, *proskuneō* is used with the meaning "do obeisance" or "fall down."

2) *Athanasius felt free to change the meaning of words when convenient.*

Another method which Athanasius used, and which, from a philological point of view represents a great weakness, is that he, straight away, gave important words new meanings. The second premise used by Athanasius in the quote above is that there is a fundamental difference between the words "to create" and "to beget" as to time. That which is created has a beginning in time; that which is begotten can be eternal. This distinction is neither found in Hebrew nor in Greek before Nicaea. He also used the words "Offspring" and "Son" in a new sense. From a philological point of view it is bad methodology to ascribe new meanings to words straight away, assuming novel, psychologically unaccommodating concepts instead of beginning examination of the referents with the words used in reference to them.

EXCURSUS ON "CREATED" AND "BEGOTTEN" ARE THEY ANTONYMS OR SYNONYMS?

Let us use a passage which, probably more than any other, was quoted by the Fathers of all parties, namely, Proverbs 8:22, to illuminate the above points.[72] Athanasius agreed with the Arians that the wisdom in Proverbs referred to Jesus Christ, and what is interesting here is that both "create" and "beget/be born" occur in parallel verses. The Hebrew word *qānā* in verse 22 is, in most instances, used in the Bible with a resultative[73] sense, as

---

[72] Justin Martyr, Clement of Alexandria, Origen, Eusebius of Caesarea, Cyril of Jerusalem, Ambrose, Cyril of Alexandria and John of Damascus, in addition to Athanasius, and practically every other Father identify the Wisdom of Proverbs 8:22ff. as the Logos. Irenaeus identifies the Wisdom with the Spirit (*Against Heresies* 20:3). Compare Wolfson, *The Philosophy of the Church Fathers*, p. 246.

[73] "Resultative" is the designation for an act leading into a state. The command "Sit down!" results in the state of being seated.

a stative with the meaning "to possess." Thus, the Vulgate translates, "The Lord possessed me in the beginning." However, in the Hebrew text there is no preposition with the meaning "in" before "beginning," and "beginning" is therefore logically an accusative object rather than adverbial. Therefore, the Septuagint translates, "The Lord created me the beginning of his ways." The Aramaic Targums and the Syriac Peshitta have similar renditions. Using normal procedures for interpretation this can only mean that the wisdom, whatever he/she/it refers to, is not eternal but had a beginning. Athanasius solves the problem of the word "created" with reference to wisdom, whom he identifies with Jesus Christ, by saying that it refers to his incarnation.[74]

But what about the words in verse 25 where the wisdom says, "Before the mountains themselves had been settled down, ahead of the hills, I was brought forth as with labor pains"? The Hebrew verb *hûl* used in this verse can mean "to bear a child with pains." Is this verb the opposite of *qānā* ("to produce")? Or, to use the Greek verbs of the Septuagint, is *gennaō* ("to beget, bear") the opposite of *ktizō* ("to create") and *ginomai* ("to come into existence, be created")? Athanasius would have us believe just that. After quoting Proverbs 8:25 he writes: "And in many passages of the divine oracles is the Son said to have been generated [*gegennesthai*], but nowhere to have come into being [*gegonenai*]."[75] As a further defense of the Nicene creed, he wrote:

> He is then by nature an Offspring, perfect from Perfect, begotten before all the hills [Prov 8:25], that is before every rational and intelligent essence, as Paul also in another place calls Him "First-born of all creation" [Col

---

[74] NPNF 4, p. 372. Athanasius used the argument that since the words refer to "the Wisdom of God," the phrase "created me" must have the meaning "begat me." Further he says that Proverbs cannot be understood literally, but the passages have a hidden meaning, which in the case of 8:22 he usess 9:1, where it is said that "wisdom has built its house," in support of his position. He believed that the "house" referred to the body of Jesus and, therefore, the words of 8:22 must refer to his incarnation.

[75] NPNF 4, p. 168.

1:15]. He shews that he is not a creature, but Offspring of the Father. For it would be inconsistent with His deity for Him to be called a creature. For all things were created by the Father through the Son, but the Son alone was eternally begotten from the Father, whence God the Word is "first-born of all creation."[76]

But it is quite clear that *hûl* in Proverbs 8:25 is a synonym of *qānā* rather than an antonym.

When we look at the way the Bible uses the words "create," "beget," "son," "offspring," and "creature," it becomes clear that Athanasius' claims are special pleading. In Psalm 90:2, for example, *hûl* ("to bear a child with pain") and *yālād* ("beget, bear") are used figuratively for the creation of the earth, thus making the words synonyms with "create" instead of antonyms: "Before the mountains themselves were born [*yālād*], Or you proceeded to bring forth as with labor pains [*hûl*] the earth."

In the rest of the Bible, when *hûl* and *yālād* are used literally or figuratively, they almost always refer to that which has been produced. One lexicon says this about *hûl*, "This idiom may be used to refer to creation or origins on a cosmic scale (Prov 8:24-25)."[77]

In the Bible the word "son" is used with a "biological" or familiar meaning. It may be used figuratively (analogically), but in such situations the literal meaning is always taken as a point of departure. There is no example of the word "son" being used with the meaning "eternal being," ascribed to it by Athanasius. It is true that Jesus Christ as "son" is contrasted with the angels who are creatures. But this does not contrast their natures, giving "son" in the case of Jesus a sense different from the familiar one; rather, the contrast relates to the *quality* of Jesus' sonship, which the Bible stresses in two ways: 1) Before Jesus came to earth he is called the "onlybegotten/unique son" (Joh 3:16) or the "onlybegotten god" (Joh 1:18); the epithet

---

[76] NPNF 4, p. 85.

[77] Gleason Archer, Harris Laird, and Bruce Waltke, eds., *Theological Wordbook of the Old Testament*, vol. 1 (Chicago: Moody Press, 1980), p. 271. Justin and Tatian used "beget" in reference to the creation of the world. See A. Harnack, *History of Dogma*, vols. 2 and 3 (New York: Dover, 1961), p. 213.

"onlybegotten" implies that there are other sons of God, but this one is special. 2) By means of his resurrection he obtained a special filial relationship with his Father. He "was declared God's Son . . . by means of a resurrection from the dead" (Rom 1:4), and "he has *become* better than the angels" (Heb 1:4). We may also note that in Hebrews 2:11 Jesus Christ is said to have brothers, also implying that others are sons of God.

3) *Athanasius condemned the Greeek philosophers but used some of their thoughts and arguments.*

What, then, is the source of Athanasius' view of God and his Son? Athanasius himself presented his teachings as a heritage from the Fathers,[78] and this is partly true. However, as we have seen, all the Fathers were influenced by Greek philosophy, and I do not hesitate to claim that Athanasius was also clearly influenced by Greek philosophy, both through the Fathers and through his own learning.[79] Justin Martyr and the other Fathers who subscribed to the two-stage view of the Son's eternal generation were probably influenced by Philo. Irenaeus, Origen and others who defended the one-stage theory were probably influenced by Neo-Platonism,[80] but Athanasius evidently got many of his views directly from Plato himself. Thus all three Platonic systems seem to have influenced the formation of the trinity doctrine.[81] One student of Athanasius' writings says, "We

---

[78] NPNF 4, p. 4.

[79] Athanasius did not consciously intended to hellenize the Christian religion, and neither did the other Fathers whom we have quoted. To the contrary, many of them, including Athanasius, made efforts to avoid this. However, by using the intellectual language of the day, perhaps without fully realizing it, they also used and adopted fundamental philosophical thoughts.

[80] It seems that Athanasius did not have any *substantial* knowledge of Neo-Platonism. See Meijering, *Orthodoxy and Platonism in Athanasius*, p. 6.

[81] As previously mentioned, all agree that there was a philosophical influence on the Fathers, but the degree of influence is seen differently. Grillmeyer, *Christ in Christian Tradition*, pp. 107, 108, who defends the trinity doctrine, writes: "The church's dogma of the Trinity and the incarnation are an attempt to maintain the mystery inherent in the basic data of the Christian revelation by a limited use of Hellenistic and contemporary concepts and

now have to deal with the fact that Athanasius, whilst constantly using philosophical arguments and language, nevertheless speaks almost exclusively negatively about Pagan philosophers."[82]

Athanasius quoted Plato by name just once,[83] but he quoted him by word at least five times,[84] and he draws on the thoughts of Plato regarding important issues, such as: 1) Time was created. Plato, *Timeaus* 38, says, "Time came into being with the heavens." Athanasius said that time was created by the Word and the Word is therefore eternal.[85] "Further, if he is called the eternal offspring of the Father, He is rightly so called. . . . For, whereas it is proper for men to beget in time, from the imperfection of their nature, God's offspring is eternal, for His nature is ever perfect."[86]

2) He uses Plato's world of the Ideas: "Athanasius clearly partly speaks about God as the Platonists speak about the divine realm of ideas."[87] Plato's Ideas are unchangeable and eternal, and, similarly, Athanasius claims that there can be no accidents in God, but that all he does in time are consequences of his eternal decisions.[88] Says Meijering:

> We regard it as highly probable that Athanasius knew this Middle-Platonic doctrine of the ideas, a doctrine which several Christian writers had already

---

language to avoid the distortions of Hellenization. To see the chronic Hellenization of Christianity in these dogmas themselves (A. Harnack) is to mistake the first intention of the dogmatic statements."

[82] Meijering, *Orthodoxy and Platonism in Athanasius*, pp. 126, 127.

[83] NPNF 4, p. 60.

[84] In NPNF 4, Athanasius quotes Plato six times, the first two are regarding the immortal soul, and the third is regarding God's nature: 1) NPNF 4, p. 6; 2) NPNF 4, p. 21; NPNF 4, p. 26 and p. 37.

[85] NPNF 4, p. 314.

[86] NPNF 4, pp. 314, 315.

[87] Meijering, *Orthodoxy and Platonism in Athanasius*, p. 68.

[88] NPNF 4, pp. 389, 390. Meijering, *Orthodoxy and Platonism in Athanasius*, p. 101.

used before him. This makes it understandable why he used in C.G.2 [Against the Pagans] terms like *ta noeta* ["the ideas"], *ta theia* ["the divine"], *ta onta* ["the existing"], and *theos* ["god"] more or less indiscriminately: if the ideas belong to the godhead, then contemplation of the true intelligible world is contemplation of God Himself.[89]

Meijering sums up Athanasius' thoughts on God's being and actions and their relation to each other, when he says:

> God is the eternal, unchangeable, always identical, real Being, says Athanasius, using both language and arguments which are also found in the Platonists. He is then confronted with the difficulty that many Biblical texts seem to contradict this ontological conception of the divine, especially of the Son. By making use of the Platonic theory that the words are secondary to the matter signified by them, he can explain those texts in such a way that they corroborate his doctrine of the ontological divinity of the Son.[90]

Thus we see that the chief defender of the Nicene creed does not start with the Biblical words to learn the concepts related to God, but starts with his own concepts of God, which seem to be partly based on Plato. By giving familiar words new meanings, and by using philosophical arguments and methods of interpretation, he is able to defend his view.

---

[89] Meijering, *Orthodoxy and Platonism in Athanasius*, p. 13.

[90] Meijering, *Orthodoxy and Platonism in Athanasius*, p. 104.

Figure 4.1

Three Platonic Systems Influencing the Trinity Doctrine

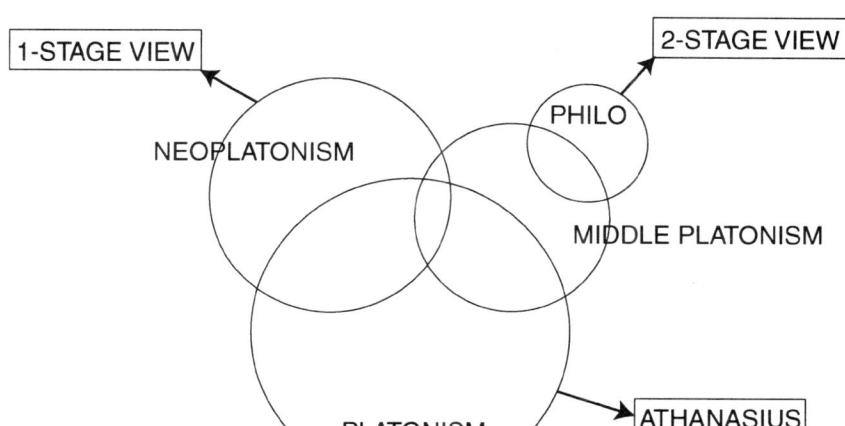

THOUGHTS AND CONCEPTIONS BY ARIUS

Arius is viewed as the heretic *par exellence*. Our knowledge of him comes from a few letters written by him and from quotes from his treatise *Thalia*, found in the writings of his opponent Athanasius. Arius was also evidently influenced by philosophical thoughts; he accepted for instance the thought in Plato's *Timaeus* that time was created. However, his writings show that he did not use a great deal of philosophical language or arguments. Some claim that Arius' belief in a created Logos can be traced back to Philo, but this is highly doubtful since he primarily used biblical passages to defend his beliefs.

Regardless of one's theological position, it is difficult to disagree with the notion that if the wisdom in Proverbs 8:22 refers to Jesus Christ, something which Athanasius also accepted, then Jesus must have been created, and there was a time when he did not exist, as Arius claimed. We may discuss whether "wisdom" really refers to Jesus, but both the two-stage and the one-stage, eternal-generation interpetation of this passage, and Athanasius' application of it to the incarnation, is mystical and forced. This is not the place to defend Arius; I just want to point out that most commentators agree that "Arius relied heavily on Biblical arguments"[91] in that he quoted a great number of texts, applying them with a literal meaning. From a philological point of view, this seems to represent a completely different objective than that of Athanasius.

I have not found a better summary of Arius' arguments than that found in a publication over sixty years old[92]:

- There is only one God who is uncreated and eternal (Deut 6:4; Luke 18:19; Joh 17:3).

- The Logos is the Son of God (Ps 45:8; Matt 12:28; 1 Cor 12:4). He is made by God from nothing, as his first creature; thus, there was a time when he did not exist (Prov 8::22; Acts 2:36; Col 1:15; Heb 3:2).

- The Son does not have a perfect knowledge of the Father, and he can change and grow morally (Luke 2:52; Matt 26:39; Heb 5:8-19; Phil 2:6; Heb 1:4). He was not perfect in knowledge (Mark 12:32; Joh 11:34; 13:31).

- The Son is lesser than the Father (John 14:28; Matt 11:27; 26:39; 27:46; 28:18; Joh 12:47; 1 Cor 15:28).

THE COUNCILS AND THE TRINITY DOCTRINE

Regarding the council of Nicaea, we have three principal sources: 1) some fragmentary reminiscences from Eustatius of Antioch; 2) some chapters written by Athanasius a generation after the council; and 3) the famous letter written by Eusebius of Caesarea, describing the council to his congregation. The

---

[91] Fortman, *The Triune God*, p. 64.

[92] J. F. Bethune-Baker, *An Introduction to the Early History of Christian Doctrine* (London, 1933), p. 161.

quarreling of two diametrically opposed views, both wanting to defend the unity of God, was the reason why the council convened in the first place. One extreme was Monarchianism, which taught that Jesus Christ was in all respects identical with the Father. The chief spokesman for this view was Sabellius.[93] One the other extreme was Arius and his friends, who taught that Jesus Christ was the first of God's creations.

The great issue before the council, however, was not the unity of God, but the Son's divinity and his eternal existence with the Father. The decision of the council was directed both against Arianism and Sabellianism, but at the same time its creed has the hallmark of compromise. After acknowledging belief in God the Father, the creeds says:

> And in one Lord, Jesus Christ, the Son of God, the only-begotten born of the Father, that is, of the substance [*ousia*] of the Father; God from God, light from light, true God from true God; begotten, not created, consubstantial [*homoousios*] with the Father. . . . And we believe in the Holy Spirit.

Why was this statement of faith accepted? The sources available suggest that emperor Constantine, to some degree, influenced the decisions, and that his primary motive was political. One commentator says this about the use of *homoousios* (consubstantiality), the keyword of the creed:

> The strong Eastern supporters of the *homoousios*, even with the addition of the Western bishops led by Hosius, were altogether in a minority as compared with the great body of Oriental bishops who thought like Eusebius [who took the position that the Father and the Son were different essences]. But with the powerful help of Constantine, only anxious for the peace of the empire, the minority succeeded in enforcing their view upon the majority, who certainly disliked Arianism, but at the same time desired no anti-Arian novelties.[94]

---

[93] Today "Sabellianism" is generally used instead of "Monarchianism."

[94] R. S. Franks, *The Doctrine of the Trinity*, p. 106. Grillmeyer, *Christ in Christian Tradition*, pp. 255-261, questions Eusebius' portrayal of Constantine,

Apart from political motivation, the spirit of compromise is seen in the choice of words. For instance, nothing is said about the divinity of The holy spirit. And the key words *ousia* ("substance") and *homoousios* ("consubstantial") were vague enough to be accepted by all parties. Says one commentator: "While different groups might read their own theologies into the creed and its key-word, Constantine himself was willing to tolerate them all on the condition that they acquiesced in his creed and tolerated each other."[95]

Let us take a closer look at the key words. The root word *ousia* ("substance," "essence") could signify the kind of substance or matter common to several individuals of a class.[96] Up to the time of the council, the word *homoousios* ("consubstantial") was used quite similarly, in the sense of *generic* unity.[97] These key-words, therefore, need not have any mystic connotations, but could simply mean that the Father and the Son had similar substances, substances of the same kind; not "the very same substance," as later Catholic theologians took it to mean.[98] But

---

who "stands *above* the council, even in questions of belief," and claims that the emperor played a more modest role. Hanson, *The Search for the Christian Doctrine of God*, pp. 152-155 and pp. 850-853, to a certain extent follows Grillmeyer, while other church historians accept the witness of Eusebius.

[95] J. N. D. Kelly, *Early Christian Doctrines*, rev. ed. (New York: Harper and Row, 1978), p. 256.

[96] Kelly, *Early Christian Doctrines*, p. 234.

[97] Kelly, *Early Christian Doctrines*, pp. 234-236. Fortman, *The Triune God*, p. 67, writes that while Catholic scholars had earlier thought that the meaning of the word at Nicaea was "of identically the same substance," "in recent years there has developed a growing tendency to question and reject this assumption."

[98] One of the expressions used, however, had definite Sabellian overtones, but it was removed from the creed at the council of Constantinople. Says Hanson, *The Search for the Christian Doctrine of God*, p. 167: "The other really remarkable point about N [the Nicene symbol] is the condemnation in the anathemas at the end of the view that the Son is "of another *hypostasis* ['person'] or *ousia* ["essence"] from the Father. This can only have been a highly ambiguous and extremely confusing statement. By the standard of later orthodoxy, as achieved at the Creed of Constantinople of 381, it is a rankly heretical (i.e. Sabellian) proposition, because the Son must be of a different *hypostasis* (i. e. 'person') from the Father."

the parties could interpret the words as they wanted.[99] The eternality of the Son, however, could not be the object of interpretation—it was explicitly affirmed in the condemnations at the end of the creed.[100] In relation to this, the council used the word "begotten" with a new and mystical sense, namely, as the opposite of "created." This is a very important point to take note of, because it is an example of how one started with a concept and actually changed the meaning of a word to conform with one's apprehension of the concept, and because it is contrary both to the secular and Biblical use of the word "begotten."

The Nicene creed did not settle the question about the unity of God once and for all, and neither did it say anything about the divinity of The holy spirit, so the creed was far from being a trinity doctrine. In the years following the council, a long series of synods produced a variety of creeds that were intended to replace or modify the Nicene symbol and to do away with phrases such as "consubstantial with the Father" and "begotten of the Father's substance."

The position of The holy spirit was undecided in the years following Nicaea, and for the first time at the council of Sirmium in 351 The holy spirit was brought up as an issue which had to be resolved. There was much vacillation among the bishops on this point, and even Athanasius did not at first speak about the Spirit as God. In 380 the church Father Gregory Nazianzus wrote about the different views of the Spirit: "But of the wise men amongst ourselves, some have conceived of him as

---

[99] Hanson, *The Search for the Christian Doctrine of God*, p. 181, points to another reason for confusion about the key terms: "The search for the Christian doctrine of God in the fourth century was in fact complicated and exasperated by semantic confusion, so that people holding different views were using the same words as those who opposed them, but, unawares, giving them different meanings from those applied to them by those opponents."

[100] The creed said (translated by Hanson, *Christian Doctrine*, p. 163): "But those who say, 'there was a time he did not exist,' and 'Before being begotten he did not exist,' and that he came into being from non-existence, or who allege that the Son of God is of another *hypostasis* or *ousia,* or is alterable or changeable, these the Catholic and Apostolic Church condemns."

an Activity, some as a Creature, some as God; and some have been uncertain which to call Him."[101]

To put an end to the heresies and schisms that were disturbing both the Church and the State, emperor Theodosius I convened a council at Constantinople in 381. Two main divisions of opinion existed: the Macedonians, also known as the Pneumatomachi, who denied the full deity of The holy spirit, and the Cappadocians, who defended it. The council reaffirmed the Nicene creed except that it omitted the words "of the substance of the Father" and "God from God," but its words about The holy spirit are amazingly vague. The holy spirit is not called "God" but "the Lord and giver of life, who proceeds from the Father, who together with the Father and the Son is adored and glorified, who spoke through the prophets."

Harnack interpreted the creed as a compromise, as "a formula of union" between the different parties,[102] but Fortman disagrees.[103] Exactly whom the Fathers wanted to reconcile by their choice of words may be open for discussion, but there can be little doubt that the words were chosen to be as unprovocative as possible. Our knowledge of the council is somewhat uncertain, but it seems that it promulgated the symbol which became known as the Nicene-Constantinopolitan Creed.

The question about the nature(s) of Jesus Christ was ignored at Nicaea, and for many years it was undecided. John wrote that the Word became flesh (Joh 1:14), but the meaning of this was interpreted quite differently. Arius and Athanasius both believed that the Logos had taken the place of the immortal soul of Jesus, the difference being that Arius stressed the human side of Jesus and Athanasius the divine side. Other bishops stressed the human side of Jesus without taking the soul into consideration, while others went to the extreme, teaching that God himself was born by a woman. Others stressed that Jesus had both a human and a divine nature, but did not agree as to how these natures were united. In 431 a council was held

---

[101] NPNF 7, p. 319.

[102] Harnack, *History of Dogma*, vol. 4, p. 98.

[103] Fortman, *The Triune God*, p. 85.

at Ephesus, which discussed how Jesus humbled himself and became man.

As was true of the the councils before it, the creed adopted at Ephesus did not resolve the issues completely, and twenty years later it was decided to convene a council in Chalcedon "to put an end to the bitter internal disputes which had occupied the period after the Council of Ephesus," to use the words of Grillmeyer.[104] A Danish church history written for seminary students says this about the council:

> After difficult discussions, which sometimes turned into fights, an agreement was reached after pressure from the emperor, about an acceptable confession, the stress of which was the words about Christ: "two natures in one person, without confusion or change," . . . By this the formation of dogma for the whole church came to an end, however, the quarreling would still last more than one century. . . . The main part of the symbol was formulated in such a way that it could be signed by the moderates on both sides. . . . With the council's dogmatic confession of compromise there was dissatisfaction, particularly in the East.[105]

The council reaffirmed the Nicene-Constantinopolitan creed, and in addition declared that Jesus was "true God and true man," and the trinity doctrine was now fully expressed. The only important thing that happened after this was the Athanasianian creed, which was formed by some unknown person(s) in the sixth century.

Approaching the end of this chapter, we have come to the point where we should gather the lines of evidence in order to reach an accurate conclusion. We started with the indisputable statement that the fully expressed doctrine of the trinity is not found in the Bible, but we considered its foundation, and discussed whether the different tenets that make up the doctrine can be found in the Bible. The essence of the trinity doctrine, as

---

[104] Grillmeyer, *Christ in Christian Tradition*, p. 541.

[105] H. Holmquist and J. Nørregård, *Kirkehistorie*, vol. 1 (Copenhagen: J. H. Schultz Forlag, 1966), p. 259.

expressed in the Athanasian creed, is that the Father, the Son and the Holy Spirit are one God in three *co-equal* persons, the three persons being *uncreated, eternal* and *almighty*. Furthermore, there is the belief that Jesus Christ is *both God and man*. Against this we may state:

- There is no passage in the Bible which even hints that Jesus (the Word or the Son) is eternal.

- Without answering for the theology of Arius, I feel that the passages he was quoting to show that the Son is inferior to his Father are quite convincing. Many more passages could be quoted showing how Jesus prayed to his Father, followed the will of the Father and acknowledged his dependence upon the Father in various ways. This argues strongly against any co-equality between the two.

- There are three, possibly four passages in the Bible that clearly apply the word "god" to Jesus Christ, namely, Isaiah 9:6, John 1:1, 1:18 and possibly John 20:28. When we study these texts we must first keep in mind the time factor. Few will deny that the Bible teaches that the life of Jesus has three "phases": he lived in heaven; he stayed on earth a little more than 30 years; and after he died, he was resurrected, and went back to heaven. The word "god" was never explicitly applied to him in a nonpejorative sense when he was on earth as a man, but two of the four passages (Joh 1:1, 18) refer to his life before he came to earth, and the third (Joh 20:28) was spoken in his presence after his resurrection, and the text from the OT (Isaiah 9:6) is prophetic.[106] Therefore, there is no passage that states that Jesus was divine (a spirit being) as well as human *at the same time*.[107] Later we will discuss how the word "god" may have different senses.

---

[106] Compare R. E. Brown, *Jesus God and Man* (New York: Macmillan, 1967), p. 36.

[107] To have different natures at different times is not necessarily a strange thought. While living on earth Christians have a human nature, but 2 Peter 1:4 contains a promise of acquiring "divine nature."

- While all the Fathers used the Bible, the evidence suggests that the trinity doctrine was gradually formed under the influence of Greek philosophy. The eternal world of the Ideas probably served as a pattern for the view that the Logos existed from eternity as the Reason in the mind of the Father. The philosophical view that time was created with the world and that God and the Ideas were unchangeable may have been the background for the view that the Son was not created and that he is eternal. The philosophical view that words are secondary compared with the entities they represent was used to neutralize any biblical passages speaking against the trinity doctrine. The creeds adopted at three important church councils condemned particular heresies, but at the same time they used phrases so vague that they could be accepted by most groups, thus bearing the hallmark of compromise.

Based on the above, there is little doubt that the trinity doctrine is a theological teaching that came into being *after* the Bible was completed.[108] In spite of the almost universal acceptance of the dogma among Christian denominations, it is philologically unsuitable as background material for Bible translation, and, therefore, it ought not to serve as criterion for what is unbiased translation, though it is often (wrongfully) used as such.

The trinity doctrine, therefore, employs words that are forced into an unnatural or non-neutral sense. The words of trinitarianism constitute a negative translation problem, because translators allow the words to influence them, and this in turn leads to Bible translations filled with ideas and concepts commensurate with trinitarianism. To solve the problem we should take a philological approach to translating the Bible, and leave doctrine, particularly those doctrines which arose

---

[108] Hanson, *The Search for the Christian Doctrine of God*, p. xviii, says about the controversies of the fourth century: "Another important point to realize about the period which forms the subject of this book is that it was not a history of the defense of an agreed and settled orthodoxy against the assaults of open heresy. On the subject which was primarily under discussion there was not as yet any orthodox doctrine."

hundreds of years after the Bible was written, out of the translation process.[109]

---

[109] We must bear in mind that the burden of proof is on those who claim that the trinity doctrine should be used as a translation principle.

CHAPTER 5

DOES THE NWT FOLLOW
ITS OWN TRANSLATION PRINCIPLES?

In this chapter and the next we are going to evaluate particular passages in the NWT, and as we do so we must keep in mind the different factors which influence a translator's choice of words and how these factors work together. In each case I will try to look at the passage through the eyes of the translators, and try to follow their way of reasoning. When discussing particular passages we will first take a look at various linguistic issues. This involves the lexical meanings of the words, how grammar and syntax narrow the possibilities that exist for understanding the clause(s), and which translation is to be preferred if only linguistic questions are taken into consideration.

Next we will consider the immediate context to see if there are semantic factors which might modify or change our linguistic preferences, and then we will similarly examine the greater context of the entire Bible. Then we will review our results in the light of relevant extra-biblical knowledge and, of course, the theology of the Bible. Finally we will take the communicative force of the translation into account. Might the the chosen rendition distort the message? After considering each passage in the light of as many of these factors as possible, then we may find ourselves in a position to make a verdict as to the quality of the passage, and determine whether the translation of it shows bias or not.

In order to effectively follow this procedure as we evaluate the NWT, we must also have a knowledge of the particular translation principles used by its translators. Because a translation is made for a particular target group, following certain translation principles, it cannot be evaluated in the light of other Bible translations or in the light of a certain theology. It can only be evaluated in the light of how faithful it is to its own translation principles, provided these principles are intelligent and balanced.

Countess' judgment regarding NWT is a very negative one. He not only claims that the translators did not stick to their own translation principles, but he also believes that some of the principles themselves can be criticized. He calls into question the translators' scholarly background, and describes the translation as a piece of work that is so biased that its text can be compared with "milk with an admixture of arsenic." According to Countess, reading the NWT "could very well prove injurious to one's health."[1]

As his own words imply, Countess' book is apologetic in nature, and such works tend to ascribe viewpoints to the opponents which they do not entertain, and then these "strawmen" are easily knocked down. Countess is no exception in this respect. In this chapter we will discuss the examples he gives of the NWT translators' violation of their own translation principles, and it will be seen that there are two outstanding strawmen in his presentation: 1) He presumes that the NWT translators follow principles which can only be met by an interlinear translation, and 2) he presumes that the translators must use such principles as strict laws from which there are no exceptions.

Both points are wrong, because, as we discussed in chapter two, an interlinear translation lacks the communicative element, because those responsible for it are merely concerned with giving the *lexical* equivalents of the words of the source language. On the other hand, a strictly literal translation, such as the NWT, strives to render the words as uniformly as possible. But communication still takes priority over literalness, and both in this kind of translation and in the idiomatic one the subjective judgement of the translators plays a most important role. This means it is impossible to make rigid laws that translators always must follow; an eclectic element must necessarily be inherent in any translation, though it is greatly reduced in a literal one. If this were not true, the Bible could better be translated by a computer rather than by a group of

---

[1] Robert Countess, *The Jehovah's Witnesses' New Testament* (Phillipsburg, NJ: Presbyterian and Reformed, 1982), p. xiv.

translators. But we know that machine translation is limited to weather forecasts and other simple material, where similar terms often occur.

THE NWT AND INTERPOLATION

The Greek text used for the NWT is that of Westcott and Hort, and it is said that when other readings are preferred, this is indicated by footnotes.[2] The translation method is thus described: "We offer no paraphrase of the Scriptures. Our endeavor all through has been to give as literal a translation as possible, where the modern English idiom allows and where a literal rendition does not for any clumsiness hide the thought."[3]

What conclusions can we draw from the above statement concerning the view of the translators regarding interpolation? Webster's defines "interpolation" as "an alteration, furbishing," and, given this meaning, the translators have bound themselves never to make an "interpolation" or "alteration." However, an *alteration* of the biblical text can be viewed differently by different people. Take, for instance, Matthew 10:29: "Do not two sparrows sell for a coin of small value? Yet not one of them will fall to the ground without your Father's [knowledge]" (brackets original to NWT). The Greek text literally says "without your father's." Thus, something must be implied. In Greek, this implicature need not be stated but English requires the addition of a noun. Is this interpolation? There are many similar examples where we have to "add" something in English in order to preserve the meaning, without actually being guilty of interpolation. Only when the translators add words that are not implied, or translate the text in a way which is contrary to lexicon, grammar or syntax are they guilty of interpolation.[4]

---

[2] NWTNT, Foreword, p. 8.

[3] NWTNT, Foreword, p. 9.

[4] Three other examples of ellipsis (something implied) are Luke 20:17, 1 Corinthians 15:5 and Hebrews 4:5. In the first example "the scriptures" is implied, and in the second "apostles" is implied. The third is a translation

Countess speaks of "the impression" the reader gets from reading the NWT's Foreword and Appendix, and from speaking with Jehovah's Witnesses. The impression of which he speaks is "that nothing extraneous shall find inclusion in the work." Then he gives examples of passages where the definite article is added and where some Greek genitive constructions are translated differently. Nobody would accuse the translators of an idiomatic Bible translation of interpolation in these instances, because in these works normal translation procedures will produce such results. To argue that the NWT is guilty of interpolation here because of Countess' "impression" that the translators have bound themselves only to translate word for word, is weak indeed. Their own translation principles, quoted above, reveal that the opposite is true. But let us take a look at some specific examples that deserve a more thorough discussion.

THE NAME "JEHOVAH" IN THE NEW TESTAMENT

Countess has a much stronger case, than in the issues we discussed above, in his criticism of the 237 occurrences of "Jehovah" in the NT text of NWT, because no Greek NT manuscript has a single occurrence of a complete form of the divine name YHWH. Therefore, the legitimate place of the divine name in the NT certainly can be questioned. However, the case is not as clearcut as Countess would have us believe.

We may illustrate the situation with an old Roman aquaduct proceeding forth from a mountainous region into a valley, and ending abruptly in the middle of the valley. If we were to see this aquaduct today and ask whether it once carried water from the mountains to the city in the other end of the valley, the answer must be that, as far as we know, this was not the case, because we see it ends in the middle of the valley. Being aware of the purpose of aquaducts, however, this answer

---

into Greek of a Hebrew oath formula, where the occurrence of the negative particle means a positive oath, "I will certainly," and the lack of it means a negative oath, "I will certainly not." The Greek text seems to be positive, thus "not" has to be supplied to give the correct idea, "They shall not enter into my rest."

is quite strange, because nobody would build such a structure just to spill the water in the middle of the plain! There is of course the possibility that the purpose was to carry water to the city on the other hillside, but for one reason or another the structure was never finished. A more likely explanation, however, would be that it was finished, but that half of it later fell down, and therefore is not seen today. To find the truth, we have to dig in the valley looking for traces of a fallen aquaduct.

Figure 5.1

Illustration of a Fallen Aquaduct

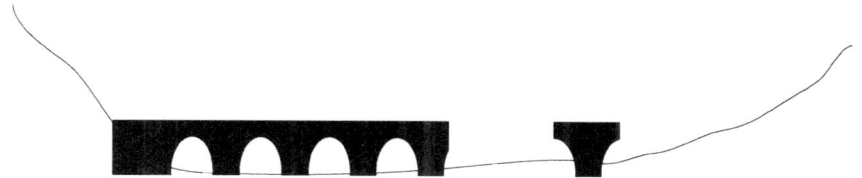

We may apply the illustration by quoting a Bible translator who suggested that the personal name of God should be found nowhere in the Bible. His name is H. Rosin, and he voiced his view at a conference for Bible translators in Djakarta in 1952, where the translation of divine names was discussed. Rosin knew that no manuscripts of the Greek NT contained the divine name, and he also believed that the translators of the Septuagint had substituted *kurios* for YHWH and that this was in fact God's providence. To use "Jehovah" or "Yahweh" in the New Testament was, for him, out of the question, and because of this he also saw a real problem in retaining Yahweh/Jehovah in the OT. He wrote:

> It might be disrespectful and disobedient, therefore, to restore something that God himself has demolished. It might mean that "Jehovah" would irrevocably become the strange God of the O.T. and that the cleavage between the two Testaments might also rend apart the church, for are not "Jehovah's witnesses" anti-Trinitarians? We therefore

feel that we should most strongly advise against a transcription of *JHWH* in a translation of the Bible.[5]

There is an important clarification that we should here make, concerning what Rosin has said above, namely, that there is just one Bible, not two. Additionally, the God of the OT is also the God of the NT.[6] If the name of God is not found in the NT, it would be inconsistent to use it in the OT. If this argument is accepted, it seems natural to suggest that the opposite must also be true. If the name of God is found in the OT, it is inconsistent if it is not also used in the NT. Thus, half of the aquaduct is standing—the divine name occurs in the Hebrew OT, but what about the other part? Did it "fall" or did it never exist?

It is essential for a faithful translator to closely follow the original text. However, in their book on Bible translation, Beekman and Callow devote an entire chapter to discussing *implicit* information, outlining situations when this kind of information should be made explicit.[7] The implicit information may be found in the immediate context, elswhere in the Bible, or it may be found outside of the Bible itself. There are three situations when implicit information should be made explicit: 1) When the grammar of the receptor language requires it; 2) when the stylistic and discourse structure of the receptor language require it; and 3) when the reader is likely to misunderstand the passage if it is left implicit.

From these observations of Beekman and Callow we may learn two things: 1) There can be situations when a translator may "add" something, without being guilty in interpolation; and 2) the basic reason for doing so is communication; the reader should not be misled by what he or she reads. True, the comments of the two authors relate to idiomatic translations. But as we have seen, even in a highly literal translation there

---

[5] H. Rosin, quoted in "Translating the Divine Names," *The Bible Translator* 3.4 (1952), pp. 180-187. The above quote is found on page 182.

[6] Acts 3:13 shows the continuity by saying, "The God of Abraham and of Isaac and of Jacob, the God of our forefathers, has glorified his servant, Jesus."

[7] John Beekman and J. Callow, *Translating the Word of God* (Grand Rapids: Zondervan, 1975), pp. 45-66.

are passages which must be translated in an idiomatic way to prevent misunderstanding. Therefore their conclusions also hold good, in principle, for literal translations.

The field which directly relates to the question of the place of "Jehovah" in the NT is not implicit information, but textual criticism. We do not possess the autographs of any of the biblical books, and even though the Greek text used as a basis for translation is reliable, all the footnotes in, for instance, the UBS Greek New Testament indicate some variation. At the outset, therefore, we cannot exclude the possibility suggested by the NWT that, as regards the divine name, the text has been changed.[8] Now we must dig for an answer.

As we proceed with our discussion we should keep in mind that the following section of this chapter (or any other part of this book) is not written to defend the renditions of the NWT or the arguments behind them. Rather, it is written to answer the question about whether or not the translators are guilty of interpolation, and thereby bias, when using "Jehovah" in the NT. The rest is up to you, the reader.

THE DIVINE NAME IN THE OLD TESTAMENT

It has been argued that the occurrences of YHWH in the post-exilic books show that the name had become less popular after the exile, or even ceased to be pronuounced. This is simply not true, as the following table reveals:

---

[8] Bart D. Ehrman, *The Orthodox corruption of Scripture: The Effect of Early Christological Controversies on the Text of the New Testament* (Oxford: Oxford University Press, 1993) has amply demonstrated how words in different NT manuscripts from the second century onward were corrupted because of doctrinal views.

Figure 5.2

Occurrences, Per Verse, of YHWH, 'Êlōhîm and 'Adōnāi in Pre-Exilic and Post-Exilic Bible Books

PRE-EXILIC	*YHWH*	*'elōhîm*	*'adōnāi*
Joshua	224	76	4
Judges	175	73	6
Isaiah	450	94	44
Hosea	46	26	0
Ruth	18	4	0
POST-EXILIC[9]	*YHWH*	*'elōhîm*	*'adōnāi*
Zechariah	133	11	1
Malachi	46	7	1
Ezra	37	55	1
Nehemiah	17	70	2
Daniel	8	22	10
Esther	0	0	0

The fact that YHWH is found in all of the post-exilic books except Esther (which also does not use *'elōhîm* nor *'adōnāi*) shows that it definitely was used during the time when the last of the OT Biblical books were written. Of particular interest is the book of Daniel, where 8 occurrences of YHWH, 17 of the 22 occurrences of *'elōhîm* and 7 of the 10 occurrences of *'adōnāi* are found in chapter 9, in connection with Daniel's prayer. This chapter clearly shows that *'elōhîm* and *'adōnāi* are not substitutes for the YHWH; rather, they are complements which are naturally used in an address to God.[10]

---

[9] The Aramaic portions of Daniel and Ezra are not counted.

[10] Most commentators date Daniel to around 165 BCE. This would then produce strong evidence for the general use of YHWH in the middle of the second century BCE. There are, however, arguments against such a late date.

It is true that in the book of Ezra *'elōhîm* occurs four times as much as YHWH, and in Nehemiah *'elōhîm* occurs three times more often than the divine name. But, when you consider what we find in Daniel, the use of the divine name in these two books does not in any way indicate that the divine name was losing importance as the personal name of God. It only shows that in these situations it was more natural for the writers of both Ezra and Nehemiah to use *'elōhîm*.[11] This is corroborated by the number of times YHWH is used by the prophets Zechariah and Malachi, which are among the latest books. This frequency of usage is even higher than that found in the books of the pre-exilic prophets.

There is another view from which we might consider this situation, namely, the frequency of the theophoric[12] elements in proper names. J. D. Fowler published a study concerning the use of *'ēl* ("god"), YHWH and other divine names/titles that occur in proper names throughout the Bible.[13] Her findings give conclusive evidence that YHWH was used during the time when the last books of the Bible were being written.

---

[11] The conclusion of Elias Bickerman (*The Jews in the Greek Age* [Cambridge, Mass.: Harvard University Press, 1988], p. 262) is that that tetragrammaton ceased to be used after the exile. He writes, "This means that from 520 BCE, that is, from the time of the restoration of the Temple, the authorities of Jerusalem refused to use the proper name of their deity in dealing with pagan authorities." But this cannot be accepted, as his findings only show that *in this situation* the name was not used.

[12] "Theophoric" has to do with names where YHWH, *'ēl* or other designations for God are included as part of another proper name, such as Nathan*el* or *Jeho*shaphat.

[13] J. D. Fowler, *Theophoric Personal Names in Ancient Hebrew: A Comparative Study* (Journal for the Study of the Old Testament, Supplement Series 49; Sheffield: Sheffield Academic Press, 1988).

Figure 5.3

The Theophoric Elements 'Êl and YHWH in Names in 5 Exilic/Post-Exilic Books of the Bible

TIME	*'ēl*	YHWH
Before the united kingdom	107	62
The united kingdom	62	71
The divided kingdom	46	194
Exile/post-exile	71	261

In the time before the united kingdom *'ēl* was twice as popular as YHWH in terms of being a theophoric element in proper names. But from the time of the exile YHWH was four times more popular than *'ēl*.[14] The name evidently continued to be used.

THE DIVINE NAME IN THE DEAD SEA SCROLLS

The material found at Qumran and the Dead Sea area consists of parts of about nine hundred manuscripts that were either written there or imported from other places. Two hundred of these are biblical manuscripts and the rest can be classified as interpretations of biblical books, apocryphal and pseudepigraphal books, phylacteries, liturgical texts, astrological texts, and a few fragments of a Greek translation of the OT. According to Charlesworth[15] there are 110 occurrences of the tetragrammaton in thirty different non-biblical manuscripts, 677 examples of *'ēl* in seventy six manuscripts, 139 examples of

---

[14] Fowler shows that the material in the book of Chronicles can be interpreted in different ways, and this may have had some influence on the above numbers. Our conclusion that YHWH was more popular as a theophoric element in proper names after the exile than it was before the exile is not affected by either interpretation.

[15] J. H. Charlesworth, *A Graphic Concordance of the Dead Sea Scrolls* (Tübingen: Mohr, 1991). This concordance is not exhaustive.

'elōhîm in twenty four manuscripts, and 51 examples of *'adōnāy*[16] in twelve manuscripts.[17] These numbers indicate a marked change in the use of the tetragrammaton compared with the OT, but, interestingly, what is used instead of the tetragrammaton is not *'adōnāy* ("Lord," equivalent to *kurios*). The preferred form was *'ēl*.[18]

The Qumran community was established in the first part of the second century BCE. *The Rule of the Community* (VI 27- VII 2), which was probably written not long after its establishment, says regarding the name of God: "Whoever enunciates the Name (which is) honoured above all [. . .] whether blaspheming, or overwhelmed by misfortune or for any other reason, {. . .} or reading a book, or blessing, will be excluded and shall not go back to the Community council."[19]

The text is broken in the middle, and it is not perfectly clear whether a person was disfellowshiped for any case of pronouncing the divine name, though this is likely. Skehan writes, "There is, therefore, at a minimum, a range of circumstances under which the divine name is not to be pronounced."[20] The data from Qumran show that some time around the start of the second century BCE there was reservation among the members of the Qumran community against pronouncing the tetragrammaton.

---

[16] The words *'ēl* and *'elōhîm* mean "God" (or, in the case of *'elōhîm*, "gods") while *'adōnāy* means "lord."

[17] In the Aramaic manuscripts we find *'alāhā* ("God") thirty-three times in many instances as a substitute for YHWH. I have looked at the eleven occurrences of the Aramaic word *mārē* ("lord") and the fifty-one occurrences of the Hebrew word *'adōnāy* ("lord"), but in no instances is there evidence that either of the two words serve as substitutes for YHWH.

[18] This is an important point to keep in mind, for when we later look for a Hebrew antecedent to the *kurios* of the NT, we will find none (see below).

[19] Florentino García Martínez, *The Dead Sea Scrolls Translated: The Qumran Texts in English*, trans. Wilfred G. E. Watson, 2d ed. (Leiden: Brill; Grand Rapids: Eerdmans, 1994), p. 11.

[20] P. W. Skehan, "The Divine Name at Qumran, in the Masada Scroll, and in the Septuagint," *Bulletin for the International Organization for Septuagint and Cognate Studies* 13 (1980), p. 15.

Can we expect that the viewpoints of the Essenes[21] at Qumran regarding the divine name were shared by the Jews at large? There is reason to believe that the answer is no. We must keep in mind that the Essenes of Qumran were a group of extremists who held certain views and practices that were not shared by other Palestinian Jews and Jews in Babylon or Egypt. That their view was idiosyncratic is also suggested by the fact that their substitution of *ʾēl* for YHWH is unprecedented among Hebrew-speaking people.

THE DIVINE NAME IN THE SEPTUAGINT

Let us now take a close look at the Septuagint (LXX), which may be representative for Alexandrian Jewry. This version is very important for our question concerning the divine name, because it was the supposed substitution of *kyrios* for the tetragrammaton in the Septuagint, in addition to its nonexistence in NT manuscripts, that has been the strongest argument in favor of the use of "the Lord" in the NT.

Countess commends NWT because it "exhibits the very important textual principle of weighing rather than counting manuscripts."[22] Using this principle means that the oldest manuscripts are normally viewed as the best textual witnesses, though they are few compared to the mass of late manuscripts used to try and establish "the Majority text." If we also apply this principle to the Septuagint manuscripts it is difficult to reach the same conclusion as Countess, namely, that the line of reasoning used by the NWT translators regarding the legitimate place of the divine name in the NT "is held together by more dogmatism than fact, by more conjecture than textual evidence."[23]

As a matter of fact, none of the published Septuagint manuscripts from the second and first centuries BCE and from

---

[21] We cannot with certainty say that the religious community at Qumran consisted entirely of Essenes, but this is the more common view.

[22] Countess, *The Jehovah's Witnesses' New Testament*, pp. 12-13.

[23] Countess, *The Jehovah's Witnesses' New Testament*, p. 27.

the first century CE contain *kurios* as a substitute for the tetragrammaton. We find the tetragrammaton in old Hebrew characters ᐅᒣᒋᐱ, 𝓂𝒽𝓂𝓏, in Aramaic script ᴎᴧ and in Greek letters as the phonetic transcription IΑω! Now we will consider these manuscripts in detail.

P Fouad 266. A few fragments of this manuscript were published during the second world war by Waddel,[24] and photographs of several additional fragments are found in the Foreword of NWTNT. There are three manuscripts in this inventory, and the tetragrammaton occurs in Aramaic script in one of them. In the other two there are no verses with the tetragrammton in the Masoretic text. The following dates have been suggested for these fragments:

Figure 5.4

Suggested Dates for P. Fouad 266

Waddel[25]	Second or first century BCE
Roberts[26]	Second or first century BCE
Kahle[27]	About 100 BCE
Dunand[28]	First century BCE, not later than 50 BCE

---

[24] W. G. Waddel, "The Tetragram in the LXX," *Journal of Theological Studies* 45 (1944), pp. 158-161.

[25] Waddel, "The Tetragram in the LXX," p. 159.

[26] B. J. Roberts, *The Old Testament Text and Versions: The Hebrew Text in Transmission and the History of the Ancient Versions* (Cardiff: University of Wales Press, 1951), p. 173.

[27] Paul Kahle, *The Cairo Geniza* (Oxford: Basil Blackwell, 1959), p. 214.

[28] F. Dunand, *Papyrus Grecs Bibliques*, Etudes de papyrologie, T.9 (Recherches d'archeologie, de philologie et d'histoire; 27; Cairo, 1966), p. 12.

Bertram[29]	Second century BCE
Stegemann[30]	Mid. of second century BC to first century BCE
Ali/Koenen[31]	Mid. of first century BCE

8HevXIIgr was found in 1952, and a few more fragments of it were found in 1961. It contains portions and fragments of the twelve minor prophets with the tetragrammaton in Old Hebrew letters. It seems that two different scribes have worked on the manuscript. The following dates have been ascribed to the script of the hand A of the manuscript:

Figure 5.5

Suggested Dates for "LXX" Manuscript 8HevXIIgr

Barthélemy [32]	Near the end of the first century CE
Barthélemy[33]	First century CE
Roberts[34]	Between 50 BCE and 50 CE

[29] G. Bertram, "Theologische Aussagen im Griechischen Alten Testament, Gottesnamen," *Zeitshrift für Die Neutestamentliche Wissenschaft* 3.4 (1978), p. 239.

[30] H. Stegemann, KURIOS O QEOS *und* KURIOS IHSOUS *Aufkommen und Ausbreitung des religiösen Gebrauchs von* KURIOS *und seine Verwendung im Neuen Testament* (Ph.D. dissertation [Habil. Masch.], Bonn., 1969), p. 155.

[31] Z. Ali and L. Koenen, *Three Rolls of the Early Septuagint: Genesis and Deuteronomy*, Papyrologische Texte und Abhandlungen, Band 27 (Bonn: Rudolf Habelt Verlag GMBH, 1980), p. 4.

[32] D. Barthélemy, "Redécouverte d'un chainon manquant de l'histoire de la Septante," *Revue Biblique* 60 (1953), pp. 18-29.

[33] D. Barthélemy, *Les devanciers d'Aquila* (VTSup 10; Leiden: Brill, 1963), p. 168.

[34] C. H. Roberts, *Manuscript, Society and Belief in Early Christian Egypt* (Oxford: The Schweich Lectures for 1977).

Parsons[35]	Later first century BCE

4QLXXLev[b] renders the divine name as IAω (*IAŌ*), and the following dates have been suggested for its composition:

Figure 5.6

Suggested Dates for 4QLXXLevb

Skehan 1957[36]	First century BCE
Kahle 1959[37]	A little later than P Fouad 266
Roberts 1977[38]	End first century BCE/first cent. CE
Parsons 1992[39]	First century BCE

In 1983 volume 50 of the Oxyrynchus Papyri was published, and there we find a Greek translation of Job 42:11-12, dated by the publishers to the early first century CE. It has the tetragrammaton in old Hebrew letters.[40] As previously stated, two of the three P. Fouad 266 manuscripts do not contain the tetragrammaton because the original Herbrew text did not have it. But there is another Septuagint manuscript, 4QLXXLev[a],

---

[35] Emanuel Tov, *The Greek Minor Prophets Scroll From Nahal Hever (8HevXIIgr)* (Discoveries in the Judean Desert 8; Oxford: Oxford University Press, 1990), p. 24.

[36] P. W. Skehan, "The Qumran Manuscripts and Textual Criticism," in *Volume du congrès, Strasbourg 1956* (VTSup 4: Leiden: Brill, 1957), pp. 148-160.

[37] Kahle, *The Cairo Geniza*, pp. 226, 227.

[38] C. H. Roberts, quoted in Skehan, "The Divine Name at Qumran, in the Masada Scroll, and in the Septuagint," p. 42, note 25.

[39] P. W. Skehan, E. Ulrich and J. E. Sanderson, *Qumran Cave 4, IV*, (Discoveries in the Judean Desert 9; Oxford: Clarendon Press, 1992), p. 11.

[40] *The Oxyrhybchus Papyri*, vol. 58 (1983 Graeco-Roman Memoirs, no. 70; London: Egypt Exploration Society, 1983), entry 3522.

which also does not contain the tetragrammaton, and this is, according to Countess, a big problem for the NWT argument:

> This fragment produces the crux for the NWT contention because this Leviticus portion contains verses which in the Hebrew Masoretic text have the Divine Name in tetragrammaton form. Verses two and thirteen have the Divine Name once each and in neither instance did יהוה or יהוה [Hebrew forms of the divine name] appear. The copyist maintained his usage of the Greek language throughout.[41]

The last sentence of the above quote is true, but at the same time it is misleading. It is true that the manuscript has only Greek letters, but what Countess does not tell his readers is that in the two verses where the Hebrew text has the tetragrammaton, the manuscript has blank spaces and no Greek letters at all! The editors of the manuscript say: "Since no occurrence of the divine name survives, it cannot be known whether IAω (as in pap4QLXXLev[b]), some other form of the Tetragrammaton, or κύριος occurred in lines 1 and 18."[42]

What, then, is the purpose of such blank spaces? In P. Fouad 266 the scribe of the Greek text evidently left blank spaces where the tetragrammaton occured in the Hebrew text, and another scribe wrote the tetragrammaton in at a later time. In this manuscript one of the blank spaces was left empty. P. J. Parsons[43] points out that this procedure was also followed in POxy656 (Genesis) from the second century CE, where *kurios* was written by a second hand. This means that the two blank spaces in the manuscript referred to by Countess in no way establish that *kurios* or a similar substitute was used for the tetragrammaton in the Septuagint in the second century BCE.

---

[41] Countess, *The Jehovah's Witnesses' New Testament*, p. 30.

[42] Skehan, Ulrich, Sanderson, *Qumran Cave 4, IV*, p. 163.

[43] Tov, *The Greek Minor Prophets Scroll from Nahal Hever*, p. 12.

What can we learn from all these Septuagint[44] fragments about the use of the divine name in writing and in speech? As far as writing is concerned, there is no example in Greek manuscripts of the use of *kurios* instead of the tetragrammaton before the middle of the second century CE. The example referred to by Countess offers nothing to contradict this point. But what about the *pronunciation* of the tetragrammaton in old Hebrew and Aramaic script and as the phonetic transcription *IAŌ*?

As to pronunciation, Stegemann[45] has gathered much information on the use of *kurios* and other divine names, and argues strongly that *IAŌ* represented the pronunciation of the divine name, and that this form was used in the original Septuagint.[46] Later, when the divine name was no longer pronounced, the tetragrammaton was used in the text. Skehan[47] has also done research on divine names, and his conclusions are quite similar to those of Stegemann. Skehan believes that the first form of the divine name in the Septuagint was *IAŌ*, and starting in the first century BCE the tetragrammaton in Aramaic script was used. Then, from the last part of the first century BCE until the fall of the Qumran settlement in 68 CE,

---

[44] The word "Septuagint" may be used differently by different commentators. We should probably say "Septuagint-like fragments" rather than "Septuagint fragments."

[45] H. Stegemann, ΚΥΡΙΟΣ Ο ΘΕΟΣ *und* ΚΥΡΙΟΣ ΙΗΣΟΥΣ *Aufkommen und Ausbreitung des religiösen Gebrauchs von* ΚΥΡΙΟΣ *und seine Verwendung im Neuen Testament*, pp. 197-201.

[46] A century or so before the translation of the Septuagint began, we find the form IAHU or IAHO in manuscripts made by Aramaic-speaking Jews on the island of Elephantine in the Nile delta. (See E. G. Kraeling's entry under "Elephantine Papyri" in *The Interpreter's Dictionary of the Bible*, vol. 2 [New York: Abingdon Press, 1962], pp. 83-84.) Remembering that the Greek "h" is a rough breathing at the beginning of a word and never occurs in the middle, then there need not be any difference between Greek *IAŌ* and Aramaic IAHU/IAHO, and that *IAŌ* is not necessarily a Greek innovation. These old witnesses to the form IAHU/O argue against the popular pronunciation Yahweh, which does not account for the U/O vowel.

[47] P.W. Skehan, *The Divine Name at Qumran, in the Masada Scroll and in the Septuagint*, Bulletin of the International Organization for Septuagint and Cognate Studies 13 (Cleveland State University, 1988), pp. 28-35.

the tetragrammaton in Paleo-Hebrew script was used. After this, *kurios* was used as a substitute for the divine name.

The conclusions of Stegemann and Skehan that *IAŌ* implies pronunciation of the divine name can hardly be disputed. Phonetic transcriptions represent pronunciation! And because we know that in the second century BCE there was some superstition at Qumran against pronouncing the divine name, it is tempting to accept the views of the two scholars that the tetragrammaton in Greek manuscripts indicate that it was not pronounced when written in Hebrew characters. But can all the data be reconciled with such views?

When we look at the ages assigned to the different manuscripts, we see that most authorities judge P. Fouad 266 to be older than 4QLXXLev[b], thus assigning a greater age to the tetragrammaton in Aramaic script than to *IAŌ*. Parsons wrote that the script of the manuscript with *IAŌ* is comparable to that of the Fouad *Deuteronomy*. He says it "may belong to the first century BCE," but it might also "extend well into the first century CE."[48] Remembering that the translation of the Septuagint probably started in the third century BCE, the manuscript with the form *IAŌ* may be two hundred years apart from the Septuagint autographs.

In 1984 Albert Pietersma[49] wrote a well reasoned article wherein he tried to contradict the evidence presented above and show that *kurios* was the original Septuagint rendition of the tetragrammaton. He took the text of the Pentateuch in later manuscripts of the Septuagint as a point of departure. In the Hebrew text, several hundred times we find the preposition *le* ("to") connected with the tetragrammaton. He argued that in the later Septuagint manuscripts we find this construction rendered as *tō kuriō* ("to the Lord") in the dative case, and to be able to give this rendition where the Hebrew text has *le* connected with the tetragrammaton, the manuscripts with *tō kuriō* must have been translated from Hebrew originals. If they

---

[48] Tov, *The Greek Minor Prophets Scroll from Nahal Hever*, p. 10.

[49] Albert Pietersma, "Kyrios or Tetragram: A Renewed Quest for the Original Septuagint," in *De Septuaginta. Studies in Honour of John William Wevers on His Sixty-Fifth Birthday*, ed. A. Pietersma and C. Cox (Toronto: Benben Publications, 1984).

were translated from Greek manuscripts containing the tetragrammaton not marked for case, they would not know where to supply *tō* in the dative case.

After Pietersma published his article, various Greek texts from among the Dead Sea Scrolls were published. In Zechariah 9:1 in 8HevXIIgr *tō* is clearly seen before the tetragrammaton in Old Hebrew script, and in Zephaniah 1:6 it is reconstructed on the basis of the length of the line.[50] This shows that *tō kuriō* very well could have been rendered on the basis of Greek manuscripts with the divine name. So Pietersma's argument is invalid.[51]

We may also refer to P. Ryl. 458, which is believed to be from the second century BCE, perhaps being the oldest Septuagint manuscript extant. In it there are no examples of divine names in any form, but it is broken at a point where the divine name would have been written. In fact, the space is so big that when Roberts published it in 1936, he suggested that *kurios* originally had been written there. Because *kurios* is never found in any manuscript of this age, it is extremely unlikely that it occurred in this manuscript, but the space is too big for the small word *IAŌ*, and Roberts later accepted the suggestion of Kahle that the tetragrammaton must have been written where the break was.[52]

The production of a manuscript with the phonetic transcription *IAŌ* from the last part of the first century BCE, suggests that the divine name was still pronounced by some at this time; and because a manuscript was used for a long time after its production, the pronunciation probably also continued. Modern Jews, when they read the Bible and come to YHWH, automatically read *'adōnāy*. Similarly, when a Greek person read a Septuagint manuscript containing the tetragrammaton, he *could* have used a substitute, perhaps *kurios*. However, the

---

[50] Tov, *The Greek Minor Prophets Scroll from Nahal Hever*, pp. 59, 77.

[51] In a lecture at the congress of The International Organization for Septuagint and Cognate Studies, in Oslo, August 1998, Emanuel Tov argued that Pietersma's point was invalid. Pietersma himself was present during the lecture.

[52] Kahle, *The Cairo Geniza*, p. 222.

likelihood that the two manuscripts with the tetragrammaton are older than the one with *IAŌ* suggests that the tetragrammaton was in fact pronounced. And regardless of how we view the pronunciation of the tetragrammaton, the age of the manuscript with *IAŌ* shows that the divine name was pronounced by some at least two hundred years after the translation of the Septuagint.

There is also another line of evidence. 8HevXIIgr is not far removed in age from the manuscripts with *IAŌ* and with the tetragrammaton in Aramaic letters; most experts give it a somewhat younger age. In Micah 1:2 this manuscript has the Greek word *kurios* as a translation for the Hebrew *'adōnāi* in a verse where the tetragrammaton in old Hebrew letters also occurs. This is important because the traditional view is that the Jews substituted the tetragrammaton with *'adōnāi* ("Lord"), and this was the reason why the Greeks used *kurios* ("Lord") instead of the tetragrammaton. Commenting on this passage, Tov expresses his belief that the manuscript probably distinguished between the tetragrammaton and *'adōnāy*.[53] And this, of course, strongly suggests that the tetragrammaton was not pronounced as *kurios*.[54] If this is true, then the reader would have read *kurios kurios*[55] in this verse, and that is not likely.

The manuscript evidence, as far as the Septuagint is concerned, suggests that persons using this translation both wrote and pronounced the divine name, and there is no compelling reason to believe that this ceased before the middle of the second century CE.

---

[53] Tov, *The Greek Minor Prophets Scroll from Nahal Hever*, p. 85.

[54] We may note that *theos* ("god") also occurs together with the tetragrammaton in Jonah 2:2 and Micah 4:5; 5:3. However, in Nahum 1:9 we find *theos instead* of the tetragrammaton that is in the Hebrew text. This may or may not be a variant.

[55] The reality of this problem is seen by the fact that the Masoretes pointed the divine name in Micah 1:2 as *Jehovih*. In the normal pointing of the tetragrammaton the vowels are borrowed from *'adōnāy* and the result is *Jehva(h)* (sometimes *Jehova[h]*). In cases where *'adōnāy* occurs immediately before YHWH, as in this verse, the Masoretes borrowed the vowels from *'elōhîm*, so they could read *'adōnāy 'elōhîm* instead of *'adōnāy 'adōnāi*.

168

THE TETRAGRAMMATON IN EARLY HEBREW AND ARAMAIC SOURCES

A need for translations from Hebrew into Aramaic arose when groups of Jews no longer understood the Hebrew language sufficiently. Oral translations were first given in the synagogues, and these were later written down. This is how the Aramaic Targums originated. The normal translation of the tetragrammaton in the Targums is YWY. Most of the Targum manuscripts that we possess today are younger than the great Septuagint codices from the fourth and fifth century, and they cannot be used to show how the tetragrammaton was handled before this time. However, in 1956 a Targum of Job was found in cave 11 at Qumran, and this manuscript was dated to the first part of the first century BCE. Fitzmeyer believes it may even be older.[56] In this manuscript *'alāhā* is written instead of the tetragrammaton.

In 1963-65 Yigael Yadin excavated Masada. Among the manuscripts that he found was one of Ecclesiasticus. This book was written about 190 BCE by Jesus ben Sira and was translated into Greek about 130 BCE. The Greek translation has been known for some time, and Hebrew fragments of the book were also found in the Cairo Geniza. While the Greek text lacks the tetragrammaton, in the Hebrew we find it either as three yods or in Aramaic script. In the 26 fragments of chapters 39-44 found at Masada, which are dated to the first half of the first century BCE we find for the most part *'elyōn* ("the most high"), but also *'ēl* ("god") and *'adōnāy* ("lord"), but not the tetragrammaton.

Stegemann concluded on this basis that the name was not found in the autograph from 190 BCE, but this conclusion is not the only possibility. The Masada fragments are a hundred years younger than the autograph, and Skehan is of the opinion that the tetragrammaton was pronounced daily in the temple in the days of Ben Sira.[57] The use of divine names is somewhat

---

[56] J. A. Fitzmeyer, *A Wandering Aramean* (Society of Biblical Literature Monograph Series 25; Missoula: Scholars Press, 1979), pp. 162, 163.

[57] P. W. Skehan and A. A. DiLella, *The Wisdom of Ben Sira* (Anchor Bible 39; New York: Doubleday, 1987), p. 554. Ecclesiasticus 50:20 reads, "The blessing

fluid in translations of Ecclesiasticus. In 5:3, for example, one Syrian manuscript has a word meaning "god," most Greek manuscripts have *kurios,* and the Latin version has "the most high." In view of the fact that a Hebrew manuscript from the twelfth century CE uses YYY to represent the tetragrammaton,[58] the original Ecclesiasticus may have contained the tetragrammaton even though the Hebrew copy from 100 BCE did not.

Josephus was originally a pharisee, and at one time he had some contact with the Essenes. During the war in 66-70 CE he deserted to the Roman enemy, and later he wrote the history of the Jews in Greek. In his writings he never used the tetragrammaton but instead used *despotēs* ("lord," "master") as a substitute; the designation *kurios* occurs twice. In his *Antiquities* (II, 12:4), which he wrote sometime in or about 93-94 CE, Josephus explains how the divine name was revealed to Moses, and then he adds, "concerning which it is not lawful for me to say any more." Because he ceased to live among his Jewish contemporaries at the end of the sixties, it is likely that his statement refers to an earlier time.

Philo of Alexandria from whom many of the Church Fathers drew, was born about 20 BCE and wrote extensively in the first part of the first century CE. He never used the tetragrammaton in his writings and he interpreted Leviticus 24:16 as a prohibition against pronouncing it. In his account of what God said to Moses, where Moses asked about God's name, Philo wrote that "no name at all can properly be used of me, to whom all existence belong."[59] His words represent the old Platonic thought that "the One" is nameless. The writings of Philo shows that in Egypt in the first part of the first century CE, there were some who did not write or pronounce the tetragrammaton.

We have already discussed some Septuagint fragments (HevXIIgr) that were found in Nahal Hever in the district of

---

of the LORD would be upon his lips and the name of the LORD would be his glory."

[58] Skehan and DiLella, *The Wisdom of Ben Sira,* p. 567.

[59] Philo, *De Vita Moses* I, sec. 75.

Bar Kochba, the last Jewish leader who led the Jews against the Romans around 130 CE. In other caves in the same area, letters to and from him have been discovered. The tetragrammaton is found in biblical fragments from these caves and in the phylacteries, but not in the letters or other documents. Bar Kochba is a typical representative of the Jews of Palestine, and it seems safe to conclude that they neither wrote nor pronounced the tetragrammaton at the beginning of the second century CE.

RABBINIC SOURCES AND THE TETRAGRAMMATON

The tractate Avoth in the Mishna tries to trace the religious tradition of the Jews back in an unbroken line to Moses by claiming that particular information was delivered from sage to sage. We would expect to find something about the divine name and why it was viewed as ineffable in this material, but there is nothing. Because of what is said in the Talmud in Tosefta Sota XIII, 8 and Yoma 39B, some researchers, including Stegemann, have drawn the conclusion that the divine name ceased to be pronounced in the time of the high priest, Simon the Just, around 200 BCE. However, the passages are not very clear, and K. Kohler wrote an article wherein he pointed out that the tradition only says that the divine name was not pronounced in *the priestly blessing* in the temple.[60] It does not say that it was never pronounced after that time. S. S. Cohon, commenting on the same question, writes:

> Tradition reports that after the death of Simon the Just (probably the contemporary of Ben Sira), whether out of considerations of reverence or possibly because of hellenistic persecution, the use of the divine name was withheld from greetings. With the passing of the danger, the old usage was reinstated.[61]

---

[60] K. Kohler, "The Tetragrammaton and Its Uses," *Journal of Jewish Lore and Philosophy* 1 (1919) pp. 26, 27.

[61] S. S. Cohon, *The Name of God: A Study in Rabbinic Theology* (Hebrew Union College Annual, 1951), p. 588.

E. M. Schuller therefore has a point when she criticizes the view of Stegemann that pronunciation of the name ceased early: "However, his evidence for 200 BCE (based mainly on Ben Sirah and on certain rabbinic passages about Simon the Just) is much less than certain, and the key texts can be interpreted in a number of different ways."[62]

Beyond what has already been referred to, neither the Mishna nor the Talmud say anything about the time when the tetragrammaton ceased to be pronounced. But the Mishna implies that even when the superstition against pronouncing the name was growing, the pronunciation was known, and it was used by some. Regarding the day of atonement it says:

> And when the priests and the people which stood in the temple court heard the expressed name come forth from the mouth of the high priest, they used to kneel and bow themselves and fall down on their faces and say, "Blessed be the Name of the glory of His kingdom forever and ever" (*Mishna*, Yoma 6:2).

There are different traditions as to how the high priest pronounced the name. One tradition says that he just whispered it; another says that he spoke so loudly that his pronunciation could be heard as far as Jericho. (*Mishna*, Tamid 3:8) In time, a fear arose about pronouncing the name, and the Mishna says, "In the temple they pronounced the name as it is written, but in the provinces by a substituted word" (*Mishna*, Sotah 7:6).

Even when the tetragrammaton was no longer frequently spoken, there were situations where common persons had to pronounce it. One tradition tells that in a court case when someone was accused of blasphemy, that is, to have pronounced the tetragrammaton, a substitute was used while all the evidence was gathered. At the end of the case the chief witness was asked privately to tell what he had heard. This must have involved using the divine name with its proper pronunciation. (*Mishna*, Sanhedrin 7:5) The gravity of blasphemy in this

---

[62] E. M. Schuller, *Non-Canonical Psalms from Qumran: A Pseudepigraphic Collection* (Harvard Semitic Studies 28, Atlanta, Georgia: Scholars Press, 1986), p. 57, note 36.

instance may be illustrated by the words of Abba Saul, who lived in the middle of the second century CE. He said that "the one who pronounces the Name with its proper letters, has not part in the world to come" (*Mishna*, Sanhedrin 10:1).[63]

So far we have discussed traditions showing that the name was not to be pronounced, or at least pronounced in a limited way. But there are also traditions that support a different conclusion. According to the Mishna it was 'ordained that a man should salute his fellow with the Name' of God, for it is written (in Ruth 2:4) "and [Boas] proceeded to say to the harvesters: 'Let YHWH be with you'" (*Mishna*, Berakhot 9:5).

Outside the Mishna and the Talmud there are rabbinic writings which contain information relevant to our discussion. L. Finkelstein discussed rabbinic traditons that could be traced back to the last few centuries BCE.[64] He quotes two passages which must have been written down while the tetragrammaton was still pronounced, by some:

> One who begins a prayer with *yodh heh* [that is, the Tetragrammaton, actually enunciating it] and ends with *yodheh* [in the doxology] is a Sage. [One who begins] with *yodh heh* and ends with *aleph lamed* [the cypher *'elōhim*] is ignorant. [One who begins] with *aleph lamed* and ends with *aleph lamed* is following another way [that is, he is a sectarian].[65]

The Morning-bathers[66] say, "We complain of you, O Pharisees because you pronounce the Name before you

---

[63] It is possible that his expression only relates to magical arts used in order to heal. This is Cohon's view. See *The Name of God: A Study in Rabbinic Theology*, pp. 592, 593.

[64] L. Finkelstein, *New Light on the Prophets* (London: Vallentine, Mitchell, 1969), pp. 9, 10.

[65] *Tosefta* Barakhot 6 (7), 20. See Saul Liberman's *Tosefta*, ed. M. S. Zuckermandel (Jerusalem, 1930).

[66] The "Morning-bathers" are probably the "Hemerobaptists," one of the seven Jewish sects that is mentioned by Hegesippus (who wrote sometime near 180 CE) and quoted by Eusebius. (See NPNF 1, pp. 198-200.) They are also mentioned by Justin (*Dialogue with Trypho*, chapter 80) as "Baptists."

bathe." The Pharisees reply, "We complain of you, O Morning-bathers because you mention the Name with a body which contains defilement."[67]

These quotes stress the same fact as does the Mishna, that the fear of pronouncing the tetragrammaton did not originate suddenly, and that there were different viewpoints among different groups of Jews as to when and under what circumstances the divine name could be pronounced. The last quote also gives an indication of the time when the discussions about the pronounciation of the divine name took place. Finkelstein pointed out that both groups who took part in the discussion must have had the custom of pronouncing the name; otherwise the text would have been meaningless. One of the groups mentioned is the Pharisees. This group probably arose in the second century BCE from the *hasidim*. At the time of John Hyrcanus (135-105 BCE) we find one of the earlist references to the Pharisees, and, therefore, the earliest time for the situation involving the Morning-bathers must have been sometime before the year 100 BCE, at a time when the Essenes had stopped pronouncing the divine name. But the situation could have occurred much later, even in the days of Jesus.

SUPERSTITION, THEOLOGY AND THE TETRAGRAMMATON

The cautious Bible translator is anxious to closely follow the original text of the Bible. However, he or she is also sensitive to all kinds of relevant background information and does not translate mechanically; rather, the translator is alert to check his translated text. Such a translator will naturally pause at James 5:9 where there is a reference to "the prophets who spoke in the name of the Lord" as most translations render it. Regardless of how we view the tetragrammaton and its place in the NT, we must admit that while this rendition is textually correct, it is

---

[67] *Tosefta* Yeadim 2:20.

factually wrong. The prophets did not speak in the name of "the Lord" but they spoke in the name of "YHWH."

Using this verse as a point of departure, we will ask why this enigmatic situation has arisen where a "correct" rendition gives the "wrong" meaning. There are three biblical passages which may have some bearing upon the question of why the Jews stopped pronouncing the divine name, namely, Leviticus 24:16, Exodus 20:7 and 3:15. The first one, Leviticus 24:16, reads, "The alien resident the same as the native should be put to death for his abusing the Name."

The verb *nāqab* has the meanings "to pierce," "to blaspheme." The Septuagint[68] and the Targum Onkelos translate the verb with the meaning "to mention [the name]," and thus become witnesses against pronouncing it. According to G. F. Moore, however, the rabbis never used this verse as proof that the tetragrammaton should not be pronounced.[69]

Exodus 20:7 reads, "You must not take up the name of Jehovah your God in a worthless way." The Hebrew phrase *Iashāw*, translated "in a worthless way" has the meaning "for nothing" or "without purpose." The rabbis of Mishnaic times used this against swearing false oaths in the name of God and against an unnecessary use of the name in prayers. But they did not use it as a proof that the name should not be used or pronunciated.[70]

The passage that was used to show that the name should not be pronounced was curiously enough the one which, in the most definite way, says that one should never stop pronouncing it, namely, Exodus 3:15. About the name YHWH it says: "this is my name to time indefinite, and this is the memorial of me to

---

[68] This translation of the Septuagint suggests that its translators did not pronounce the name of God. We should, however, keep in mind that this rendering is found in manuscripts from the second century CE and onwards. Whether it was also rendered in this way in the original Septuagint is unknown. The phonetic transcription *IAŌ* in earlier Septuagint manuscripts argues against the later Septuagint and Targum Onkelos rendering.

[69] G. F. Moore, *Judaism in the First Centuries of the Christian Era: The Age of the Tannaim Judaism*, vol. 1 (Cambridge: Cambridge University Press, 1955), p. 428.

[70] Finkelstein, *New Light on the Prophets*, p. 428.

generation after generation." There is a parallelism in the verse between "my name" and "the memorial" and between "to time indefinite" and "to generation after generation." This reduces the possibilities for misinterpretation.

The Jewish sages, however, used the words to prove that the divine name should not be pronounced. They offered these different lines of reasoning:

- The word *'ōlām* is written defectively,[71] and therefore the noun *'ōlām* (time indefinite) is not meant but the verb *'ālam*, which means "to conceal," to hide." The name must be concealed and therefore it should not be pronounced.

- A later meaning of the noun *'ōlām* is used. In the OT the noun refers to "a long time where the length is not stated" or to "eternity." The Aramaic noun *'ālam* often stresses the quality of time; it is even used of "people." An extension of this meaning is also found in the Mishna, for instance, in the often recurring phrase *'ōlām habbā* ("the world to come"). If the meaning of *'ōlām* in Exodus 3:15 is "world order," it may be claimed that it refers to "the world to come." In this world the name will be pronounced for ever, but in the present world we must not pronounce it.

- "This is my name for ever (to time indefinite)" refers to a righteous person who will get "a monument" (Isaiah 56:5) in Jerusalem in the world to come. He will also get an everlasting "name." This indicates that the meaning of the ineffable name will then be revealed to him, and he will reap its benefits for ever. Exodus 3:15, therefore, does not refer to the pronunciation of the divine name in this world.[72]

---

[71] When the Bible was written, Hebrew lacked vowels, but a few consonants were used as vowels. In the word *'ōlām* the consonant "w" may be used to designate the vowel "o." This is called "plene writing." If the vowels in a word are just implied, the writing is "defective."

[72] See M. M. Kasher, *The Encyclopedia of Biblical Interpretation*, vol. 2 (New York: American Biblical Encyclopedia Society, 1967), p. 109.

- The clause "and this is the memorial of me to generation after generation" means that in some generations the name would be a memorial and thus be pronounced, in other generations it would not be pronounced.

My objective is to find, observe and then describe the philological setting; and theological arguments are restricted as much as possible. When I elucidate the rabbinic interpretations of Exodus 3:15 it is to show that these viewpoints cannot be the reason why the divine name, at some point in time, was no longer pronounced. The interpretations that we have just considered are so idiosyncratic and forced that they seem to represent retrospective explanations of what is perceived to be a problematic text; the text itself (Exod 3:15) could hardly be considered the foundation for this position against pronouncing the divine name. We may also note that the Septuagint and the Samaritan Pentateuch take the words in their normal sense. Therefore, we should look for a source other than the OT for reasons why some took a stand against pronouncing the divine name.

A principal argument against the pronunciation of the divine name, both in ancient and modern times, is that it is so high and elusive that it is ineffable (unutterable or beyond expression). By showing it this kind of respect, one will achieve the same result that formerly was achieved by pronouncing and using it, namely, a stressing of God's unique position. Related to this viewpoint is the desire to protect the name from magical use. Witchcraft became quite widespread in Palestine, and this can be traced back to the Egyptian magical arts.[73]

Those practicing magical arts viewed a name as having an intrinsic potential; by using the name, one could exercise power over the one bearing the name. In the Pseudephigraphal book of 1 Enoch (69:13-25) it speaks about "the concealed name," indicating a magical influence around 100 BCE. It was a widespread opinion that by using the tetragrammaton one could heal sick persons. The form *IAŌ*, both alone and in

---

[73] Cohon, *The Name of God*, pp. 592-598.

combinations with other letters, is very common in magical papyri; I have seen it used frequently for magical purposes in the papyri collection at the University library of Oslo. One reason for ceasing to pronounce the tetragrammaton may thus have been to prevent its use in magical arts.[74]

It seems, however, that foreign religious and philosophical influence, related to the question of whether or not it was right to use a proper name for the grand creator of the universe, was the main reason why the pronunciation of the divine name fell into disuse. The article "Nameless gods"[75] shows that gods without proper names are a phenomenon in religons all over the world. The gods were often described through their acts, often with adjectives and substantivized adjectives. Later on the god received a proper name, but in time it was viewed so holy that nobody pronounced it. Thus, in both the first and last stage of the worship of the god, namelessness occured. The article mentions two such phenomena not far from Palestine, the Canaanite god Ba'al and the Egyptian Amen-Ra, "whose name is concealed for all his creatures" according to a hymn.

That Canaanite religion influenced the Jews is clear both from the Bible and from archaeology; some Egyptian influence is also quite likely. However, the most pronounced influence in the last half of the existence of the second temple was that of Greek philosophy. A. Marmorstein[76] wrote a entire book where he discusses this influence, and he concludes that Hellenistic influence was the principal reason why the divine name ceased to be pronunced. Nobody will deny a strong Hellenistic influence on the Jews from the second century BCE onward. The need to translate the Bible into Greek shows the important role played by the Greek language for Egyptian Jews. And several new religious viewpoints, such as the immortality of the soul, were aquired from the Greeks during this period.

Marmorstein tells us that "Greek philosophy, Jewish Alexandrian theology, Christian apology and Gnostic lore

---

[74] See Cohon, *The Name of God*, pp. 592-598.

[75] In *Hastings Encyclopedia of Religion and Ethics*, vol. 9, (1908).

[76] A. Marmorstein, *The Old Rabbinic Doctrine of God* (London: Oxford University Press, 1927).

concur in the idea of God's *namelssness*. That God has no name was taught by Aristotle, Seneca, Maxim of Tyre, Celsus and Hermes Trismegistus."[77] Of those names mentioned by Marmorstein, the last four were evidently influenced by the first, namely, by Aristotle (and Greek thought). But the surrender to Greek ideas did not occur without a struggle:

> We notice a far-reaching difference between Palestinian and Alexandrian theology concerning the Tetragrammaton. A bitter struggle between Hellenists and Hasidim [the forerunners of the Pharisees] centered around the pronunciation of the Divine Name. A similar controversy arose afterwards around the use of the name Elohim and even as to the substitution of the tetragrammaton.[78]

Marmorstein, himself a rabbi, reached his conclusion after a thorough study of rabbinic litterature. To the best of my knowledge, no important discoveries affecting his conclusions have been done in the 60 years since he wrote his book. Thus, his principal conclusion appears to be on solid ground.

THE TETRAGRAMMATON AND THE NEW TESTAMENT

What about the view of Jesus and of his followers Peter, James, John and Paul? Did they use and pronounce the divine name? We do not know! But we must add that neither do we know whether the man in the street pronounced the tetragrammaton at this time. In fact, we do not even know with certainty in what language Jesus spoke with his disciples; we do not know whether it was Aramaic or Hebrew, or possibly even Greek, at times. The popular view is that the divine name in the first century CE had for a long time been out of use among the Jews. But, as we have seen, this is unfounded. Might there be

---

[77] Marmorstein, *The Old Rabbinic Doctrine of God*, p. 17.

[78] Marmorstein, *The Old Rabbinic Doctrine of God*, p. 13.

some clues in the NT text itself that could shed some light on whether or not the divine name was used by Jesus and his followers?

As evidence that YHWH was no longer pronounced we find 6 examples of the word "heaven" (Matt 21:25; Luke 15:18, 21; 20:4) and 2 instances of "power" (Matt 26:64; Mark 14:62) as references to God. The words of Luke 22:69, however, suggest that "power" may be an abbreviation rather than a designation for God. The particular use of "heaven" in the aforementioned passages is also found in Daniel (compare Daniel 4:25, 26), a book that contains the tetragrammaton and that was written during a time when the tetragrammaton was still pronounced. As respects the principal designations for God, there are 1317 occurrences of *theos* and 717 of *kurios* in the Greek NT. Looking at all these, I found that 630 instances of *theos* and 134 instances of *kurios* are referrences to God.[79] There are between 50 and 100 other instances of *kurios* were it is difficult to know whether Jesus or God is the referent.

In looking at the situations where the two words are used, there can be no doubt that the normal designation for the creator in the days of Jesus, both among the people and among those writing the NT, was *'elōhîm* in Hebrew and *theos* in Greek, both meaning "god." But this does not necessarily mean that the name YHWH was not used.[80] When a British person speaks about "the queen" everybody knows which queen he or she means, and if he or she should have the opportunity to talk to her, the person would likely address her as "Your Majesty." To a foreigner, however, the British person might refer to her as "Queen Elizabeth."

---

[79] Genitive constructions where something is owned by God and quotes from the OT are not included in these figures.

[80] The NT data indicate that it was common to use different designations for God. In Luke 1 and 2 we find 16 occurrences of *kurios* (which may originally have been YHWH) and 13 occurrences of *theos* (1:6, 8, 9, 11, 15, 19, 25, 26, 28, 30, 32, 35, 37, 38, 46, 47, 49, 58, 66, 68, 76, 78; 2:9, 13, 14, 20, 22, 23, 24, 28, 29, 38, 39, 40). In the speech of Stephen in Acts 7 we find "the God of glory" (verse 2), "God" (verses 6, 7, 9, 17, 25, 35, 37, 42, 45, 46, 55, 56); "the Lord (*kurios*, verses 31, 33, 49, 60), and "the most high" (verse 48).

One NT example which may indicate that the personal name of God was used when necessary is Mark 11:3. Here we find *ho kurios* as the referent in the Greek text and not *theos*, the usual designation for God. The words *ho kurios* are definite and must correspond to a definite noun phrase or to a proper name in Hebrew (or Aramaic) which is the language the disciples spoke. The use of a definite noun phrase presupposes that those who heard it mentioned would have a knowledge of the identity of the person or thing to whom/which it referred. If the disciples had approached a person who had no knowledge of "the Lord" their request for the colt might have been resisted. However, a Jew living in the first century CE would have had a knowledge of the God of Israel, and because the disciples needed to make sure that they were not perceived as theives, a reference to God would help them secure the colt, but a reference to a vague or unknown "Lord" may not have succeeded, apart from divine intervention.

Thus, in Mark 11:3 *ho kurios* most likely stands for the personal name of God. In contrast, Jesus is addressed as *ho didaskalos* ("teacher," Mark 14:14). Corroborating the preceding reasoning is the fact that the people, acording to Mark 11:9, cry, "Blessed is he who comes in the name of *kurios*." In this case *kurios* must represent YHWH because the people are here quoting from the OT, which uses YHWH.

There is no copy of the NT text where YHWH is written, but *kurios* (or sometimes *theos*) is written where we would expect to find YHWH, if it was used. The traditional explanation is that the Jews in the first century CE used a substitute word for YHWH and this substitute was translated by *kurios*. This explanation has two serious problems. The first problem is that there is no Hebrew or Aramaic word that was used as a substitute for YHWH, which naturally would have been translated by *kurios*. The Hebrew word which, like *kurios*, means "lord" is *'adōnāy* and the Aramaic equivalent is *marē/marî*, but there is no evidence that either of these words were used as substitutes for YHWH, either. In the Hebrew Bible *'adōnāy* is used for God about 900 times but not *in place of* YHWH. All the occurrences of *kurios* in the Septuagint are of no help because this word does not occur in any manuscript as a name of God before the second century CE. In the Dead Sea

Scrolls[81] only 47 examples of *'adōnāy* are found and 8 of *marî*, compared with 677 examples of *'ēl* and 139 occurrences of *'elōhîm*. So there is absolutely no evidence for the use of a Hebrew or Aramaic equivalent to *kurios* before or in the first century CE.[82]

The second problem is that of confusion. Naturally, an author writes to be understood, but the use of the one word *kurios* for two different individuals is really confusing, and this is the case when "God" and "Jesus" are found together with *kurios* (see Acts 11:20, 21; 1 Cor 11:23; 1 Thess 4:15,16). The use of one "name"[83] for a father and his son, to the point where it results in confusion over their identities, is unprecedented in the Bible, and suggests that everything is not well with the text, and that the word *kurios* may not originally have been used for God. In support of this there is evidence that *kurios* in the NT translates *two* different Hebrew (or Aramaic) words, and not just one. Take for instance John 21:7, where John says regarding Jesus, "It is the Lord [*ho kurios*]." In Matthew 4:7 we also find *ho kurios* in this quote from the OT, "You must not put *ho kurios* your God to the test." If John had used the same Hebrew or Aramaic word in 21:7 that Jesus used in Matthew 4:7 the result would have been complete confusion. If John had said, "It is *adōnāy*" and *'adōnāy* was used as a substitute for YHWH, he could rightly have been construed to mean, "It is YHWH."[84] So,

---

[81] According to Charlesworth's concordance, which, again, is not exhaustive.

[82] For an attempt to reveal a semitic background for *kurios*, see J. Fitzmeyer, "The Semitic Background of the New Testament *Kyrios*-Title," in *The Wandering Aramean: Collected Essays* (Society of Biblical Literature Monograph Series 25; Missoula: Scholars Press, 1979).

[83] The word *kurios* is an appellative rather than a proper name. But in reference to God it is used as a substitute for a proper name, and when the same word is also used as a title or designation for Jesus we might say that the same "name" is used for two individuals.

[84] The argument relates to the time when Jesus was on earth. In Acts 2:36 it is said that "God made him both Lord [*kurios*] and Christ"—God made Jesus "Lord" in a special sense. However, during his earthly sojourn he was called "Lord" in the ordinary sense of "master" and "teacher." (Matt 14:28, 30; 15:22, 25, 27) The disciples also used the word in this sense, and, additionally, they referred to Jesus as "the Lord," that is, 'their Lord,' the Lord whom they knew.

in all the instances where *kurios* is used in addressing or referring to Jesus (most likely also in the instances where *kurios* is used together with the word "Jesus") a Hebrew word other than *'adōnāy* was spoken or was in the minds of the Hebrew authors.[85] But there is more evidence to consider.

Acts 4:24, 29 are part of a prayer to God. Here we find the words *despota* and *kurie*.[86] The first word, *despota*, is found 11 times in the Septuagint, always translating *'adōnāy* (except in Dan 9:11 where it possibly translates *'elōhîm* ["God"]). The meaning of *despota* is "Lord" and in Acts 4:24 it is most likely a rendition of *'adōnāy*. But if this is true, the word *kurios* in verse 29 can hardly represent *'adōnāy*, and there are few alternatives except YHWH. We should also think of Revelation 11:17, 15:3 and 16:7, where God is addressed three times as *kurie ho theos* (= "the Lord God"). Revelation is very much dependent upon the OT, and in its Hebrew text we find *'adōnāy 'elōhîm* ("Lord God") only five times while we find YHWH *'elōhîm* 817 times. The Septuagint manuscripts (dated from the second century CE onward) have 178 examples of *kurios theos* and 817 examples of *kurios ho theos* in verses where YHWH is part of the original. It is therefore quite likely that YHWH was written in the original manuscript of Revelation, something which is corroborated by the words of Revelation 15:4, where the importance of God's name is stressed and by the three occurrences of *hallēlouia* ("praise Jah") in 19:3, 4, 6.

But how shall we explain the discrepancy between the number of occurrences of the divine name in the OT and the

---

[85] The versions give credence to the "confusion" argument. In Syriac the normal reference to God is *marya* ("the Lord"), and this is the word we find in the Peshitta of Matthew 4:7. In John 21:7, however, we find *maran* ("our Lord") in both places where the Greek text has *ho kurios*, and this cannot be taken in reference to God. In Ethiopic (Ge'ez) the normal designation for God is *'egzi'abher* ("the Lord of the land"), and this is what we find in Matthew 4:7. In John 21:7 we find *'egziena'* ("our Lord") in both places. In the Arabic manuscript Sinai 69 from the eleventh century CE we find *rabbaka wa-ilahaka* ("your Lord and your God") in Matthew 4:7 but *rabbuna* ("our Lord") in the first instance in John 21:7, and *al-rabb* ("the Lord") in the second instance.

[86] The two words are the vocative case (direct address) of *despotēs* and *kurios* respectively.

much smaller number of possible uses of the name in the NT? Even the NWT has only 237 instances of "Jehovah" in the NT (plus possibly 72 others) compared with almost 7000 in the OT? There could be several reasons for this: 1) The proper name of God was no longer important; 2) veneration for Jesus suppressed the Jewish name of God; and 3) there were pragmatic reasons for the discrepancy.

A study of how Jesus is addressed and referred to from Romans through Revelation seems to suggest that 3) is the correct explanation. In going through the material, I found 282 examples of the name Jesus, and of these, 202 occur together with the word *christos* ("Christ"), 106 occur with the word *kurios* ("Lord"), sometimes in addition to *christos* and sometimes not. There are 450 examples of *christos* in these books, and, therefore, there are 248 examples of "Christ" used alone as a title for Jesus. Additionally, there are 356 examples of *kurios* ("lord"), and substracting the 106 used in connection with Jesus, we find 250 examples of "lord" used as a title. If it is correct, as the NWT sees it, that 117 of the occurrences of *kurios* refer to YHWH, there are 133 examples of the lone title *kurios* applied to Jesus. The result is that we find 192 examples where Jesus is identified by name and 381 instances where only his title is used.

In OT times it was of primary importance to show the difference between the YHWH and other gods. "Thus says YHWH" was the identifying word of the prophets. For Paul and others who wrote to the Christian congregations, it was of primary importance to stress that one born by a woman, Jesus Christ, was the savior of mankind. Jesus has the central position in the NT, and therefore his name was on the minds of the NT writers more often than YHWH, as issues of controversy revolved around Jesus and his role in YHWH's purpose. But this in no way means that the name of Jesus' Father was removed. To the contrary. The one who accepts the Son will also accept the Father, as 1 John 2:23 says, there is no meaning in the concept "son" without the concept "father."

From the above numbers we can see that when a person is called by a title descriptive of his position more often than he is called by his own name, the person is no less significant in the minds of those persons who show a preference for using the title(s). Thus, we see that a title is used for Jesus one and a half times as often (381 versus 282) as his personal name. The word *theos* occurs 845 times from Romans to Revelation, compared with 117 (plus possibly 52 more) cases of YHWH. This means that the title *theos* occurs 5 to 7 times as often as does God's personal name YHWH. In view of the stress being put on the name "Jesus" and because at least the Jewish members of the congregations knew the Father well, it is not unusual that a title of God was used much more frequently than his personal name. But in no way does this argue against his name being found in the NT autographs. If it is correct, as the NWT sees it, that 110[87] of the occurrences of *kurios* refer to YHWH, there are 140 examples[88] of the lone title *kurios* applied to Jesus. The result is that we find 192 examples where Jesus is identified by name and 388 instances where only his title is used.

In summary we might say that the OT says that the name of God should always be used (Exod 3:15; Mal 1:11) and there is absolutely nothing in any of its books suggesting that the name would eventaully cease to be used by God's worshipers. Jesus was against those traditions that came from outside the Scriptures, particularly those which nullified the sacred text. (Joh 10:35; Matt 15:8, 9) Thus, even if some or all the people in his day viewed the name as ineffable, there is no reason for him to have adopted this same view. To the contrary, he regularly stressed the importance of God's name (Joh 17:4-7; Matt 6:9). In the synagogue of Nazareth Jesus was given the book of Isaiah to read. (Luke 4:17, 18) If we possessed no other information than what Luke wrote, nobody would doubt that Jesus pronounced the divine name when he read from this text. The almost universal view that he did not pronounce the name is, as we have seen, based on faulty evidence. We therefore have good reason to believe that Jesus pronounced the divine name and that Luke wrote it down in his Gospel account. The relatively few instances where it may have been written in the NT do not contradict this.

---

[87] In the following places NWT translates *theos* as "Jehovah": Romans 4:3; Galatians 3:6, Colossians 3:16; Hebrews 2:13; James 2:2 (twice) and 2 Peter 3:12.

[88] In several instances is it difficult to determine the referent, so some of these 140 examples might be in reference to YHWH.

EVIDENCE FROM THE GREEK NT MANUSCRIPTS

Regardless of how we interpret the "internal evidence" of the NT, we have the manuscript evidence speaking in favor of "the Lord" and not "YHWH." This evidence should be given more weight than the internal evidence. However, there is also evidence which, when taken together with the "internal evidence," may even overrule the manuscript evidence. This evidence comes in the form of small textual changes that have been made in the NT manuscripts.

Let us take the text of the Septuagint as a point of departure. In the great codices from the fourth and fifth centuries CE, which contain the entire Septuagint, and in the Chester Beatty papyri, which Frederick Kenyon dates to the middle of the second century CE, we do not find either the tetragrammaton nor *IAŌ*, but where the tetragrammaton occurs in the Hebrew text we find κϛ and sometimes θϛ with a horizontal bar above them. These letters are abbreviations for *kurios* ("lord") and *theos* ("god"); other divine designations have also been abbreviated. If we compare this with the Septuagint manuscripts that were written between the second century BCE and the first century CE, we can see a clear difference as to the treatment of the divine name.

In a commentary on the publication of P Fouad 266 by F. Dunand, professor G. D. Kilpatrick[89] mentioned the period 70-135 CE and pointed out that three important changes occurred in this period: 1) the change from scroll to codex; 2) the tetragrammaton was replaced by *kurios*; and 3) abbreviations for *nomina sacra* ("sacred names") were introduced. So there can be no doubt that someone changed the text of the Septuagint, removed the divine name, and substituted abbreviations for it and other divine designations.

Looking at the *nomina sacra* in the NT manuscripts from the second and third centuries, we find the same abbreviations as we do in the Septuagint manuscripts. It is impossible that the NT autographs originally contained the abbreviated forms of

---

[89] G. D. Kilpatrick, *Etudes de Papyrologie Tome Neuvieme*, Le Caire, Imprimiere de L'Institut Francais d'Archaéologie Orientale (1971), pp. 221, 222.

kurios and other divine designations, so the abbreviations must have been introduced at some later time. Since we know that in the Septuagint the original form was the tetragrammaton or *IAŌ*, it is reasonable to conclude that this *may* also have been the case with the NT manuscripts. Keeping in mind that Jesus and his followers simply had no reason to avoid using the divine name, and seen in the light of all the evidence presented so far, the view that the tetragrammaton was found in the NT autographs has strong support.[90] In any case, the abbreviations used in place of the divine name shows that the NT text has in fact been altered.

But there is one problem we have not discussed: the age of P[46], P[64] and other early NT manuscripts. These manuscripts have recently been redated by Kim and Thiede. Formerly they were dated to 150 and 200 CE respectively, but these two researchers have dated them to the last quarter of the first century CE. Kim discusses the shape of particular letters and writes, "This strongly suggests that P[46] was written some time before the reign of emperor Domitian."[91]

Emperor Domitian reigned between 81 and 96 CE, and because P[46] has the abbreviations κϛ and θϛ, a verification of this date would be a severe blow to the opinion that the tetragrammaton (or *IAŌ*) was written in the NT autographs. Regarding another NT manuscript Thiede writes: "For our present purpose, we may proffer a tentative suggestion: the material from Nahal Hever, Herculaneum and Qumran could point towards a first-century date for the Magdalen Gr. 17/P. Barc. 1."[92]

---

[90] Compare George Howard, "The Tetragram and the New Testament," *Journal of Biblical Literature* 96 (1977), pp. 63-84. Howard has gathered much of the relevant material, and he concludes that the tetragrammaton occurred in the New Testament. He has reaffirmed this view in *The Anchor Bible Dictionary* (1992), under the heading "Names of God in the OT, Yahweh (deity)."

[91] Y. K. Kim, "Palaeographical Dating of P[46] to the Later First Century," *Biblica* 69 (1988), pp. 248-261.

[92] C. P. Thiede, 1995, "Papyrus Magdalen Greek 17 (Gregory-Aland P64): A Reappraisal," *Tyndale Bulletin* 46 (1995), p. 37.

However, there are several reasons why these revised dates cannot be viewed as conclusive. First of all, because of the individual handwriting it is impossible to date an old manuscript with exactness by studying the shapes of the letters alone. Regarding the three Septuagint manuscripts that we discussed in detail earlier (see above, pages 167-174), there is a discrepancy in the datings of more than one hundred years. Parsons commented on this paleographic dating and said that, "The reader who surveys the bibliography will not need to be warned that such evidence is shifting sand."[93] He gave the following two reasons for this view:

> (a) A scribe may have a working life of 50 years; in that time he may not change his script. Therefore, even if a style can be assumed to show a linear diachronic development, not all practitioners will develop with it.; very precise datings are risky. (b) Occasionally we can point to certain examples of archaising writing; thus POxy L 3529, which I should have assigned on palaeographic evidence to the early Roman period, is shown by its content to date after A.D. 307.

We may note that the editorial committee for the fourth edition of the United Bible Societies Greek New Testament[94] disagrees with Kim's dating. S. Peterson from the University of Pennsylvania has written an article about Thiede's dating, and she concludes: "In the absence of more data, such as the Barcelona fragments might provide, these fragments do not provide any firm evidence for the existence of *nomina sacra* in either Roberts's date of ca. 200, or Thiede's 1st century dating."[95]

We should also mention four other lines of evidence in favor of the continued use of the tetragrammaton during the

---

[93] Peter J. Parsons in E. Tov's *The Greek Minor Prophets Scroll*, pp. 22, 23.

[94] *The Greek New Testament*, 4th ed., Revised, eds. Barbara and Kurt Aland, Johannes Karavidopoulos, Carlo Martini, and Bruce Metzger (Stuttgart: United Bible Societies, 1993), Introduction, p. 8.

[95] S. Peterson, http://ccat.sas.upenn.edu/~petersig/theide2.txt, "Media Papyri: An Examination of Carsten Thiede's Rediscovered Fragments" (1995) Electronically published by the author.

time when the NT was written, yes even into and beyond the second century CE.

First, we have the following Greek translations of the OT made from the second century CE onward: Aquila (c. 130), Theodotion (sometine during the second century), Symmachus (near the end of the second century), Quinta and Sexta (undated). The first three, and possibly all five translations, were used in Origen's Hexapla. All of these translations have the tetragrammaton in the form of the Greek letters ΠΙΠΙ (PIPI).[96]

Second, we have the Syriac Bible manuscripts. Around 600 CE, Paul of Tella made a strictly literal translation of Origen's Hexapla into Syriac. This is called the Syro-Hexapla. In 2 Kings 18:6 (and in other places) we find MARYA (a technical term for God meaning, "the Lord") in the text, and PIPI in the margin. In Isaiah 1:2 we find MARYA in the text and YHYH in the margin.[97] If we look at other old non-Hexaplaric Syriac manuscripts, we find MARYA in the main text but PIPI[98] and HEHE[99] in the margin. Keeping in mind that the Syro-Hexapla also has the divine name in the margin and MARYA in the main text, while the Vorlage (underlying text) has it in the main text, the presence of the divine name in the margin of so many Syriac manuscripts suggests that the original Syriac also had the divine name in the main text. Thus, the Syriac evidence parallels the Greek evidence: the Septuagint manuscripts from the second century CE have κς in the main text while earlier manuscripts have some form of the divine name. Moreover, the divine name occurs in two forms in the margin of Syriac manuscripts, one resembling the tetragrammaton in Aramaic script (PIPI) and the other in an old Hebrew script (HEHE).

---

[96] See Adrian Schenker, *Psalmen in den Hexapla*, STUDI E TESTI 295 (Citta Del Vatticano, 1980), pp. 422, 423, 458, 486.

[97] See Henricus Middeldorpf, *Codex Syriaco-Hexaplaris* (Berolini: Th. Chr. Fr. Enslin, 1835).

[98] In Cod. Reg. Paris. Syr V, fol. 4-90, from the eigth century CE we find 410 examples of PIPI.

[99] We find examples of HEHE in the margin of Codex Ambrosianus, an important manuscript from the sixth or seventh century, and in Codex Curzonianus.

This suggests that Greek Septuagint manuscripts with the tetragrammaton in both scripts were in circulation and were used by the Syriac translators.[100]

Third, we have the words from the Talmud about the "Minim," who were probably identical with or at least included the Christians:

> The blank spaces and the Books of the Minim, we may not save them from a fire. R. Jose said: On weekdays one must cut out the tetragrammata which they contain, hide them, and burn the rest. R. Tarfon said: May I bury my son if I would not burn them together with their tetragrammata if they came to my hand.[101]

Fourth, there exist a great number of extrabiblical papyri with a magical tendency where *IAŌ* often is mentioned. In one papyri from the fourth century we find the words, *IAŌ Sabaōt, Adonai Elōai* and in another of same age we find *IAŌ Sabaōt, Adōnai, Eloē*.[102] Since the last three words are transcriptions of titles applied to YHWH in the Hebrew Bible, it is logical that *IAŌ* is a transcription of the divine name in Hebrew. Thus the papyri serve as individual witnesses, in addition to the Elephantine papyri. The use of *IAŌ* in the Septuagint manuscript 4QLXXLevb can be traced back to a Hebrew form that was in use between the fourth century BCE, and the foruth century CE.

---

[100] See Stegemann, ΚΥΡΙΟΣ Ο ΘΕΟΣ *und* ΚΥΡΙΟΣ ΙΗΣΟΥΣ *Aufkommen und Ausbreitung des religiösen Gebrauchs von* ΚΥΡΙΟΣ *und seine Verwendung im Neuen Testament*, pp. 122-124. Stegemann's conclusion is that the original Syriac translation of the OT contained the tetragrammaton.

[101] Talmud Shabbat 13 (14:5). L. H. Schiffmann, *Who was a Jew? Rabbinic and Halakhic Perspectives on the Jewish Chritian Schism* (New Jersey: Ktav Publishing House, 1985), p. 62, applies this to Christian Gospels and R. Travers Herford, *Christianity in Talmud and Midrash* (New Jersey: Reference Books Publishers, 1966) agrees that the "Minim" were the Christians. R. Jose lived around 150 CE.

[102] S. Eitrem *Papyri Osloenses*, Fasc. I. (Oslo: Jacob Dybwad, 1925), pp. 16, 44, 83, 111. The form *IAEŌ* is found on page 8.

We may summarize and compare the evidence for the use and substitution of the divine name by considering the following two charts:

Figure 5.7

Use of Substitutes for the Divine Name in Ancient Manuscripts

Second cent. BCE	The Qumran community uses *'el*
First cent. BCE	The Job Targum uses *'alāhā*
"	Ben Sira's Ecclesiasticus uses different words
First cent. CE	Philo uses *theos* and *kurios*
"	Josephus uses *despotēs*
Second cent. CE	Manuscripts of the LXX and the NT use *nomina sacra* (for example, κς and θς).

Figure 5.8

Use of the Divine Name in Ancient Manuscripts

Second cent. BCE	LXX manuscripts use the tetragrammaton or *IAŌ*
First cent. BCE	The "Morning-Bathers" and the Pharisees used and pronounced the divine name (the tetragrammaton)
"	LXX manuscripts used the tetragrammaton or *IAŌ*
First cent. CE	LXX manuscripts use the tetragrammaton or *IAŌ*
Second cent. CE	Aquila, Origen and the Minim used the tetragrammaton
Third cent. CE and later	Origen used the tetragrammaton; Syriac manuscripts have PIPI and HEHE.

THE FORM "JEHOVAH" IN NWT

After this review of the evidence regarding YHWH and the NT, we may now return to the crux of the matter, which is thus expressed by Countess: "NWT has introduced 'Jehovah' into the Greek Scriptures for the sole purpose of wiping out any vestige of Jesus Christ's identity with Jehovah."[103]

Once again theology is strongly involved in a matter which on the surface seems to be a question of textual criticism and translation theory. It is of course quite problematic for those believing in the trinity doctrine to have two proper names for God in the NT, that is, both Jesus and Jehovah. The reason this is a problem for those who believe in the trinity is because such a use of two different personal names seems to indicate two different individuals. But if "the Lord" is used for both individuals then it is much easier to assimilate this useage to trinitarainism.

Even though I conclude that the bulk of the evidence speaks in favor of the view that Jesus and his followers used the divine name, I will take a neutral stand as to whether or not it should be included in the NT, because such a conclusion should be drawn by the translators themselves. The question I am asking here is whether the introduction of "Jehovah" into the NT in 1950 by the NWT translators, and the retaining of it in later editions, is an example of religious bias or if it can be defended from a philological point of view.

My view is that even though a literal translation should almost never choose a rendition which is not explicitly textually attested, there may be exceptions, and this is a situation which may be exceptional.[104] All the rabbinic material was available in 1950, and four years earlier the first evidence for the occurrence

---

[103] Countess, *The Jehovah's Witnesses' New Testament*, p. 33.

[104] The Bible translation in the Madagassian language, published by the Norwegian Bible Society, also uses the divine name in the form of "Jehovah" in the NT. The same is true with scores of other translations made by missionaries. The reason for the inclusion of the divine name in these translations is, of course, the target groups. In the minds of various Christian missionaries this is the best way to defend Christian monotheism and also differentiate between the God of the Bible and other gods.

of the divine name in the Septuagint was published. Those responsible for the NWT evidently researched the matter thoroughly. In fact, they even sent representatives to Egypt to photograph the Septuagint manuscripts.[105]

According to the NWT Foreword, the translators have not committed themselves to follow the Greek text of Westcott and Hort in all instances, but to notify the reader when they have deviated from this text.[106] YHWH is not found in the text of Westcott and Hort, and a lengthy discussion about why Jehovah is supplied is found in the NWT Preface. By this the interests of the readers, as far as "informed consent" is concerned, are well served. One may disagree with the conclusions of the translators, but it is difficult to claim that their arguments do not have the characteristics of sound scientific methodology.

CONSISTENCY IN THE CHOICE OF THE FORM "JEHOVAH"

The name Jehovah occurs 237 times in the NT portion of the NWT, and an additionally 72 times in the margins. Because the extant Greek manuscripts lack the tetragrammaton, each occurrence of Jehovah is based on the judgement of the translators. In the Foreword of NWTNT (page 20) we are told, "To avoid overstepping the bounds of a translator into the field of exegesis, we have tried to be most cautious about rendering the divine name, always carefully considering the Hebrew Scriptures."

Countess takes this to mean that the translators have put themselves under obligation only to use Jehovah where there is an OT quotation containing the tetragrammaton.[107] But this is nowhere stated in the NWT, and, obviously, this was not in the mind of the translators. To the contrary, they say that they have

---

[105] NWTNT was the first to publish photographs of these fragments.

[106] NWTNT, p. 8, says:, "Where we have varied from the reading of the Westcott and Hort text, our footnotes show the basis for our preferred reading."

[107] Countess, *The Jehovah's Witnesses' New Testament*, p. 34.

consulted other Hebrew versions of the NT to control their own judgement and have looked to the context for further insight. This is, of course, a normal procedure for translators, because they cannot follow rigid rules applying to every situation; rather, they must take all factors into consideration and then make their decision.

There is, however, one criticism made by Countess which we should seriously consider. He refers to passages in the NT which are quotes from the OT that contain the tetragrammaton where "the Lord" is used in the NWTNT and not "Jehovah," because the texts are applied in some sense to Jesus Christ. The question must be posed whether these renditions are examples of bias on the part of the translators.

Countess uses the words of John 19:37 (quoted from Zechariah 12:10) as an example of words referring to God in the OT, but which are applied to Jesus in the NT. He says "there can, then, be no denying His identification *in some way* [his italics] with Jehovah."[108] But here there is a textual problem in the OT verse indicating that the words may not be referring to God.[109] If God is the one referred to, then I agree with what Countess says on this point. Still, I ask: What kind of identification is made? When discussing this question, we should keep in mind that our horizon of understanding is greatly affected by our belief in, or denial of the trinity doctrine. We should therefore strive to review the material in a balanced way.

Let us first of all point out the unique position of Jesus according to the Bible, as *almost* being on par with God himself in different situations. The words of Revelation 5:13, that the blessing and honor and glory and might belongs to the One sitting on the throne *and* to the Lamb, would have been pure blasphemy in the ears of an orthodox Jew. And the reference in Revelation 22:1, 3, to the throne of God "and of the Lamb," would not be less offensive. Jesus is in the NT portrayed as having the most central position in YHWH's purpose, and in

---

[108] Countess, *The Jehovah's Witnesses' New Testament*, p. 38.

[109] Theodotion's Greek translation has "the one" instead of "me" just as we find in John's text. This could indicate that the reference is not to God.

Revelation 19:10 it is even said that bearing witness to Jesus is what inspires prophesying; thus he is the center of all the prophetic words in the Bible. He, therefore, can fill any position in God's universe, and represent his Father in any purpose. This is something to keep in mind when we are looking at the various quotes that are applied to Jesus.

As we consider how the NT quotes the OT, we must stress that an "ontological" identity between the persons mentioned in the quotes is not at all obvious. In Hosea 11:1 the reference in both the Masoretic text and the Septuagint is Israel. But in Matthew 2:15 the words are applied to Jesus. Will anybody suggest that Jesus is ontologically identical to Israel? In Jeremiah 31:15, Rachel, representing the ten-tribe kingdom, is portrayed as weeping over her sons, yet Matthew 2:17, 18 applies the words to the murder of the small children in Bethlehem after Jesus' birth, and those who wept over them.

Then there is the identification of John the baptist with the prophet Elijah. Malachi 4:5 prophecied that Elijah the prophet would come before the great and fear-inspiring day of YHWH. Jesus quoted these words in Matthew 17:12 and said that "Elijah has already come." Verse 13 tells us that the disciples perceived that he spoke about John the baptist. In Matthew 11:14 Jesus states the matter clearly, "He himself is Elijah who is destined to come." There can hardly be a more direct way to express ontological identity than to say that John the baptist *is* Elijah! But this is not what is meant, because John was neither the resurrected nor the reincarnated Elijah. But John did the same work as Elijah, under circumstances which were comparable to those of Elijah.

We could also quote the prophecy of Habakkuk 1:5, 6 referring to the Chaldeans, which was fulfilled not many years after the prophecy was given. However, Paul quotes this prophecy in Acts 13:40, 41, indicating that it would get a second fulfillment through a people playing the same role as the Chaldeans, but who were not identical with them. Given the background of the unique position of Jesus and how prophecies may be applied without any ontological identity, let us look at some prophecies that originally referred to YHWH but which are applied to Jesus in the NT.

The most interesting prophecy in our context is Psalm 68. The one referred to in this Psalm is YHWH, a fact which is already stressed in verse 1. The Psalm tells how God went forth before his people (verse 7), women were telling the good news of victory (verse 11), the Almighty One scattered the kings (verse 14), YHWH had come from Sinai into the holy place (verse 17), and how he had ascended on high, had carried away captives and had taken gifts in/among men (verse 18). We are also told how the enemies had seen God's processions into the holy place (verse 24), how the singers went in front, then maidens with tambourines (verse 25), and how the congregated throngs blessed God (verse 26).

How did YHWH do all these things? Not by being personally present on earth, but through a proxy, namely, the king sitting on his throne (1 Chr 29:23), in this case probably David. David conquered his enemies, took captives and then led them in a triumphal procession up to the holy place. But because David acted as the representative of YHWH, it could be said that YHWH did all of this.

The Psalm is quoted in Ephesians 4:8-10 and Paul applies the words about YHWH in the Psalm to Jesus. Does this mean that there is an ontological identity between Jesus and YHWH? Not at all! In both cases *two* individuals are affected. In the past, David actually performed the acts but YHWH was given the honor. In the first century CE Jesus actually performed the work but YHWH is again given the honor. If Ephesians 4:8-10 is taken to mean that there is an ontological identity between Jesus and YHWH, the consequence is that there should be an ontological identity between David and YHWH, also. This quote from Psalm 68 only tells us that Jesus acted as YHWH's representative. This fact is stated frequently in the NT (Joh 7:16, 17; 12:49, 50; Heb 1:1-3; 3:1).

This situation may be viewed as a pattern or precedence for any other situation where words or actions are applied to YHWH in the OT, and the same words and actions are applied to Jesus in the NT. This need mean nothing more than a functional unity; it does not necessarily involve ontological unity. Additional evidence supporting this reasoning is found in Genesis 18:13, where it is said that YHWH visited Abraham as a visible person and spoke to him. Evidently it was the angel of

YHWH and not YHWH himself who personally acted. We are also told that that YHWH was present at Sinai, gave the law to Moses and spoke with a loud voice to the people. But Paul says in Galatians 3:19 that it was God's angel who actually did all of this.

Let us now return to Countess and consider his view that NWT is consistent in only 95 percent of its renderings of *kurios* in the NT,[110] or as he says about the rendering of 1 Peter 3:15a and its footnote, *"As it now stands NWT is guilty of a flagrant violation of its dogmatically stated principle as touching the Divine Name* [his italics]."[111]

1 Peter 2:3 and 3:15 quote Psalm 34:8 and Isaiah 8:12, respectively. The Masoretic text has the tetragrammaton in both places. All the other occurrences of the tetragrammaton in quotes are translated by NWT as "Jehovah," but in these two passages they use "the Lord." This is because the reference is to Jesus Christ.

Does this "inconsistency" in rendering indicate bias on the part of its translators? My opinion is that Countess has overstated his case. For any translator, the immediate context is the final criterion for what words should be used. Any stated translation principles should yield to the context, as it is more important. The truth is, the NWT translators time and again appeal to the context.

Again, the translators' procedure to look to the OT for agreement when they would use Jehovah in the NT is important, but not so important as the context. Because it is indisputable that the one referred to in 1 Peter 2:3 and 3:15 is Jesus Christ, it is legitimate to use "the Lord." Countess would have the translators use "Jehovah" because he believes in the trinity doctrine, but this would be tantamount to Sabellianism. Because the trinity doctrine is post-biblical, the burden of proof is not those who abstain from using the dogma as a translation principle, but rather on those who claim it should be used as such.

---

[110] Countess, *The Jehovah's Witnesses' New Testament*, p. 34.

[111] Countess, *The Jehovah's Witnesses' New Testament*, p. 37.

CONCLUSION

We have seen that Countess makes demands on the NWT translators that can only be met by an interlinear translation. He assumes that the translators have bound themselves by rigid rules and thus have renounced their personal judgement. The NWT Foreword explicitly states that this is not the case.

From a philological point of view, therefore, Countess has not been successful in showing bias on the part of the NWT translators. His examples of "interpolations" may be classified as "implicit information being made explicit." Regarding the most controversial question of interpolation, the place of "Jehovah" in the NT, there is much data to show that the NWT's use of the divine name, scientifically speaking, is well founded.

CHAPTER 6

AN ANALYSIS OF DISPUTED PASSAGES

When you consider the different books and articles that are critical to NWT, most of the criticisms are in reference to passages that have doctrinal implications. Among those passages most frequently discussed, those related to the trinity doctrine comprise the largest group. Bowman's entire book, for example, discusses trinity questions, and much of Countess' book deals with similar questions. Thus, in this chapter I will primarily deal with passages of christological import.[1] Fortunately a discussion of the disputed passages in different ways will also throw light on the role played by theology and bias in Bible translation.

Of those passages that will be discussed, John 1:1 has primarily to do with Greek grammar and syntax relating to nouns, while John 8:58 illustrates the problem translators are faced with when they must deal with three completely different verbal systems at the same time. Colossians 1:15-20 shows the importance of taking the context into consideration. Philippians 2:6 deals with lexical semantics, how the context may help in understanding a word that occurs but once, and also with Greek grammar. The holy spirit as *parakletos* ("advocate," "helper") illustrates the difference between grammatical gender and sex, the discussion of *parousia* ("presence") throws light upon the role of theology in lexical semantics, and Acts 20:28 and 1 Corinthians 15:29 relates to the question of faithfulness toward the original text. 1 Corinthians 11:24 is a passage where the

---

[1] Murray J. Harris' work, *Jesus as God: The New Testament Use of* Theos *in Reference to Jesus* (Grand Rapids: Baker, 1992), will be quoted throughout this discussion. This is probably the most exhaustive book ever written about the Biblical witness to Jesus as *theos*. Its strength is the sound grammatical and linguistic analysis presented and it also gives the principal viewpoints for each verse discussed. Its weakness is that the scholarly discussion is interspersed with statements of faith, which the reader may misconstrue as balanced scientific conclusions.

theology of the NWT translators is the most important factor influencing their rendering.

WAS THE WORD "A GOD" OR "GOD"?

Of those texts that are usually criticized in NWT, none has created a greater controversy than John 1:1. Therefore, we will consider this passage at length. First, word meaning will be discussed, particularly the meaning and use of *theos*. Then syntactical questions relating to the verse as a small, bounded linguistic unit will be illuminated. Finally the greater context will be taken into consideration, and we will consider how the different renditions of this verse might impact the readers' understanding.

THE PROBLEM

Figure 6.1

John 1:1 in Three Different Translations

NWT	"In [the] beginning the Word was, and the Word was with God, and the Word was a god."
NRSV	"In the beginning was the Word, and the Word was with God, and the Word was God."
Goodspeed	"In the beginning the Word existed. The Word was with God and the Word was divine."
Greek text	*ēn arkhē* ("in the beginning") *ēn* ("was") *ho logos* ("the word"), *kai* ("and") *ho logos* ("the word") *ēn* ("was") *pros* ("with") *ton theon* ("the god"), *kai* ("and") *theos* ("god" or "a god") *ēn* ("was") *ho logos* ("the word")

The words *ho* and *ton* represent the Greek article, and the important linguistic question as respects the clauses quoted above is why the Greek article is lacking before the last occurrence of *theos*. Is there a semantic reason for this? Does it signal a difference in meaning between *ton theon*[2] (the one with whom the Word was) and *theos* (the designation for the Word)? Or is this merely a matter of syntax, that is, does the word order require an anarthrous *theos* without signaling any semantic difference between *theos* and *ho theos*?

The NWT rendering "and the Word was a god" implies a semantic difference between *theos* and *ho theos*, and this has been attacked from two angles: Countess and Kubo and Specht accuse NWT of downright bias, while Bowman argues that the NWT rendering is grammatically possible, but he concludes that the resulting theology is faulty. This, therefore, is an ideal situation for further illumination of the principal subject of this book.

QUESTIONS RELATED TO WORD MEANING

The first problem we encounter when seeking to understand John 1:1 is that terms such as "articular," "anarthrous," "definite," "indefinite," "generic," and "specific" are used with different senses by different authors. Bowman has a very good discussion of some of these fundamental terms, and I agree with much what he says regarding their use.[3] But in order to properly handle the issues, we should make a distinction between semantic and pragmatic factors.

Regarding semantic meaning, it cannot be cancelled without contradiction or reinforced without redundancy. We might illustrate this with the verb "plod," the adverb "slowly" and the adjective "tired." The four clauses below show that

---

[2] The phrases *ton theon* and *ho theos* both mean "the god." The difference is that *ton theon* is the object in the clause and therefore in the accusative case, while the form *ho theos* is the subject of the clause, the subject being in the nominative case.

[3] Robert M. Bowman, Jr., *Jehovah's Witnesses, Jesus Christ, and the Gospel of John* (Grand Rapids: Baker, 1989), pp. 28-34.

"slowly" is part of the semantic meaning of "plod," but this is not so with "tired."[4]

1) Elsie plodded along, *but not slowly.*

2) Elsie plodded along *slowly.*

3) Margaret plodded along, although she was not tired.

4) Margaret plodded along; she was very tired.

Sentence 1) is contradictory and sentence 2) is redundant, indicating that "slowly" is a part of the semantic meaning of "plod." Sentences 3) and 4) show that "tired" can be cancelled or reinforced; thus, its nature is pragmatic rather than semantic.

Which factors are semantic and which are pragmatic in relation to the Greek words of John 1:1? Or, to put it differently, with reference to the terms mentioned on the previous page, are they part of the semantic meaning of the key words, or is their nature pragmatic? The first step in the search for an answer to this question is to define the terms and find their basis.

It is rather easy to differentiate between the terms "arthrous" (or "articular") and "anarthrous" (or "nonarticular"), because it involves an objective or grammatical question. All nouns having the article are "arthrous" and those lacking the article are anarthrous. If we were to proceed by using the original triangle, we might look at the bottomline and ask about the relationship between "the word" and the "reference" (or "referent"). In this case we need to discuss the terms "count noun" and "noncount noun."[5]

As the names imply, the first group contains nouns that can be counted and that can be used in the plural, because they are "generic"; they are members of a class or kind ("genus"). Examples are "boy," "car," "lake" and "angel." The group of

---

[4] The examples are based on Mari Broman Olsen's *A Semantic and Pragmatic Model of Lexical and Grammatical Aspect* (New York and London: Garland Publishing, 1997), p. 17.

[5] For a fine discussion of these terms, see *Collins Cobuild English Grammar* (London: HarperCollins, 1993), pp. 6-13.

"noncount nouns" refers to general things such as qualities, substances, processes and topics; some examples include "beauty," "food," "travel," and "violence."

When we take a closer look at the "count noun" group, we find a derived subgroup that contains "singular nouns."[6] A "singular noun" behaves like the singular form of a count noun and it always has a determiner, usually the article, because it denotes one particular entity that is unique. It cannot be used in the plural. The same noun can in one context be used as a generic "count noun," and in another context it can be used as a "singular noun." One example is the noun "moon." We can speak of "a moon" and "seven moons" but if we add the article and speak about "the moon," then the word will, in a context relating to our earth, be a "singular noun."[7] Thus, a "singular noun" is marked by the article or a similar determiner and our basis for identifying it as such has to do with our knowledge of the world and in some instances our knowledge of the context.

So far we have discussed terms that can be identified by the help of grammar, or by a knowledge of the world, which is sometimes combined with what is known from the context. Let us now discuss two terms where the context is the most important tool in terms of identification, namely, "definite" and "indefinite." All "singular nouns" are definite but that is also the case with many ordinary "count nouns." What is definite refers to a particular, identifiable person, thing or property, while what is indefinite does not. This means that a noun that is definite must have been mentioned earlier in the context or must be known by the audience. It need not be unique, as is true regarding a "singular noun." All kinds of nouns can be definite, even "noncount nouns." We can, for example, speak of "his courage" or "the food," both being "noncount nouns."

---

[6] The *Collins English Grammar* mentioned in note 5 uses this term. Others prefer "invariable singular nouns."

[7] The opposite is also possible, in some instances. Even a proper name which, of course, is similar to a singular noun, can be changed into a generic count noun. We read in Deuteronomy 6:4, "Listen, O Israel: Jehovah our God is one Jehovah." This is definitely the most natural way to translate the verse. Here "Jehovah" seems to be used as a count noun, evidently in contrast to the different Baals.

Nouns that, in English, are definite are usually marked by a determiner, usually the article. But the context is more important than such a determiner. Bowman is therefore correct when he says that in the clause (in American English) "I am going to the hospital" the noun "the hospital," even though it is used with the article, is also indefinite, because it can refer to more than one hospital. However, if a physician who works at a particular hospital leaves for work and says, "I am going to the hospital," then "the hospital" is definite because that particular hospital where he works is meant. And, similarly, in the clause "I am going home" the noun "home," even though it does not have the article, is definite because one particular home is meant. Thus, it is true that indefinite nouns often lack the article (or some other determiner) and definite nouns often have it, but this is not always the case.

Let us then apply the terms used above to the key words of John 1:1. The words *theos* and *logos* both have the article and therefore both are articular. From the objective fact that both words are articular, can we draw just any conclusion regarding their *lexical* contents, that is, can we know anything definite about the nature of the persons they denote? The answer is no, because the addition of the article to a Greek noun does not add any new meaning to the word; its function is to make visible a part of the word's meaning. The pragmatic nature of any discussion about the key words of John 1:1 can also be seen if we look at *theos* and *logos* without taking into account their articles. Both words are count nouns because we can speak of many gods and many words, but the important question is whether they are, in this verse, generic or specific, that is, whether or not they are "singular nouns."

Looking at *ho logos*, we can see from verses 14 and 18 that the referent is the prehuman Jesus Christ, and *ho logos* must, in this case, be a designation or a title. Nowhere else does *logos* denote a person other than Jesus, so there can be little doubt that *ho logos* is a "singular noun." But what about *ho theos*? The word is articular and definite, even though this is the first time it is mentioned in John's gospel. Nobody else but the creator could be referred to in this context, in this way. However, in the Bible the word *theos* is also used for persons other than the creator, and therefore neither "creator" nor

"YHWH" could be a part of its semantic meaning. The nature of John's use of *ho theos* is, therefore, a pragmatic question, not a semantic one. The word *theos* is a count noun, and John uses it in one of two ways: either in a generic sense or as a "singular noun."[8]

We might illustrate this point by use of the OT. Here we find that *ĕlōhim*, the Hebrew equivalent to *theos*, is used in a generic sense. The word is plural in form but is used for the creator and for singular gods. The gods in opposition to YHWH could be viewed either as lifeless gods or as living gods represented by idols. Isaiah 44 shows that there is but one living God, and carved images are lifeless. We find the same contrast in Psalm 115:2-5 and 135:14-19. However, in the account of Elisha and the Ba'al prophets in 1 Kings 18 it is evident that the Ba'al worshipers believed in the existence of Ba'al, apart from his statue. This was also the way the nations around Israel viewed their Gods. It is interesting to note that Moses referred to living gods behind the images (*shēdim*, Deut 32:17), and we find the same view expressed in Psalm 106:36-37. So while YHWH was the proper name of the God of Israel, the semantic meaning of *ĕlōhim* makes it a generic count noun (or an appellative).

In about one fourth of the occurrences of *ĕlōhim*, the word occurs with the article as *ha ĕlōhim*. As an example, consider 1 Kings 18:21.[9] NWT reads, "If Jehovah is the [true] God, go following him; but if Ba'al is, go following him." There can be no doubt that *ha ĕlōhim* in this instance is generic, and that the epithet "true" is fitting. The word *ĕlōhim* is plural but its function is singular, and, therefore, we *could* view its occurrence together with the article as an example of a "singular

---

[8] Rien Op Den Brouw has written an interesting article entitled "The Problem of the Missing Article in the Use of 'God,'" *Religious Studies* 30 (1994), pp. 17-27. Brouw's article helps the reader learn more about the difference between semantics and pragmatics, and about how different combinations of factors such as lexical meaning, grammar, syntax and context may give different senses to "God." Because his objective is the Judeo-Christian religion rather than the text of the OT or NT, his conclusions are not directly relevant to our discussion.

[9] The Septuagint uses *ho theos* in this verse.

noun." However, because the normal contrast in the OT is between YHWH and false gods, we can conclude that the above example represents the *normal* meaning, and that *ha ̓elōhim* is often generic and may be translated as in the NWT. On the other hand, we have an anarthrous example of *̓elōhim* that seems to function as a "singular noun" in Psalm 96:1, 9.[10]

Proceeding to the NT, we find that Paul used words in his letter to a Greek congregation (1 Cor 8:5, 6; 10:20) that reveal the mindset of the members of that congregation as one that could grasp the contrast between the one living God and lifeless gods representing demons (*daimoniois*)! For the Greek mind the word *daimonios* could either mean "god or goddess," or "divine spirit" (see Liddell and Scott and BAGD). The Greek Christians, therefore, also believed in the existence of many gods. In NT, *theos* occurs 1,317 times, and of these 995 have the article immediately preceding it.[11] There are 322 examples of *theos* without the article. Because there is no inherent semantic contrast between the articular and the anarthrous *theos*, the question about the meaning of *theos* in some passages is pragmatic, and thus the context becomes essential.[12]

Returning to *ho theos* in John 1:1, there are two possible senses: Either the word is a "singular noun,"[13] serving as the title or designation "God," which is semantically equivalent to a proper noun, or it has the often-used, generic sense of *ha ̓elōhim* in the OT, namely, "the true God." The sense of *ho theos* is not essential to its translation in John 1:1b; it should be translated as "God." But its sense does have a bearing on the

---

[10] The Septuagint uses *ho theos* and *theos* in these verses.

[11] Many of these could be considered anaphoric.

[12] If we compare Luke 20:37, 38 with Matthew 22:32 we find examples of both an articular and anarthrous *theos* denoting YHWH, both being used in a generic sense. In Luke there are two uses of an articular *theos* and two anarthrous uses, the last occurrence of which is fittingly translated by NWT as "a God." In Matthew all four occurrences are articular. These references have no direct bearing on John 1:1, because in John there are two different persons mentioned. Rather, these references emphasize the importance of the context.

[13] Brouw, "The Problem of the Missing Article in the Use of 'God,'" uses "title-phrase" instead of "singular noun."

understanding of the contrast between *ho theos* in 1:1b and *theos* in 1:1c. If John uses *ho theos* in a generic sense what he does is compare the godship of *ho theos* with that of *theos* (the *logos*), just as the Israelite mind could compare the godship of *ha ʾelōhim* with the godship of the angels or that of demonic gods, or even to that of lifeless idols (which do not have real godship apart from that attributed to them by their worshipers). If John uses *ho theos* as a "singular noun" then the contrast could be viewed as one between two beings who can legitimately be called *theos*. Thus, the generic sense would put a greater stress on quality, both being members of the group of *theoi* ("gods"), though in a qualitatively different way. The definite use would stress personality.

I would like to add one additional observation, in order not to be misunderstood. In the above discussion there are no traces either of polytheism[14] or of henotheism.[15] As will be shown later, the angels are occasionally called "gods," but this is not their usual designation. This designation is not used in a *religious* sense, as is the case with the pantheons of gods found in the Babylonian, Greco-Roman and other ancient (and modern) religious systems. The angels are "gods" in a purely generic sense—they are simply sons of YHWH, and the designation "gods" had no higher *religious* value to worshipers of YHWH than the designation "angels" (though the two descriptions highlight different attributes and functions). Also, the "belief" of Paul and others in many gods did not amount to "belief" in a religious sense; rather, it was a "belief" in the sense of "acknowledgement." Only when more than one god is worshiped in a religious sense can we speak of polytheism, and only when one supreme god is worshiped and the worshiper believes in the existence of other gods in a religious sense can we speak of henotheism.

---

[14] Webster defines polytheism as "belief in or worship of many Gods, or of more than one god: opposed to *monotheism.*"

[15] Also from Webster, we find these definitions for henotheism: "1. A religious doctrine attributing supreme power to one of several divinities in turn. 2. Belief in one god, without denying the existence of others."

THE MEANING OF *THEOS*
AND THE CONCEPT OF ETERNALITY

John 1:1 has one example of the articular *ho theos*, which was the subject of our discussion above, and one example of an anarthrous *theos*. Because the words occur inside the same small linguistic unit, and because they refer to two different beings, the occurrence of the article in one instance and the lack of it in the other seems to have some significance. Bowman admits that the articular *theos* in 1:1b and the anarthrous *theos* in 1:1c are used "in two distinct senses,"[16] but it is very important for him to show that both senses are in full agreement with the trinity doctrine, and thereby justifying the rendering of 1:1c as "and the Word was God." He does this by arguing that the verse shows that Jesus is eternal and that *theos* in 1:1c cannot mean "anything less than it means in 1:1b."[17] Now we will carefully consider each of these arguments.

THE VERB "TO BE" IN JOHN 1:1a

"In the beginning *was* [*ēn*] the word." How should we understand the force of the verb "was"? Bowman draws the right conclusion as to its force, but his premises for doing so are wrong, in that he confuses *Aktionsart* with aspect.[18] The verb *eimi* is stative, and though it is viewed as "aspectually vague,"[19] the imperfect of the verb can hardly mean anything else but the subject's *existence* in the past. Of the 389 examples of the third person imperfect of this verb in the NT, all are compatible with the common definition of stative verbs as "a state that continues." Therefore, the meaning of the first clause of John 1:1 seems to be that at the point of time described as "the beginning" the Word existed (or was existing).

---

[16] Bowman, *Jehovah's Witnesses*, p. 26.

[17] Bowman, *Jehovah's Witnesses*, p. 42.

[18] Bowman, *Jehovah's Witnesses*, p. 23. See *Excursus on Greek and Hebrew Verbs*, pp. 79-94, for a discussion of "aspect."

[19] Porter, *Verbal Aspect in the Greek of the New Testament*, p. 449.

However, Bowman, in defending the trinity doctrine, wants us to believe that the Word is eternal. His argument is that the "beginning" in John 1:1 is the same as the one mentioned in Genesis 1:1, referring to the creation of the universe. Further, because "it appears certain that time began with the creation of the physical universe," when the universe was created (Gen 1:1), the Word must be eternal.[20]

This line of reasoning is highly speculative, building on the old Greek philosophical thought (*Timaeus* of Plato) that time was created with the universe.[21] I intend to limit the discussion of theological and philosophical questions as much as possible, but because I, in the chapter on the trinity, claimed that the Bible nowhere says that Jesus is eternal, some comments must be made regarding Bowman's view.

First of all, I ask: How can we define "time"? If we use the triangle, it is very difficult to differentiate between its *meaning*, *concept* and *reference*. This is so because "time" is a loose concept with very elusive borders; actually, it is an abstraction.[22] This can be illustrated by the saying "time flies." By this we mean that everything around us and in the universe is "moving" forwards, and we ourselves are moving further away from the moment of our birth. But this "movement" is not directly

---

[20] Bowman, *Jehovah's Witnesses*, pp. 22, 23. A similar argument is found in Harris, *Jesus as God*, p. 54, and it is an example of a statement of faith in the middle of fine scholarly arguments. Harris uses three premises: 1) The "beginning" mentioned in John 1:1 is identical with the beginning mentioned in Gen 1:1; 2) Nothing was created before this "beginning"; and (3) time did not exist before this "beginning." His point 1) may be true, though John 8:44 and 1 John 1:1 show that "the beginning" may refer to things other than the creation of the world. He errs regarding 2) because there is nothing in Genesis which indicates that spirit beings are included in the words "the heavens and the earth." As will be shown, his view of time is Platonic and cannot be defended.

[21] Einstein's view of time has, from one point of view some similarity with Plato's view, but by and large it is different. We should also keep in mind that Einstein's theory regarding time is speculative and very difficult to substantiate.

[22] The progress of any phenomenon that undergoes regular changes may be used to measure time. The measurement involves two quantities: an event and the duration of a particular phenomenon after that event.

connected to "time"; rather, it is an illustration that can help us get some understanding of the abstract concept. Thus, "time" is nothing more than a symbol of that which we have an indistinct apprehension of in our mind. Therefore, to me, it seems meaningless to say that time was created at a certain point (In this sentence it is tempting to add "in time" after "a certain point"!), and it is even more nonsensical to contrast time with eternality.

We may illustrate this further with the words "everlasting life," and with candor I could state, "Nobody will ever get everlasting life!" This may seem to be the creed of an atheist, but the point is that nobody will ever reach a point (in time) where he or she can look back and say, "I have lived forever." This is so because "everlasting life" is a *concept*. The words are used in the Bible, and the meaning is to live and live and live and continue to live. But when was "to continue to live" created? Such a question is nonsensical. The Bible tells that everlasting life was *instituted* by God through Jesus Christ, but not that it was created at a certain point in time.

If we, from the expression in John 1:1a, namely, that the Word "was" in the beginning, can draw the conclusion that the Words is eternal, what about the angels? The rabbis interpreted the words, "Let us create man in our image" in Genesis 1:26 as an instance where God spoke to the angels,[23] and the words of Job 38:4-7 show that the angels, too, 'were' in the beginning (that is, if Job 38:4-7 refers to the creation of the universe). But from this should we draw the conclusion that the angels also are eternal? If we follow Bowman's line of reasoning it seems difficult to avoid this conclusion. But this contradicts Paul's words in Colossians 1:16-17 that the angels (if they are in fact the "thrones," "lordships," and "authorities" of whom Paul speaks, though they surely can be assumed under the "the things invisible") were created by God through Jesus Christ. Regarding the expression "in the beginning was the Word," all we can say with reasonable certainty is that at the particular point of time called "the beginning" the Word existed. This is a far cry from saying "the Word is eternal."

---

[23] M. M. Kasher, *Encyclopedia of Biblical Interpretation*, vol. 1, pp. 58, 59.

THE USE OF "G-god" IN THE BIBLE

There is no question that *ho logos* ("the Word") in John 1:1c is the subject and that *theos* is predicate nominative. This means that while *ho logos* is a "singular noun" applied to the prehuman Jesus Christ and *ho theos* of 1:1b is either a "singular noun" or a generic count noun[24] used in reference to YHWH, the anarthrous *theos* of 1:1c is a generic count noun that tells us something *about* the person denoted by *ho logos*. But what does it tell us?

Bowman speaks about the use of *theos* in the NT, and according to him there are just two possibilities: either the word *theos* means the true God (this is the case in 1400 instances) or it means false gods (this is the case in only 6 instances);[25] there is no third alternative. He then reasons that because the Word is not a false god, he must be (the) true God, and therefore this must be the meaning of the anarthrous *theos* in 1:1c.

But are these arguments well founded? Is it possible to restrict the references of *theos* as Bowman does? Not at all! The words *theos/ elōhim* are also applied to a third group. It is true that the alleged material applying the words to others than the creator and false gods is somewhat slim; actually there are about 10 instances. But it is equally true that the alleged Biblical evidence that Jesus is called God also consists of ten examples, and when textual and grammatical issues are brought into the equation, these ten can be reduced to only two, maybe three examples. So in both cases we are discussing the exceptions rather than the rule.

Let us take a look at the evidence. BAGD defines *theos* as "God, god," and then shows that the word is used "of divine beings generally," "with reference to Christ," "of the true God," "of that which is worthy of reverence or respect," and "of the devil," thus allowing for more than two groups.

It is difficult to establish the etymology for the words *elōhim* or *theos*. If we try to find common elements in the application of these words, we may find "object of worship" as a

---

[24] Bowman, *Jehovah's Witnesses*, p. 43, believes it is generic.

[25] Bowman, *Jehovah's Witnesses*, p. 59.

common denominator between the creator and false gods. However, this element is not extant in all uses of the word. "One possessing superhuman authority" might be a more common element found in the use of these words. But this description is not necessarily the right one either. As we saw in Chapter 1, words/concepts have fuzzy edges, and their application in different contexts must be seen against some prototypical concept. So instead of drawing an absolute line of demarcation around the "god" at the outset, we should keep a prototypical concept in our minds, and by means of this we should try to find the meaning of the different applications of the word. Since Bowman tries to restrict the references of the word "god," let us take a look at some Biblical applications of this word other than those for "the true God" and those for "false gods."

In Psalm 82:1, 6 earthly judges are called *ĕlōhim* ("gods"). Jesus referred to this passage in John 10:34 and confirmed that human beings could be called "gods." In Exodus 4:16 it is said that Moses would serve as "god" for Aaron, and Exodus 7:1 tells that Moses should serve as "god" for Pharaoh. Setting aside any concepts we might give to the words *ĕlōhim/theos*, we must admit that these 6 instances neither refer to the creator nor to false gods. And, further, Psalm 8:6 speaks of somone having been made a little less than *ĕlōhim* ("god[s]"). The Septuagint translates *ĕlōhim* here as *angelous* ("angels"), and Hebrews 2:7, in its quote of this verse, also uses "angels." Thus we have an example where *ĕlōhim* is applied to the heavenly angels. Two other Psalms evidently also apply *ĕlōhim* to the angels, namely, Psalm 97:7 and 138:1.[26] Therefore, we have 10 examples where *ĕlōhim/theos* is applied to persons other than to the almighty God and to false gods.

Thus, we may conclude that Bowman's attempt to limit the anarthrous *theos* in 1:1c to "the true God" has failed, and at this point, since we are discussing lexical semantics, we must

---

[26] Gleason Archer and Gregory Chirichigno, *Old Testament Quotations in the New Testament* (Chicago: Moody Press, 1983), p. 59, comments on the quote of Psalm 8:6 from Hebrews 2:7, pointing out that *benei ĕlōhim* ("sons of God") often is used in the sense of angels (Deut 32:43, 4QDt[a], Job 1:6; 2:1; Psalm 29:1; 89:6.) They also agree that angels are called gods in Ps 97:7 and 138:1.

return to the characteristics of the word itself, which are simple: The word *theos* is a count noun, and in 1:1c it is anarthrous and indefinite. It may have uses appropriate to our descriptively referring to any member of a set of superhuman, spirit persons—including the Almighty One; therefore, uses other than for our referring to the Almighty One need not mean reference to false gods—to those who by nature are not gods.

THE IMMEDIATE LINGUISTIC CONTEXT

The first verse of John's first chapter consists of three co-ordinated clauses constituting one sentence. This is a small, linguistically bounded unit and constitutes the immediate linguistic context. When we proceed beyond the borders of this unit, then we also leave linguistics behind and engage in discourse analysis, contextual studies, or theology. Bible translators will also use these tools, but they should keep in mind that such evidence is secondary compared to the lingusitc evidence from the verse itself. The most important linguistic question is the role played by the Greek article, so let us consider this matter in detail.

THE ARTICLE IN OTHER LANGUAGES

In English we have the definite article "the" and the indefinite articles "a" and "an." We know that the use or non-use the article in an English clause may significantly affect the meaning of the clause. But this is not true in all languages. For example, in Accadian, the Semitic language in which we have the oldest documents, there is no article at all, neither definite nor indefinite. The same is true in Classical Ethiopic, another Semitic language, and also in Latin, which is an Indo-European language. How, then, could people speaking these languages differentiate between nouns which were definite and those which were not? There were some clues. For example, proper names, common nouns previously mentioned and nouns governed by demonstratives were definite, but other nouns might be definite or indefinite. Thus, the context was very important.

In Biblical Hebrew there is an article which has an important function. However, in the Psalms the use of the article is sparse, and the rule of thumb is that when the article occurs, the noun is definite, but when it is not found, the noun may either be definite or indefinite. In Biblical Aramaic there is also a definite article[27] by the help of which one may differentiate between definite and indefinite objects. In time the Aramaic language developed into the Syriac dialects, the most important being an Eastern and a Western one. The article was used in the script in both dialects but in time its *meaning* became lost, to the effect that nouns had the article in script, but whether the noun was definite or not could only be ascertained by help of the context.

RULES FOR THE USE OF THE GREEK ARTICLE

The above sketch of the definite article in some languages teaches us an important lesson, namely, that the ways of marking definiteness or indefiniteness are quite elusive, and regardless of the different uses of the article, the *context* is a most important factor.[28]

As a deciding factor for the translation of John 1:1 the rule of E. C. Colwell is often cited.[29] He tabulated all the predicate nouns in the NT which he assessed to be definite, 244 articular ones and 123 anarthrous ones. Regarding the articular nouns he

---

[27] The "definite article" (or the equivalent of the definite article) in Aramaic occurs at the end of the word; for example the last *ā* in *'abbā*, and a noun with the article is said to be in the "determined state" rather than being referred to as a noun with the definite article.

[28] The "Definition of Terms" in Bowman, *Jehovah's Witnesses*, pp. 28-35, is most illuminating. He is correct in his differention between what is articular and definite and between what is anarthrous and indefinite. His concern here is to lay the foundation for an understanding of the anarthrous *theos* in John 1:1.

[29] E. C. Colwell, "A Definite Rule for the Use of the Article in the Greek New Testament," *Journal of Biblical Literature* 52 (1933), pp. 12-21.

found that 229 (94%) occurred *after* the verb and 15 (6%) *before* the verb. As to the anarthrous nouns he found that 26 (21%) occurred *after* the verb and 97 (79%) *before* the verb. Based on this material he formulated some tentative rules, of which 2b states that definite predicate nouns preceding the verb usually do not have the article. This is what has become known as "Colwell's rule," and it has been widely used to show that the rendition "a god" is incorrect.

Bowman has a discussion of Colwell's rule which is qualitatively very good, showing insights which are completely lacking in most other discussions of the application of this rule to John 1:1. Indeed, because the rule applies only to nouns that, by other means, have *already* been determined to be definite Bowman correctly notes that "to argue that a noun must be definite because of Colwell's rule, therefore, is logically fallacious."[30] Regarding the rule and the NWT, Bowman writes: "Where Colwell's rule can and has been severely abused is in the popular evangelical apologetic argument that the rule alone refutes the JW rendering 'a god.' Such an argument goes far beyond what Colwell himself, careful scholar as he was, said."[31]

Another scholar who has contributed a fine study of all the anarthrous predicate nouns in John is Paul S. Dixon. His conclusion is that in 96 percent of the cases where the predicate

---

[30] Bowman, *Jehovah's Witnesses*, p. 67. Harris, *Jesus as God*, pp. 61, 62, 310-313, also has an informative discussion of Colwell's rule, where he reveals his reservations about applying the rule to John 1:1.

[31] Bowman, *Jehovah's Witnesses*, p. 69. Contrary to what Bowman says, Colwell himself laid the foundation for the misuse of his rule by applying it to John 1:1 (See page 21 of Colwell's *JBL* article.) Bruce M. Metzger, "The Jehovah's Witnesses and Jesus Christ," *Theology Today* 10.1 (April 1953), pp. 65-85, also must share some of the responsibility for the general abuse of the rule. He stated that the translators of the NWT, by translating "the Word was a god," overlooked entirely "an established rule of Greek grammar which *necessitates* [my italics] the rendering . . . and the Word was God." Metzger is a respected scholar who has done much good work with the Greek text of the NT. His words may have been written because of his theological differences with Jehovah's Witnesses. I think he would have expressed himself more cautiously today. However, such inaccurate statements are still used as authoritative, for instance, by Robert Countess, *The Jehovah's Witnesses' New Testament* (Phillipsburg, NJ: Presbyterian and Reformed, 1982), p. 53.

nominatives precede the verb they are *qualitative* and not definite or indefinite. He writes:

> Colwell's rule cannot be applied to [John 1:1] as an argument for definiteness. Colwell's rule says that definite predicate nominatives preceding the verb usually are anarthrous. The rule asserts nothing about definiteness. It does not say that anarthrous predicate nominatives preceding the verb usually are definite. This is the converse of the rule, and as such is not necessarily valid.[32]

When discussing and applying rules such as those given by Colwell, Dixon, and others, we should keep in mind that rules are made by help of induction, that is, the rule is a result of the interpretation of many sets of data, all pointing in the same direction. This is usually how rules are made concerning dead languages, but due to their nature the *problem of induction* is also at work.

We can illustrate this problem by considering the colors of a swan. If we observe that swans in our area are white, and we travel to other areas and only find white swans, then from this we may inductively establish the rule: all swans are white. The more white swans we observe, the more confidence we have in the rule. However, a showing of hundreds of thousands of white swans does not *prove* the rule, because induction can never prove anything. But the opposite is possible, just one black swan will falsify it.

Because language is very flexible and there may be great personal variation, one or two examples which are contrary to a rule do not falsify it. But what we may learn from the swan illustration is that rules—even when they are built on sound methodology—are not conclusive, and when methodological blunders occur they are even less secure. Colwell's rule is not relevant to the understanding of the anarthrous *theos* in John 1:1c. Dixon's rule is clearly relevant, suggesting that *theos* is

---

[32] Paul Stephen Dixon, "The Significance of the Anarthrous Predicate Nominative in John" (Th.M. thesis, Dallas Theological Seminary, 1975), p. 55. Dixon contends (page 31 of his thesis) that "the significance of the anarthrous predicate nominative [in pre-copulative constructions] is qualitativeness."

exclusively qualitative, having the meaning "divine." However, his study is weak as respects methodology, because he presumes that qualitativeness on the one hand and definiteness and indefiniteness on the other are mutually exclusive, that is, no predicate nominative can have two of the characteristics at the same time. This is clearly wrong because count nouns denoting persons such as *theos* and *logos*, must be either definite or indefinite, and a stress of qualitativeness is an *additional* characteristic, not an alternative one. Dixon's assessment of qualitativeness in relation to most predicate nouns occurring before the verb is basically correct, but it must be qualified by assessing definiteness/indefiniteness in each case.

In discussing John 1:1, J. Gwyn Griffiths refers to Dr. Strachan, who ascribes an adjectival force to the anarthrous *theos*. He also refers to Dr. Temple, who similarly understood a force "not far from adjectival." Griffiths then concludes:

> It may be suggested that neither of these statements is confirmed by general usage in classical or Hellenistic Greek. Nouns which shed their articles do not thereby become adjectives; nor is it easy to see how the predicative use of a noun, in which the omission of the article is normal, tends to give the noun adjectival force.[33]

Harner's study[34] is based on sound methodology, and he shows explicitly that predicate nouns may be both definite and qualitative and others may be indefinite and qualitative. According to him, John has 53 examples of anarthrous predicate nominatives occurring before the verb.[35] He writes that 26 of

---

[33] J. Gwyn Griffiths, "A Note on the Anarthrous Predicate in Hellenistic Greek," *The Expository Times* 62 (1951), p. 315.

[34] Philip B. Harner, "Qualitative Anarthrous Predicate Nouns: Mark 15:39 and John 1:1," *Journal of Biblical Literature* 92 (1973), pp. 75-87.

[35] Harner, "Qualitative Anarthrous Predicate Nouns: Mark 15:39 and John 1:1," pp. 82-83. He gives the following examples: John 1:1, 12, 14, 49; 2:9; 3:4; 3:6; 3:29; 4:9, 19; 5:27; 6:63, 70; 7:12; 8:31, 33, 34, 37, 39, 42, 44, 48, 54; 9:5, 8, 17, 24, 25, 27, 28, 31; 10:1, 2, 8, 13, 33, 34, 36; 11:49, 51; 12:6, 36, 50; 13:35; 15:14; 17:17; 18:26, 35, 37; 19:21.

these are clearly indefinite and 11 others may be indefinite.[36] We even find two examples where predicate nominatives preceding the verb have the article.[37]

Harner's article is important because it shows that, from a strictly linguistic point of view, the absence of the article before *theos* in John 1:1 is not decisive in determining whether *theos* should be translated "God," "a god," or "divine." There is no linguistic rule *demanding* either of the alternatives! With this, Bowman agrees.[38] However, this does not mean that all has been said, because if we add to the linguistic data what the context says, then clearly there are preferences as to how the words should be translated. The important point, therefore, is that because rules are general and apply to the whole textual corpus, they alone cannot have the final word regarding a particular question related to a particular clause. For the translation of particular passages the immediate context is the most important factor.

THE ANARTHROUS THEOS IN JOHN 1:1C

Perhaps the most important objection Countess makes against NWT is his criticism of NWT renderings for *theos*. He writes:

> In the New Testament there are 282 occurrences of the anarthrous θεός. At sixteen places NWT has either a god, god, gods or godly. Sixteen out of 282 means that the translators were faithful to *their* translation principle only six percent of the time. *To be ninety-four percent*

---

[36] John 1:14; 2:9; 6:63; 7:12; 8:31, 44, 48; 9:8, 24, 25, 27, 28; 10:1, 8, 34; 12:6, 36; 18:35.

[37] John 6:51; 15:1. Kubo and Specht, *So Many Versions?* p. 99 write: "However, since in this verse [John 1:1] in Greek *theos* (God) is a predicate noun and precedes the verb and subject, it is definite, since a definite predicate noun when it precedes the verb never takes an article in Greek." John 6:51 and 15:1 show that this claim is in error.

[38] Bowman, *Jehovah's Witnesses*, p. 62.

> *unfaithful hardly commends a translation to careful readers!*[39]

If Countess' claim is correct, we have a blatant example of bias on the part of the NWT translators. However, it is he who is "ninetyfour percent unfaithful," as it were. Reading through the explanation given in NWT's Appendix which provides the translator's reasons for choosing the rendering "a god," two key arguments are evident: syntactical and contextual, but no lexical-grammatical ones. To put it differently, it is nowhere said that *theos*, or any other word without the article in every case, must be rendered either with the indefinite article or with no article, in English.

It is said that the rendering "a god" builds on two important factors: 1) The word *theos* occurs a total of three times in verses 1 and 2—twice with the article and once without. Because of the contrast with the articular *theos* the occurrence without the article must have some semantic significance. 2) The Word is said to be "with God," and it is unreasonable to say that the Word was the God with whom he existed.[40]

Again, it is necessary to emphasize that we cannot demand that a literal translation follows the procedures of an interlinear translation. Thus, Countess' long tables (in his Appendix) regarding NWT's renderings of *theos* with and without the article, though they are interesting in terms of a general review, are worthless as examples of bias. What they do show is that the translators have not translated mechanically, but that they have consistently taken the context into consideration. Before Countess can use the tables to show evidence of bias, he must

---

[39] Robert Countess, *The Jehovah's Witnesses' New Testament*, pp. 54-55.

[40] Harris, *Jesus as God*, p. 61, says regarding this point: "If θεός were taken as subject and as equivalent to ὁ θεός ("God was the Word"), the clause would contradict what precedes ('the Word was with God,' distinguishing two persons) and would reduce the λόγος to merely a divine attribute." The use of the phrase "distingusihing two persons" accords with Harris' belief in the trinity doctrine. He would hardly have said "distinguishing two individuals (according to their respective godships)," which would contradict the trinity doctrine.

produce evidence that the translators have committed themselves to *always* rendering anarthrous Greek nouns with anarthrous English nouns.

Harris' arguments also show the weakness of Countess' claims of bias on the part of the NWT translators.[41] According to him, John's Gospel uses *theos* for the Father in each occurrence except John 1:1, 18 and 20:28. To use "God" with a capital letter in 81 out of 83 occurrences, even in those instances where the article is not present, is therefore quite natural.

Harris' third example above is John 20:28, where *ho theos* is used.[42] In this passage it is not possible to claim that the article has semantic importance, and that Jesus is therefore identical with *ho theos* in John 1:1, because the article is grammatically required.[43] There is of course a possibility that it has semantic importance, but there is no way to know for sure. Because the phrase has a posessive pronoun ("my"), the word *theos* must be definite, and in Greek it cannot stand without the article. We may illustrate this with the English possessive pronoun. If I say "my book," the reference is definite. If I am referring to this particular book and I phrase my words differently, I could say, "this book of mine" or "the book of mine" However, I cannot say "book of mine," and if I say "a book of mine" the reference is indefinite. Thus, a definite reference in English containing the possessive pronoun also requires the definite article or a demonstrative pronoun. In

---

[41] Harris, *Jesus as God*, p. 53.

[42] Theodore of Mopsuestia (4th century CE) and others have claimed that the exclamation of Thomas was addressed to the Father and not to the Son. This seems to be ruled out by the preceding clause showing that the words were directed "toward him [= Jesus]" (see Harris, *Jesus as God*, pp. 108-109). However, in all 88 instances in the gospels, where Jesus is addressed as "Lord," the vocative form *kurie* is used and not the nominative form *kurios*. And, similarly, in the Septuagint and in the NT, where God is addressed, in all instances except Revelation 4:11, we find *kurie*. (The grammar of Revelation often differs from standard Greek.) If the words of John 20:28 were directed only to Jesus, it is rather strange that the nominative form *kurios* and not the vocative form *kurie* was used.

[43] C. F. D. Moule, *An Idiom Book of New Testament Greek*, 2d ed. (Cambridge: Cambridge University Press, 1959), pp. 116-117.

Greek all kinds of references including a possessive pronoun require the article.

We cannot know exactly what Thomas meant with his exclamation. Those believing in the trinity can hardly argue that Thomas meant that Jesus was the same as *ho theos*, with whom the Word is said to be in John 1:1, because this would be tantamount to Sabellianism. Thus, Thomas' words do not add anything to our understanding of the word *theos* when used of Jesus in John 1:1c, 18.

THE GREATER CONTEXT

The Word is mentioned twice in John 1:1 and once in verse 14, where the text reveals that the Word became Jesus Christ. In reading through the book of John, there can be no doubt that, in the mind of John, God and Jesus Christ were two different individuals. It is John who reports these words of Jesus, "the Father is greater than I am." (14:28) He also relates Jesus' words, "I am ascending to my Father and your Father and to my God and your God." (20:17) In John, Jesus also refers to "the only true God, and the one whom you sent forth, Jesus Christ." (17:3) There are also scores of passages where Jesus expresses his dependence upon God.

We also find the portrayal of two different individuals in John 1:1, 2, where twice the Word is said to be "with God." Regarding this, Bowman correctly writes: "The Word certainly cannot be with 'God' and be 'God' unless the term *God* somehow changes significance from the first to the second usage."[44] It is this difference in meaning that NWT tries to communicate with the rendering "and the Word was a god," while in the reading "and the Word was God" there is no such

---

[44] Bowman, *Jehovah's Witnesses*, pp. 25-26. Harris, *Jesus as God*, pp. 61, 69, agrees that there is a difference between the Word (*theos*) and God (*ho theos*). He says they are two different "persons," an expression which accords with the trinity doctrine. However, elementary logic would imply that a person who is "with" another person is also a different *individual*. But to say that the Word and God were two different individuals would contradict the trinity doctrine.

difference, but it must be *postulated* (by Bowman and other trinitarians) that a difference is implicit!

Of the 10 passages that potentially call Jesus "God," three are found in the Gospel of John, and two of these (possibly the third, also) are the only ones left when the dust of textual criticism settles and translation possibilities are evaluated.[45] One of these, John 1:18, which occurs in the Prologue of John, is a good confirmation of the rendering "a god" in verse 1, because Jesus is here called "the only-begotten/uniquely derived god."[46] There are some differences in the Greek manuscripts regarding this phrase, but the committee appointed by the United Bible Societies to evaluate textual variants in the Greek NT[47] chose the rendering *monogenēs theos* (an "onlybegotten/uniquely derived god") as the most probable reading.

Bart Ehrmann argues in favor of *huios* ("son") instead of *theos*, so the phrase would read "the uniquely derived son."[48] He argues for *ho monogenēs huios* ("the onlybegotten/uniquely derived son") because it is the reading of both the Western, the Byzantine and Caesarean text families. His principal argument against *theos*, however, seems to be the *meaning* of the phrase. He says:

> By definition there can be only *one* μονογενής: the word means "unique," "one of a kind." The problem, of course,

---

[45] G. H. Boobyer, "Jesus as 'THEOS' in the New Testament," *Bulletin of John Ryllands Library* 50 (1967-68), p. 253, writes: "First there is the rarity of New Testament references to Jesus as 'God' ('theos'). Some nine or ten passages occur in which Jesus is, or might be, alluded to as as 'God' ('theos'). Usually cited are John i. 1, 18; xx. 28; Romans ix. 5; 2 Thessalonians i. 12; 1 Timothy iii. 16; Titus ii. 13; Hebrews i. 8f.; 2 Peter i. 1 and 1 John v. 20. Two or three of these, however, are highly dubious, and, of the remainder, varying degrees of textual or exegetical uncertainty attach to all save one, which is Thomas' adoring acclaim of the risen Jesus in John xx. 28 as 'My Lord and my God!'"

[46] "The unique god" is also possible, but "unique" is not a primary meaning of *monogenēs*. See Harris, *Jesus as God*, p. 85.

[47] Bruce M. Metzger, *A Textual Commentary on the Greek New Testament*, 4th ed. (Stuttgart: United Bible Societies, 1994), p. 169.

[48] B. D. Ehrmann, *The Orthodox Corruption of Scripture* (New York: Oxford University Press, 1993), p. 80.

is that Jesus can be the *unique* God only if there is no other God; but for the Fourth Gospel, the Father is God as well. Indeed, even in this passage the μονογενής is said to reside in the bosom of the Father. How can the μονογενής θεός, the unique God,[49] stand in such a relationship to (another) God?[50]

If we accept Ehrman's arguments for *huios* over *theos* and adopt the reading "the uniquely derived son," then the verse has no bearing on the question about the meaning of *theos* when it is applied to Jesus. If we, on the other hand, accept the reading of NA27, which has the strongest textual basis, we need to explain the relationship between the adjective *monogenēs* and the substantive *theos*. Harris refers to one Bible translation (NASB) and 16 commentators who take *monogenēs* as an adjective qualifying *theos*, suggesting the rendering "the only begotten God," or something similar.[51] He refers to 7 other translations (TCNT, NAB, NIV [1973 and 1978 eds.], NRSV, NAB, Goodspeed and Phillips) and 9 commentators who take *monogenēs* as a substantivized adjective ("God, the only Son" or something similar), and two translations (NIV [1984] and GNB [1966 and 1971 eds.]) and 15 commentators who in different ways avoid using *monogenēs* as an adjective qualifying *theos* ("the only One, who is the same as God" or something similar).

The word *monogenēs* is an adjective and there are two strong arguments against viewing it as substantivized or taking it in any other way than as a modifier for *theos*: 1) Any adjective can be substantivized but there is no example of this in the NT when it immediately precedes a noun in the same gender, number and case.[52] In such a situation it always qualifies the noun. 2) John uses very simple language, easy to understand. Says Büchsel, "[μονογενὴς θεὸς] can only mean 'an

---

[49] There is no compelling reason to exclude the meaning "only-begotten," which occurs in most translations (compare Harris, *Jesus as God*, pp. 84, 85). However, this word also contains an element of uniqueness.

[50] Ehrmann, *The Orthodox Corruption of Scripture*, p. 80.

[51] Harris, *Jesus as God*, p. 88.

[52] Ehrmann, *The Orthodox Corruption of Scripture*, p. 81.

only-begotten God'; to render 'an only-begotten, one who is God' is an exegetical invention. It can hardly be credited of [John], who is distinguished by monumental simplicity of expression."[53]

Instead of being impossible because of its meaning, the phrase "the unique god/uniquely derived god" (or "the only-begotten god") may turn out to be just the opposite, namely, a parallel to "a god" in 1:1. Regardless of whether we take *monogenēs* to mean "unique," "only-begotten" or "uniquely derived," it implies "the generation/derivation of only one of its kind." Here we will stress the word "kind." In the expression "the only-begotten son," "son" is generic. The implication is that there are others who may be called "son," but only one is "only-begotten."[54] Similarly, the expressions "the presiding overseer" and "the commanding general" both imply that there are other overseers and generals. If there was just one, an epithet such as "presiding" or "commanding" would not be necessary.

The words of John 1:18, therefore, may imply that apart from the Father, others may be called "gods," but of these only one is "the only-begotten/uniquely derived god." Thus we have a parallel between verse 1 where "a god" is said to be "with God" and verse 18 where "the only-begotten/uniquely derived god" is said to be "in the bosom of the Father."[55]

THE TRANSLATION OF JOHN 1:1

Since this verse is, theologically speaking, very important, translators should consider word meaning, grammatical and syntactical questions, and the context. But translators must also

---

[53] F. Büchsel, "μονογενής," TDNT 4 (Grand Rapids: Eerdmans, 1967), p. 740, note 14.

[54] Even when "only-begotten/uniquely derived" seems to be almost identical with "only," as with the son of the widow referred to in Luke 7:12, the implication is valid. The boy was the only son of the widow, but not the only one who could be called "son."

[55] We may also add John 17:5 where Jesus speaks of his relation to God before the creation of the world as "beside you," which hardly can mean anything else but a spatial relationship between the two.

consider the implications that their choice of words will have on the understanding of who Jesus Christ is. The translator who works on a literal translation has a few choices, either to translate "the Word was God," "the Word was divine," "the Word was a god" or "the Word was a divine being."[56]

If we set aside our theological learning, and only consider linguistic and contextual matters, we find that there is a clear preference in the choice of renderings. Still, a comment from *The Translator's New Testament* may be representative for the view of most translators:

> There is a distinction in the Greek here between "with God" and "God." In the first instance the article is used and this makes the reference specific. In the second instance there is no article and it is difficult to believe that the omission is not significant. In effect it gives an adjectival quality to the second use of *Theos* (God) so that the phrase means "The Word was divine."[57]

Bowman agrees with the above statement concerning "adjectival quality," but not with the rendering, "The Word was divine." He says that the anarthrous *theos* is "qualitative," and that those arguing that "*theos* is definite are in error."[58] He also says that "for JW's to translate 'a god' is in one sense grammatically possible, but *only if they are willing to adopt a pagan interpretation of the entire verse* [his italics]."[59]

The above quotes drive home the point that all persons with a reasonable knowledge of New Testament Greek should

---

[56] I am indebted to Greg Stafford, *Jehovah's Witnesses Defended* (Huntington Beach, CA: Elihu Books, 1998), p. 220, for this suggestion. The second edition of this publication (see note 178 below) contains additional information on this subject.

[57] *The Translator's New Testament* (London: The British and Foreign Bible Society, 1973), p. 451.

[58] Bowman, *Jehovah's Witnesses*, p. 42. Those who were in error must include Metzger, "The Jehovah's Witnesses and Jesus Christ," p. 75; Kubo and Specht, *So Many Versions?* p. 99; and Countess, *The Jehovah's Witnesses' New Testament*, p. 56.

[59] Bowman, *Jehovah's Witnesses*, p. 62.

know that the rendering "a god" is a legitimate rendering from a grammatical and syntactical point of view. This rendering (or, "the Word was divine," "the Word was a divine being") is even preferable because of the lack of article and because the Word is said to be "with God." Bowman's argument, quoted above, clearly shows that the reason for his objection to the NWT rendering is exclusively theological and not grammatical or syntactical.[60]

Let us, then, look more closely at the translation alternatives, and at the same time take the interests of the readers into account. First of all, we must admit, as do both Bowman and Harris, that *any* translation of the anarthrous *theos* could create problems for the readers, because the words have connotations which may give the readers an inaccurate impression.

Regarding the Greek of John 1:1, Bowman writes that if John had supplied the Greek article before the second occurrence of *theos* in this verse, which would then have produced the clause *kai ho theos ēn ho logos* ("and the God was the Word"), the only possible understanding would have been that the Word was identical with God in every resepect, which is pure Sabellianism. But is it not true that the rendering "and the word was God," in English, also conveys Sabellianism, without further qualification? Since English does not have the definite article before "God" in "the word was with God" nor in "the word was God," there is absolutely no evident distinction between them.

We find in Kubo and Specht an indirect confirmation of this view. They quote Titus 2:13 in the KJV ("of the great god and our saviour Jesus Christ"), RSV ("our great God and saviour Jesus Christ"), the NEB ("our great God and Saviour Jesus Christ") and the NWT "of the great God and of our savior Christ Jesus." They then conclude: "The first three translations are similar and make God and Jesus Christ the same *person*

---

[60] Harris, *Jesus as God*, p. 60, says, "from the point of view of grammar alone Θεὸς ἦν ὁ λόγος could be rendered "the word was a god." He also says, "But the theeological context, viz., John's monotheism, makes this rendering of 1:1c impossible."

[italics mine], although it is ambiguous in the KJV."[61] Their observation is, of course, true, and the same must be true of the translation "the word was God" for John 1:1. Harris has an even more illuminating comment along the same lines. He writes:

> From this sample of paraphrases it is clear that in the translation "the Word was God" the term *God* is being used to denote his nature or essence and not his person. But in normal English usage "God" is a proper noun, referring to the person of the Father or corporately to the three persons of the Godhead. Moreover "the Word was God" suggests that "the Word" and "God" are convertible terms, that the proposition is reciprocating. But the Word is neither the Father nor the Trinity. Therefore few will doubt that this time-honored translation needs careful exegesis, since it places a distinctive sense upon a common English word. The rendering cannot stand without explanation.[62]

Anyone reading the clause "the Word was God," perhaps with exception to those with a good knowledge of and trust in the trinity, will get the understanding that the Word is identical with God Almighty. In any case, in such a translation the qualitative or indefinite nature of the anarthrous *theos* is not effectively communicated. Without an explanation the readers will be completely misled, and even with an explanation they might still be confused. If the translator recognizes that the rendering "the Word was God" is indeed confusing, and if he or she also refuses to use the trinity doctrine as a translation principle because it is post-Biblical, then "the Word was God" is completely out of the question.

---

[61] Kubo and Specht, *So Many Versions?* p. 101.

[62] Harris, *Jesus as God*, p. 69. This quote also shows how the belief in the trinity doctrine can saturate scholarly discussions. Harris admits that the rendering "the Word was God" is likely to be misunderstood and needs explanation, but still he prefers this rendering. The rendering "the Word was a god" comes in the same class of renderings which can be misunderstood and needs an explanation, but this rendering he categorically rejects (p. 60). There is little doubt that the reason for this rejection is due to Harris' personal view of Jesus and John's monotheism.

The rendering "the Word was divine" prevents the reader from Sabellianism, but at the same time it has some drawbacks. The Greek word is a noun and some nuances may be lost if it is transformed into an adjective; it may be too weak to convey what John meant by using *theos*. Additionally, NT Greek has an adjective that means "divine" (*theios*) which John did not choose; and when it is not aboslutely necessary, it is a service to the reader not to render two Greek words by the same English word.

What about the NWT rendering, "and the Word was a god"? Countess objects to this rendering, saying that Jesus then becomes "'a god' in a pantheon of lesser divinities,"[63] and Bowman uses almost the same words in his objection to this translation.[64] Both claims are somewhat slanted. While it is true that the rendering "a god" *may* be interpeted in a Greek, pagan sense, both authors know very well that such an interpetation is miles apart from the view of the NWT translators. And this is not the only way to interprete the phrase "a god"!

However, it is true that the expression "a god" implies that there is more than one who deserves the designation "god," and because God is the object of worship, some readers may wonder if several gods should be worshiped. But it need not mean more than that "god" may be used qualitatively, with a more restricted meaning than when used for Almighty God.[65] The problem here is finding words which adequately describe the world where God lives without having to add an explanation. To help the reader, therefore, footnotes and other explanations are sometimes necessary. Whatever translation of John 1:1 we offer, there may be some unfortunate connotations, but

---

[63] Countess, *The Jehovah's Witnesses' New Testament*, p. 44.

[64] Bowman, *Jehovah's Witnesses*, p. 62.

[65] Griffiths, "A Note on the Anarthrous Predicate in Hellenistic Greek," p. 315, argues that the rendition "a god" might catch the adjectival force of the anarthrous *theos*: "Taken by itself, the sentence καὶ θεὸς ἦν ὁ λόγος could admittedly bear either of two meanings: (1) 'And the Word was (the) God' or (2) 'and the Word was (a) God.' It is possible to argue that translation (2) brings the predicative noun nearer to the position of an adjective."

compared with the two alternatives "God" and "divine," "a god" or "a divine being" seem to be the best choices.[66]

In view of the above, when it comes to John 1:1 we conclude that the translation "a god" is not the result of a bias on the part of the NWT translators. True, they translate in accordance with their theology, but this is true of every other translation; and this is legitimate so long as translation principles are not violated. Linguistically speaking the rendering "a god" is just as likely as "God." Grammatically speaking there is a preference for "a god" because of the contrast between the arthrous and anarthrous *theos*. Contextually the preference for "a god" is even stronger, because an individual who is said to be "with" another individual cannot be identical with this other individual. The rendering "a god," like most if not all other renderings, has connotations which may give the reader some wrong impressions, but in a literal translation, apart from "god" (in contrast with "the God"), it seems to be the best choice after all.

THE MEANING OF *EGŌ EIMI* IN JOHN 8:58

In this passage NWT reads, "Before Abraham came into existence, I have been." TEV reads, "Before Abraham was born 'I am.'" The last two Greek words ("I am") are the crux of the passage, being translated from the Greek *egō eimi* (the personal pronoun "I" together with the present of the auxiliary "to be"). The question is whether these words are used in an everyday sense, as reflected in the NWT, or whether they are used in a mystical, theological sense, as reflected by the TEV.

---

[66] An alternative rendering would be, "And the Word was with God, and god was the Word." An implication of several gods is less pronounced in this rendering, but explanations are still needed to show the difference between "God" with capital letter and "god" with a lower case letter.

GRAMMATICAL CONSIDERATIONS

To get a full understanding of this passage (and the other *egō eimi* passages as well) we must take three different verbal systems into account.[67] Jesus uttered the words in Hebrew (or Aramaic), they were written down in New Testament Greek, and they have been translated into English. Thus, right from the start we are faced with a problem, namely, that these three languages are very different. As to what is grammaticalized, Hebrew (and Biblical Aramaic) does not have tenses, but only aspects; Greek has two conjugations that only code for aspect, one that codes for tense, one that codes for both aspect and time and one stative conjugation.[68] English has only tenses and no grammaticalized aspects.[69] Thus there are many pitfalls for the one attempting to translate or interpret the passage.

The English reader is first of all interested in the *tense* of the verb in John 8:58. Tense is defined as a grammaticalization of location in time. What then is English present, the tense used most when translating the passages containing *egō eimi*? Speaking schematically, it is a point on a time line diagram representing the present moment, or the intersection between past time and future time. However, it is relatively rare for actions to coincide exactly with the present moment; therefore, present tense situations for the most part "occupy a much longer period of time than the present moment, but nonetheless include the present moment within them."[70] To state it differently, English present may occupy a part of the past as well as of the future but always including the present moment; it can be used for the distant future but hardly including a definite reference point in the distant past.

The Greek present is different from the English present because it is an aspect and not a tense. It portrays a part of the

---

[67] See the *Excursus on Hebrew and Greek Verbs*, p. 71, 72.

[68] What this book calls "conjugations" (aorist, present, etc.) are usually called "tenses," which is really a misnomer.

[69] See *Excursus on Hebrew and Greek Verbs*, p. 72, note 2.

[70] B. Comrie, *Tense* (Cambridge: Cambridge University Press, 1985), p. 37.

action, not including the end,[71] and is evidently timeless.[72] Greek future probably has about the same meaning as English future, thus being a grammaticalized tense, and the Greek imperfect normally makes visible a sequence of a continuous action in the past. The Greek present stands between the two and usually describes actions which often are translated by English present or present continuous.

Bowman writes that the literal translation of *egō eimi* in John 8:58 is "I am" and that the NWT rendering "I have been" is an attempt to harmonize the passage with the antitrinitarian doctrine of the translators.[73] He even says with reference to the context that the rendering "I have been . . . is not accurate."[74] The premise for the claim that only "I am" is a literal translation usually involves the belief that Greek present is a tense with the same meaning as English present, but as we have seen, this is not the case. In fact, in one sense it is accurate to claim, as I do here, that the choice of English *tense* has nothing to do with being a literal translation. Any English equivalent of *eimi* (to be), regardless of its tense, is a literal translation. Thus "I have been" is just as literal as "I am."[75] To find the best way to render *egō eimi* into English we must look in two directions: 1) at the original words of Jesus and 2) at the context.

JESUS' ORIGINAL WORDS

We know that both Hebrew and Aramaic were spoken in Palestine at the time of Jesus. In his daily conversations he

---

[71] Except in resultative situations, that is, when an action ends with a resulting state following. The resultant state is unbounded.

[72] A. T. Robertson, *A Grammar of the Greek New Testament in the Light of Historical Research* (Nashville: Broadman Press, 1934), pp. 881, 882; S. Porter, *Verbal Aspect in the Greek of the New Testament* (New York: Peter Lang, 1993), p. 78.

[73] Bowman, *Jehovah's Witnesses*, p. 89.

[74] Bowman, *Jehovah's Witnesses* , p. 111.

[75] It is true that *eimi*, in most cases, will be translated by the present tense in English, but when the context demands it other tenses can be and are used.

probably spoke Hebrew, which does not have tenses but only aspects. Jesus lived in the period between Classical Hebrew and Mischnaic Hebrew, but there is no evidence that the tense-system of Mishnaic Hebrew was at work during this time. If he spoke Aramaic, the verbal system would have been somewhat different from Classical Hebrew, with participles playing a much greater role; but Biblical Aramaic also does not have a tense system. How, then, did Jesus express the words which John translated with the Greek phrase *egō eimi*?

A participle of the Hebrew verb *hāyā* ("to be")[76] is used only twice in the Hebrew text of the Bible,[77] and of the 50 occurrences of the first person singular of the verb in the Hebrew imperfect, all cases, except possibly 5,[78] have future meaning. So Jesus' use of the Hebrew participle or imperfect is unlikely. The perfect of the first person singular occurs 63 times, but a search revealed only two instances where the Septuagint translated them by *eimi*,[79] and one instance by *egō eimi*.[80] Jesus could have used the Hebrew perfect, *'anî hayîtî* (or just *hayîtî*) as one Hebrew New Testament[81] translates John 8:58. But it is more likely that he used the words found in another Hebrew New Testament, namely, *'anî hû*,[82] or that he simply used the single pronoun *'anî*. The word *'ani* means "I" and *hû* means "he." In Hebrew the pronoun *hû* could be used as a copula (with

---

[76] As will be shown later, *hāyā* is different both from the Greek *eimi* and the English "to be." It is not a copulative verb but emphasizes existence rather than mere being. In a few instances it is used in way similar to a copulative verb.

[77] Exodus 9:3 and Proverbs 13:19.

[78] Job 3:16; 10:19; 12:4; 17:6 and Ruth 2:13.

[79] Job 11:4 and Exodus 2:22.

[80] Job 30:9. There are 18 instances (all with enclitic *waw*) that are assessed as having future meaning, 28 as having past meaning and 17 as having present meaning. Of the last mentioned, 3 are viewed as imperfects of *eimi* and 11 as active or passive aorists of *ginomai* ("to come into existence").

[81] Published by The Bible Society in Israel and translated by Norman Henry Snaith.

[82] *The New Testament in Hebrew and English.* Published by The Society for Distributing the Holy Scriptures to the Jews, Edgware, Middlesex, England.

the meaning *is,* or more rarely *was* or *will be*) in clauses without any verb. The pronoun *hû* was also used for emphasis (*'anî hû,* "it is I" or "I am the one"). In the Septuagint all 9 occurrences of *'anî hû*[83] are translated by *egō eimi.* However, in 160 other instances the words *egō eimi* in the Septuagint translate the lone Hebrew pronoun *'ani* (or *'anōkhî*).[84]

Jesus therefore could have used the perfect *hayîtî,* the nominal clause *'anî hû* or the lone pronoun *'anî.*[85] But regardless of what he actually used, two important points should be kept in mind:

1) *All three expressions were normal Hebrew without any element of mysticism.*

2) *None of the three expressions contain any element of tense.*

Therefore, we conclude that both the original words of Jesus and the Greek rendering made by John did not contain any grammatical element pinpointing time. Thus, the context must decide, and the task of the English translator is to find a rendering of "to be" which is consistent with the context of Jesus' statement.

DOES EIMI, WITH PRIN, POINT BACKWARDS?

The greater context will be considered in detail later on in this section, but what clues do we get from the verse itself? The time element in the verse is evident, *"before* Abraham came into existence." The Greek word translated "before" is *prin,* and both the Hebrew New Testaments referred to in notes 80 and 81 have *beṭērem* where the Greek text has *prin.* Both the Hebrew and

---

[83] Two instances have *'anōkhî,* a variant of *'ani.*

[84] There are two examples of *'ehyē* rendered by *egō eimi* in the LXX, namely, Exodus 3:14 and Hosea 1:9.

[85] The Aramaic equivalents in Targum Onkelos/Jonathan for the last two is *'anā hû* and *'anā.* The Hebrew perfect may be expressed in different ways in Aramaic.

the Greek words mean "before," and *semantically* speaking the phrase "before Abraham" must refer to a time when Abraham was not yet born. How long this "time" was cannot be determined from the grammar or the syntax; it may or may not involve an eternal reference.

At this point Bowman has a curious argument, which according to him "is critical and somewhat new."[86] He says that because of the phrase *prin Abraam genesthai* the expression *egō eimi* "does not point forward from Abraham's birth up to the time of Jesus' speaking," but instead "points *backward* from Abraham's birth to the more distant past." Then he puts it another way, saying that "a clause beginning with *prin* cannot specify 'duration' up to the present, since it refers to a period *prior* to the past event specified in the clause."

Where this rule comes from is not stated. What Bowman overlooks is that the Greek verb *eimi* is both stative[87] and is imperfective; a combination which would signify a situation having duration.[88] Says Fanning, "the present aspect with STATES denotes the *continuing existence* of the subject in the condition indicated by the verb."[89]

The subject of the verse is "I," that is, Jesus, and it is too modest to say it is "somewhat new" to claim that *eimi* refers to the continuing existence of Jesus *backwards* from the birth of Abraham into the distant past. Grammatically speaking it would have been completely new, and if it were truthfully shown that the continuing existence of states could be reversed, it would really revolutionize the study of aspects. But Bowman

---

[86] Bowman, *Jehovah's Witnesses*, p. 110.

[87] A stative describes a state rather than an action. The Hebrew *hāyā* is a stative and *'anî hû* also represents a state.

[88] Robertson, *A Grammar of the Greek New Testament*, p. 864, speaks of "PUNCTILIAR (AORISTIC) PRESENT," and he also mentions *eimi* in this context. However, Robertson held the old, erroneous view of aspect where it was confused with *Aktionsart*. In addition, John 8:58 does not fit his description of a punctliar present. Fanning, *Verbal Aspect in New Tesament Greek*, 1990, p. 113, lists the following states: "Verbs of existence, identity, or class-membership," "εἰμί as intransitive (not as copula or with location phrase)."

[89] Fanning, *Verbal Aspect in New Tesament Greek*, p. 137.

does not give any examples for his novel view. However, examples of continuing existence in a forward sense, also in clauses with the Greek *prin* or the Hebrew *beṭerem* ("before"), can be found.

In the apocryphal book of Susanna, which late manuscripts of the Septuagint add to the book of Daniel,[90] we find the following Greek parallel to our passage: "O Lord God, the eternal, the one who knows [*eidōs*[91]] all things before [*prin*] they spring forth; you know [*oidas*[92]] that I did not do [*epoiēsa*[93]] this."

The Greek verb *oida* is stative and is formally a perfect, but the verb is generally used as a present. The first occurrence of it in the sentence is as an active participle. It is obvious that the knowledge God has about these things, before they spring forth,[94] is not directed backwards nor does it cease at some point before they spring forth. Therefore, Susanna uses the same stative verb when she says, "You know" (at present). What God knew before things took place he also continued to know afterwards, so *prin* in this case does not exclude "duration up to the present."

Let us look at another example. The two Hebrew New Testaments quoted in notes 62 and 63 use the word *beṭerem* where the Septuagint has *prin*. In Jeremiah 1:5 we find this word used twice in a construction quite similar to John 8:58. The Septuagint in both places has *pro tou*, a phrase with basically the same meaning as *prin*. "Before [*pro tou*] I formed you [*plasai*[95]] in the belly I knew you [*epistamai*[96]] and before

---

[90] Daniel 13:35, according to the *o'* text of the book. Septuaginta *Vetus Testamentum Graecum Auctoritate Societatis Litterarum Gottingensis editum*, vol. XVI pars 2 Susanna - Daniel - Bel et Draco, 1954 Göttingen - Vandenhoeck & Ruprecht, p. 85. (The symbol *o'* stands for the Septuagint text of Daniel.)

[91] Active participle of *oida*.

[92] Perfect indicative with present meaning.

[93] Aorist indicative with past meaning.

[94] This is how the author of Susanna views it.

[95] Aorist infinitive; Hebrew has imperfect.

[96] Present indicative; Hebrew has perfect.

[*pro tou*] you came forth [*ekselthein*[97]] from the womb I sanctified you [*hegiaka*[98]]."

To "know" is a state of the mind, and the Greek present must indicate a continuing state. The Hebrew perfect has exactly the same meaning.[99] And both in Hebrew and in Greek we find the preposition "before," referring to a time in the past prior to the birth of Jeremiah. From this time to the time when God uttered the words, he knew Jeremiah. It is similar with the parallel clause. To "sanctify" is an act leading into a state. Here a Greek perfect is used, indicating even more definitely that a clause beginning with "before" can signify a state with duration into the present.

THE TRANSLATION OF EGŌ EIMI

But how should *egō eimi* be translated into English? As already mentioned, Greek has a verbal conjugation called "perfect," which may be defined as "a state or condition resulting from a completed action."[100] It is often translated with English perfect, but the two may not match exactly. As a matter of fact, the Greek *eimi*, being stative, has no perfect form, so John could not have chosen a perfect for *eimi*, but he did choose the imperfective aspect of Greek present to portray a state lasting from the past and continuing into the present.[101]

English has no grammaticalized imperfective aspect which may portray an action or state that began before a certain point in the past, and which continues into the present. But it does have a present tense which covers situations including the present moment. The English present tense, however, cannot be

---

[97] Aorist infinitive; Hebrew has imperfect.

[98] Perfect indicative; Hebrew also has perfect.

[99] H. W. F. Gesenius, *Gesenius' Hebrew Grammar*, ed. E. Kautzsch, trans. A. E. Cowley, 2d Eng. ed. (Oxford: Clarendon Press, 1980), sec. 106, 2 (a).

[100] Fanning, *Verbal Aspect*, p. 103.

[101] Fanning, *Verbal Aspect*, p. 21, and others call this the "Present of Past Action Still in Progress."

extended to include a time before a particular point in the past, so English and Greek present may be mutually exclusive in situations where both past and present are combined.

How, then, should we translate the *egō eimi* of John 8:58, into English? Let us consider the alternatives in the light of the following parameters: "grammaticality," "intelligibility," "faithful conveyance of the message," and "addition of elements."

1) *"Before Abraham came into being, I was."* This rendition is grammatically correct, it is intelligible and it does not add any elements that are not found in the text itself. But because the state is confined to the past, before Abraham came into being and Jesus still lived when he expressed his preexistence, the message is distorted. English preterite cannot include a state which is still in effect.

2) *"Before Abraham came into being, I am."* This is the rendition found in most translations of John 8:58, and it is the one preferred by Bowman. But it is the least attractive one, for several reasons. It is ungrammatical because English present tense cannot start before a definite point in the past. It is unintelligible and does not convey the message, because an element of mysticism must be added to defend its place in an English translation. Since there are no mystical connotations in the Greek text, it adds foreign elements.

3) *"Before Abraham came into being, I have been."* This is the rendition found in the NWT and some other translations, including the early marginal reading offered by the *New American Standard Bible*. It is ungrammatical because English perfect cannot be used to portray a state which is anchored to a particular point in the past.[102] It is, however, intelligible and therefore it conveys

---

[102] The linguist Carlota Smith, in *The Parameter of Aspect* (Studies in Linguistics and Philosophy 43; London: Kluwer Academic, 1991), p. 149, says, "perfect sentences with specifying adverbials do not appear in English; a sentence such as '*Sam has arrived yesterday*' is ungrammatical, though quite intelligible."

the message. It also does not add any mystical or foreign elements.

The truth is, there is no way to translate this Greek passage into English in a strictly literal way, because Greek is an aspectual language and English is not. In comparing the above translations, we can see that 2), which is the most popular choice, does not fulfill any of the four requirements, while 1) and 3) fulfill three out of the four. My personal preference is for 3), rather than 1), since 3) does not distort the message as does 1).

I recently discussed the problem of translating this passage with two leading Norwegian linguists. Both of them chose 3) without hesitation, for they viewed an ungrammatical but intelligible rendition as better than those who which do not convey the message. While there are faults with the NWT rendition from an English grammatical point of view, in no way does it convey any bias on the part of the translators. By reading this literal translation of the passage, the readers have an opportunity to interpret John's record of what Jesus said for themselves.[103]

There is, however, one way to avoid the problems mentioned above, and that is to allow the addition of just a small element which in no way qualifies as interpolation. This is done by K. L. McKay in his superb translation, "I have been in existence since before Abraham was born."[104]

---

[103] NWTREF gives the reader another advantage in its Appendix 6F, where additional information about the passage is given. The Appendix also gives English translations of three Syriac versions from the fourth or fifth century. One of the versions corresponds to the English "I have been" and two others correspond to "I was." There are also English translations of the Old Georgian and the Old Ethiopic versions, both from the sixth century, and both of them correspond to the English rendering, "I was." The Ethiopic and the Syriac versions are compatible with the NWT rendering because the perfect of these ancient languages do not have the same restrictions as the English preterite. The Syriac Peshitta, both its Eastern and Western versions, has the rendering *'ena itai* ("I am/was/will be") which is completely time indifferent.

[104] K. L. McKay, *A New Syntax of the Verb in New Testament Greek* (New York: Peter Lang, 1994), p. 42.

One point, however, where Bowman is right, is in his criticism of the footnote in the 1950 edition of NWT, for its use of the words "the perfect indefinite tense."[105] Even though the semantic contents of the phrase may be fitting, and the term can be found in old English grammars, it was not standard grammatical terminology in 1950, and therefore does not contribute much to the readers' understanding of the passage or the translation offered. In NWTREF (page 1582) "the perfect indefinite tense" is changed to "perfect indicative."

SUPPOSED OLD TESTAMENT PARALLELS

Bowman highlights what he views as important OT parallels to Jesus' words in John 8:58. The first proposed parallel we will consider is Psalm 90:2.

IS PSALM 90:2 PARALLEL TO JOHN 8:58?

Below we consider NWT's translation of the Hebrew text of this verse, followed by Brenton's translation of the Septuagint text:

NWT's Translation of the Hebrew of Psalm 90:2

> Before the mountains themselves were born, Or you proceeded to bring forth as with labor pains the earth and the productive land. Even from time indefinite to time indefinite you are God.

LXX Translation of Psalm 90:2

> Before the mountains existed, and *before* the earth and the world were formed, even from age to age, Thou art.

---

[105] Bowman, *Jehovah's Witnesses*, p. 91.

The principal difference is that the Hebrew text has "God" as predicate nominative in the last clause, while the Septuagint simply says *su ei* ("you are") without any predicate nominative. "The parallels between this text and John 8:58 are remarkable" writes Bowman, and in this he is correct. "You are" (*su ei*) in the Psalm is indeed parallel to "I am" (*egō eimi*)[106] in John 8:58, and "were born" (*ginomai*) is parallel to "was born" (*ginomai*). The use of slightly different prepositions does not alter this otherwise harmonious picture. The Hebrew noun *'ōlām* and the Greek *aiōn* have the meaning of "time indefinite," but sometimes they can be used to convey eternality. Psalm 90:2 evidently says that God is eternal.

In spite of the aforementioned similarities between these two scriptures, much of what Bowman says about them is hard to accept, and easy to dispute. He argues, "To be consistent, then, they [Jehovah's Witnesses] have to admit that John 8:58 just as clearly affirms the eternality of Jesus."[107] Bowman's premise evidently is the same as the one used for John 1:1, namely, that time was created with the universe. Only if this is true is his conclusion justified, but, as was earlier shown, this is a philosophical thought which cannot be substantiated. The Psalmist compares the short life of men with that of God, who is eternal. In verse 1 he places God within the timeframe of the generations of mankind. In verse 2 he expands on this thought, pointing out that God existed before the universe was created, and then comes his climax: God is from everlasting to everlasting! There is neither a linguistic nor a semantic reason to claim that the clause "before the mountains were brought forth" necessarily implies God's eternal existence, since even the angels existed before the creation of the universe (Job 38:7).

If we compare Psalm 90:2 with John 8:58 we do in fact find a difference in the temporal descriptions given. Speaking

---

[106] I use "I am" here as a simple representation of these present verbs, without taking the context into consideration. This is not the only way they can be translated. That *egō eimi* is said to be equal to "I am" cannot be used as an argument for such a rendering in John 8:58, for there are other factors to consider. Some of these factors have been considered already, and others will be discussed later in this section.

[107] Bowman, *Jehovah's Witnesses*, p. 118.

syntactically of the Psalm, the time adverbial "from everlasting [age] to everlasting [age]" gives the anchor points for the words *su ei*, a fact which, semantically speaking, indicates that the time covered by *su ei* is from everlasting to everlasting (compare 1 Chr 29:10). This means that past, present and future are gathered together by this expression, or that it is independent of any time measure. Speaking syntactically of John's words, we may say that the time adverbial "before Abraham" is the past anchor point of *egō eimi* while Jesus' speech time represents the other point; speaking semantically, this indicates that the time covered by *egō eimi* runs from some unspecified point before Abraham was born, up to the time when Jesus' words were spoken. This means that past and present are gathered together by the expression, but not the future. So compared with Psalm 90:2 this is a completely different situation.

Because Greek present is not a tense but an aspect, which can give different meanings when used with verbs with different *Aktionsart* in clauses with different kinds of subjects and objects, it can be used in both in Psalm 90:2 and in John 8:58. Those understanding Greek in the first century CE would have no problem understanding the meaning of both of these passages. If we are going to translate these texts into English, since English does not have aspects similar to those in Greek, but only tenses, the verbs of both passages must be translated differently.

Using present tense in the Psalm creates no problems. The words "from everlasting [age] to everlasting [age] you are" gather the present, past and future into a single expression. But when we have a clause with the preposition "before," referring to a particular time in the past, to use the present tense would be ungrammatical in English. An act or a state anchored to a particular time in the remote past cannot be expressed by English present. So while there are indeed parallels between John 8:58 and Psalm 90:2, there are also considerable differences.

IS EXODUS 3:14 PARALLEL TO JOHN 8:58?

In discussing Exodus 3:14, we may also learn an important lesson from Psalm 90:2, something which evidently has not occurred to Bowman. There are two words in the Hebrew text of the Psalm and two in the Greek. However, the two Greek words are not a translation of the two Hebrew words, but of one of the Hebrew words and of another which is implied. The Hebrew word which is not translated by the Septuagint is the predicative nominative "God." The Hebrew text literally says "You (are) God" while the Septuagint has the rendering "You are." Bowman is aware of this, but there is another important point which he does not stress.

One of the premises on which he builds when he parallels Exodus 3:14 and John 8:58 is that *hāyā* ("to be/exist") in Hebrew is equivalent to *eimi* ("to be") in Greek, and herein lies a problem, for this is not necessarily true. The linking verb (copula) "to be" is usually implied in Hebrew, not written. Therefore, the Greek *eimi* does not have a written equivalent in Hebrew, and it does not correspond to *hāyā*.

A few statistics might help illustrate this point. Apart from consecutive perfect and imperfect, the meaning of which may be open for discussion, there are a total of 493 occurrences of *hāyā* in the Hebrew OT, compared with 6469 occurrences of *eimi* in the Septuagint and 2462 occurrences of *eimi* in the NT. The reason why *eimi* is used 13 times more frequently than *hāyā* is because *eimi* serves as copula while *hāyā* does not. Therefore, when *hāyā* is used there is often a stress on *existence*, which is normally lacking in the Greek *eimi*. Bowman has not considered this, but it has a bearing on his attempt to parallel John 8:58 and Exodus 3:14.

The crucial words of Exodus 3:14 are *'ehyē 'ashēr 'ehyē* ("I will be what I will be"), or, as NWT reads, "I shall prove to be what I shall prove to be." In the following verse the personal name of God is expressed by the four consonants YHWH, and Bowman, Countess, and others claim that Jesus applied this name to himself.

There is a similarity between *'ehyē* and YHWH in that two of the consonants (H and H) are identical, and the third

242

(W) is probably identical.[108] So, what is the meaning of YHWH? It is near impossible to determine with certainty the etymology of such an ancient word; we simply do not know! One suggestion is that the name represents the causative form of *hayā*, meaning, "he causes to be." This may very well be the case. Against this, however, it may be argued that a causative form (hiphil) of *hayā* is unprecedented, and that a third person singular is strange indeed for the personal name of God. We would have expected *"I* cause to be" rather than *"he* causes to be," just as we see in the *'ehyē* ("*I* will be") of the following verse. Because the *'ehyē*-clause *describes* God and YHWH *names* God, it is not unreasonable to think that there is some connection between them, but what that connection is may be difficult to determine, with certainty.

The Septuagint translation of *'ehyē 'ashēr 'ehyē* is *egō eimi ho ōn*. The words *ho ōn* are the present participle of *eimi* together with the article, so the clause may be translated, as Brenton does, "I am The Being." It is important to note that the second occurrence of *'ehyē* is translated by *ho ōn*, which is the predicate nominative of the clause. When the Septuagint in the next verse refers to the person of the previous verse, it uses the predicate nominative *ho ōn*, which now serves as the subject, "The Being [*ho ōn*] has sent me."

If Jesus, by help of the Septuagint translation, had claimed identity with YHWH, he could either have said, "I am YHWH" or "I am God" (as shown in Chapter 5, the Septuagint contained God's name in Jesus' day), or he could have said "I am The Being [*ho ōn*]." The word *eimi* in Exodus 3:14 is merely a linking verb, and cannot be claimed to represent a point of reference, even an important one. So here there is no link to John 8:58.

---

[108] The verb *hāyā* has a *yod* as the second consonant, while YHWH has a *waw* in the second position. In Aramaic a *waw* is used in the equivalent verb, and such a verb with *waw* also occurs five times in the Hebrew text (Gen 27:29; Isa 16:4; Eccl 2:22; 11:3 and Neh 6:6). The wife of Adam, in Genesis 3:20, is called *hawwā* ("the living one," with *het*, not *he*, as the first consonant) though we might have expected *hāyā*. The names in Genesis 5 and 10 reveal that the Hebrew behind them was slightly different from the Hebrew of the Masoretic text.

Scholars in the field of translating literature know that because languages are different there are times when certain nuances found in a source-language word do not have an exact equivalent in the receptor language. If this is the case, a careful translator of an idiomatic translation should try to create the same effect somewhere else in the clause, or even in the next clause. This is probably what the Septuagint translator tried to do in Exodus 3:14. As already noted, *hāyā* is not a linking verb, even though it, in a few instances, is used like one. But it does indicate existence or emphasis. There is no equivalent verb in Greek, so the translator lets all the emphasis materialize in the expression *ho ōn*. In a way, this expression accounts for both occurrences of *'ehyē* in the Hebrew text, while *eimi* in the same clause is just a linking verb (copula). The *eimi* of John 8:58, on the other hand, is probably a translation of a nominal clause with an implied copula (the lone *'anî*) or a nominal clause with an expressed copula (*'anî hû*, "I am"). In either nominal clause a predicate nominative is lacking (though one could be implied from the context), and therefore *existence* on the part of the subject is expressed. But this existence is expressed syntactically while the existence signaled by *hāyā* is expressed lexically. If this reasoning is correct, the difference between *egō eimi* used in John 8:58 and in Exodus 3:14 becomes even more profound.

IS *'ANÎ HÛ* IN ISAIAH PARALLEL TO *EGŌ EIMI* IN JOHN?

Bowman also sees a parallel between *'anî hû* in Isaiah and *egō eimi* in John, but his case is not conclusive in this instance, either. He admits that David's use of *'anî hû* "is completely nontheological,"[109] and this implies that the words are normal, without any mystical connotations. However, when God uses the words through Isaiah, Bowman claims that the words are substitutes for the divine name, and that Jesus uses *egō eimi* in this same sense.

---

[109] Bowman, *Jehovah's Witnesses*, p. 120.

There are 8 occurrences of *'anî hû* in the Hebrew OT. In Isaiah 52:6 the words definitely have a demonstrative force, indicated by the relative particle pointing back to *hû*. The rendering of NWT in this case is quite appropriate, "Look! It is I." To render *'anî hû* by "I am" in this passage would be strange, if not impossible. In 1 Chronicles 21:17 the same words are used by David, and they also have a demonstrative force, though another relative particle is used here, compared with Isaiah 52:6.

Also, consider Isaiah 42:8, *'anî YHWH hû shemî* ("I [am] YHWH, that [is] my name). If *'anî hû* is a substitute for the divine name, YHWH would be superfluous in this verse. In Isaiah 46:4 there are four occurrences of *'anî* in the same verse, in addition to *'anî hû*. In Isaiah 48:12 there are two more occurrences, all of these used to emphasize the subject, God. Several other texts (Isa 43:10, 13; 52:6; Deut 32:39) are also compatible with the NWT translation, "I am the same one." An element of mysticism is not visible anywhere in these texts.

The conclusion, therefore, regarding *egō eimi* in John 8:58, is that theology has been very much involved in the translation of these words, to the effect that the most popular rendering, "Before Abraham was born, 'I am,'" (which we find in TEV), is both ungrammatical, unintelligible, and adds an element of mysticism which is not found in the Greek text. On the other hand, NWT represents the best that can be achieved by a strictly literal translation: it is literal and it does not add any foreign elements. But its weakness is that it is ungrammatical. Thus, it may be that in this case even a strictly literal translation should concede to add the one word ("since") that, in English, would allow for a grammatical and intelligible translation, such as the one offered by McKay.

COLOSSIANS CHAPTER ONE AND NWT'S USE OF "OTHER"

A considerable controversy has been raised about NWT's use of "other," in brackets, in Colossians 1:16-17, because whether or not this word is used in these texts is said to have a bearing on the position of Jesus Christ in relation to creation. NWT also brackets "other" in Colossians 1:20, but few dispute the use of other in this text. NWT's translation of verses 16-17 and 20 is as follows:

> Because by means of him all [other] things were created in the heavens and upon the earth . . . All [other] things have been created through him and for him. Also he is before all [other] things. And by means of him all [other] things were made to exist. . . . and through him to reconcile again to himself all [other] things.

IS JESUS CHRIST INCLUDED IN CREATION? OR IS HE THE SOURCE OR SUPERIOR TO ALL OF CREATION?

The critical verse in the context of Colossians 1:16-17 is verse 15. Let us look at three different renderings of this verse:

Figure 6.2

Translations of Colossians 1:15

RSV	He is the image of the invisible God, the first-born of all creation.
TEV	Christ is the visible likeness of the invisible God. He is the firstborn Son, superior to all created things.
C. B. Williams	Yes, He is the exact likeness of the unseen God, His first-born Son who existed before any created thing.

One can only wonder how it is possible to translate the three Greek words *prōtotokos pasēs ktiseōs* so differently: one version includes Jesus in creation and the other two exclude him by making him either superior to creation, or highlighting his existence *prior to* creation. This is a particularly useful comparison for purposes of this discussion since there is a clear preference in the translation of the verse. One book on translation puts it this way: "'The first-born Son, superior to all created things' represents a three-word phrase in Greek, 'first-born of all creation.' Translated literally (as RSV), it implies that Christ is included in the created universe, which is inconsistent with the context of the whole passage."[110]

Quite a few translations render the words "literally," but why do so many deviate from such a rendering? It is because of their theology, a fact which is revealed by at least one commentator:

> *The first-born of all creation.* The meaning of the word *first-born (prōtotokos)* is crucial for a right understanding of Paul's conception of Christ. The real problem is whether or not this word implies that Christ was included in creation, whether in other words there is any sense in which Christ can be described as a created being. If the word is considered out of context, it would be possible to make a case for the inclusive meaning as paralleled, for instance, in Rom. 8:29. But the context makes clear that Christ is the agent of creation, which at once places Him above it. In this case the word *first-born* must be understood in the sense of "supreme" rather than in the temporal sense "born before."[111]

Most writers arguing against a "literal" rendering of this verse point out that such a rendering is inconsistent with their understanding of Jesus Christ. One experienced writer wrote that such a rendering is inconsistent with 1) the words that follow "firstborn," 2) the conception of Christ as the divine pre-existent Wisdom, and 3) the Christian redemption where a redeemer from among the creatures is not possible.[112] Christian redemption is outside the scope of this book, but let us study the two other points.

---

[110] R. G. Bratcher and E. A. Nida, *A Translators Handbook on Paul's Letters to Colossians and to Philemon* (Stuttgart: United Bible Societies, 1977), p. 22.

[111] Donald Guthrie, *The New Bible Commentary*, Revised ed. (London: Inter-Varsity Press, 1970), p. 1144.

[112] C. F. D. Moule, *The Epistles of Paul the Apostle to the Colossians and to Philemon* (Cambridge: Cambridge University Press, 1968), pp. 63, 64.

IS THERE A PARALLEL BETWEEN COLOSSIANS 1 AND PROVERBS CHAPTER 8?

It is somewhat surprising that Moule appeals to the conception of Christ as the divine pre-existent *wisdom*. True, the church Fathers almost unanimously applied Proverbs 8 to Jesus Christ, but if this view is accepted, it is very difficult to escape the conclusion that Jesus was the first one created by God, the exact opposite of Moule's opinion. However, I agree with Moule that the translation of Colossians 1:15-20 must be seen in the light of what is said about wisdom in Proverbs 8. Let us now compare the two.

Both Proverbs 8 and Colossians 1 and 2 discuss creation. In Proverbs 8:27-31 wisdom is portrayed as a master-worker who was present with God and who had a part in the creative process. Colossians 1:16 (TEV) says about Jesus: "For through him God created everything in heaven and on earth, the seen and the unseen things, including spiritual powers, lords, rulers, and authorities. God created the whole universe through him and for him." Similarly, John 1:3 reads, "through him God made all things." In the NT Jesus is nowhere called "creator"; rather, he is always portrayed as the "mediator" in connection with creation. As far as a parallel concept, Colossians 1:16 fits very well wisdom's description as a "master-worker" in Proverbs 8:30.

A closer look at the context of Colossians 1 and 2 reveals another parallel with Proverbs 8, namely, the close association of "wisdom" to Jesus in Colossians 2:3. Jesus seems to apply the concept of wisdom to himself in Matthew 11:19 and 12:42, and in 1 Corinthians 1:24, 30 Paul applies it directly to Jesus.

A third parallel may be seen between Proverbs 8:22, 25 and Colossians 1:15, which, according to the RSV read, respectively:

> The LORD created me at the beginning of his work, the first of his acts of old. Before the mountains had been shaped, before the hills, I was brought forth.

> He is the image of the invisible God, the first-born of all creation.

To suggest a parallel between words in the NT and words in the OT where there is no direct quotation, may be somewhat elusive. For example, while one German commentator[113] has no doubt that there exists a link between Proverbs 8 and Colossians 1 and 2, another commentator[114] rejects this connection. Thus, it is up to the reader to evaluate the three parallel points listed above. However, if Paul had the pre-existent wisdom in mind, as suggested by Moule, the figure was both the intermediate agent of creation and at the same time a created being.

THE MEANING OF PRŌTOTOKOS

The three important Greek words of Colossians 1:15 are *prōtotokos* ("first-born"), *pasēs* (a genitive form of "all") and *ktiseōs* (a genitive form of "creation" or "creature"). The genitive case in Greek may have several meanings. Grammatically it is possible to include the firstborn in creation and it is also grammatically possible to exclude this one from creation. The situation is not, however, as ambiguous as it may seem. The different meanings of the genitive are not equally probable; the meaning which would exclude the firstborn from creation is much less likely than the one that includes him among the created order. But, more important, the lexical meaning of the words may reduce the possibilities even further. In fact, the problem may be solved by our answering just one question: What is the meaning of *prōtotokos* in this context?

The word occurs 128 times in the Septuagint and 8 times in the NT. The only *lexical* meaning ascribed to the word in Liddell and Scott, BAGD and NIDNTT is "firstborn." Michaelis gives his views in TDNT[115] as to which of the word's root elements the different contexts stress, but this is just speculation. With all their ingenuity, those seeking a meaning other than

---

[113] E. Lohse, *A Commentary on the Epistles to the Colossians and to Philemon* (Hermeneia Series; Philadelphia, Fortress Press, 1971), p. 48.

[114] W. Michaelis, "πρωτότοκος," TDNT 6 (Grand Rapids: Eerdmans, 1968), p. 879.

[115] Michaelis, "πρωτότοκος," pp. 871-881.

"the one who is born first" are able to list just one example, and that is Psalm 89:28, "And I will make him the firstborn, the highest of the kings of the earth."

This Psalm, however, does not give a new *lexical* meaning to *prōtotokos*, but simply tells about *the result* of God putting the mentioned person in the position of a firstborn (compare 1 Chr 26:1 and 2 Chr 21:3).[116] As an illustration we may point to the fact that the priests in Israel would also serve as physicians, but this did not add the meaning "physician" to the word "priest." Having gone through all the Biblical passages that use *prōtotokos*, I have found no example which has the meaning "supreme" or even something similar, not even a passage which *might* be construed with such a meaning! Rather, in all of the examples used of individuals, in a sense other than where one is "placed" as though he were the firstborn, they take as a point of departure the notion of one who is born first. In Colossians 1:18, for example, we find the expression "firstborn from the dead," evidently meaning "the first one to experience a resurrection with the prospect of never dying again."

How, then, are we to view the different translations of the important phrase in 1:15? It appears that a general tendency among some modern translators is to follow the suggestion of Bratcher and Nida, "He is the first-born Son, superior to all created things."[117] But this rendering is a paraphrase rather than a translation, and it deserves to be classified as a biased translation. The justification for calling the rendering biased is not because it is theological in nature, building as it does on belief in the trinity. Indeed, in this verse it is legitimate to use one's theology (though it should not be the principal factor behind one's translation) because there are just two possibilities: either to include Jesus in the creation or to exclude him from the created order. But what can be criticized is the deviation from normal translation procedures.

---

[116] This was explained a hundred years ago by T. K. Abbott, *A Critical and Exegetical Commentary on the Epistles to the Ephesians and to the Colossians* (ICC; Edinburgh: T. & T. Clark, 1977), p. 211.

[117] Bratcher and Nida, *A Translator's Handbook on Paul's Letters to the Colossians and to Philemon*, p. 22.

To state the case more explicitly, we may point out that the phrase "all created things" in the suggested translation is a literal rendering of the two Greek words *pasēs ktiseōs*. But how is *prōtotokos* translated? As "the firstborn, superior to"! So we see that *prōtotokos* is first rendered literally as "the firstborn," the only sense in which it is used in the NT and the Septuagint, but then *prōtotokos* is translated a second time, with a completely different meaning, which is not even a lexical meaning of the word, namely, "superior to."[118] In this there is a deviation from normal translation procedure. Additionally, there is a question about the grammar of Bratcher and Nida's translation of Colossians 1:15. The three Greek words *prōtotokos pasēs ktiseōs* make a Greek genitive construction ('all-creation's firstborn') where the second and third words are subordinated to the first, as its modifiers. It is questionable for a translator to change the subordination to co-ordination by making the phrase "superior to all created things" in apposition to "the first-born Son."

What we are here discussing is to what degree theology and bias have influenced the NWT translators. Regarding Colossians 1:15, we have not found any basis for the claim that bias is at work in the NWT translation of this passage. No, but I have pointed out that one of the more preferred renderings is biased. Let us, then, consider the evidence in favor of NWT's rendering of this verse:

- In the same verse Jesus is called "the image of the invisible God." An image is something different and temporally distinct from the original.

- Paul may possibly have alluded to the wisdom in Proverbs Chapter 8. Three parallels are possible: 1) in Colossians chapters 2 "wisdom" is applied to Jesus; 2) the function of a master-worker or agent in creation is found in both places; and 3) wisdom is portrayed

---

[118] If anyone objects to the portrayal of one word being translated twice with different meanings, we may instead say that *prōtotokos* is translated once literally, and then a phrase, which neither explicitly nor implicitly is found in the Greek text of the verse, is added.

as the one who was created first by God, while Jesus is called the "the firstborn of all creation."

- The only lexical meaning of *prōtotokos* is "firstborn," and the word is used in this same way in Colossians 1:18.

- If *prōtotokos* is taken with the meaning "firstborn," it implies membership in a group with others who are born later, as in Romans 8:29, where Jesus is said to be the "firstborn among many brothers." The literal meaning of *prōtotokos* seems to exclude all the different Greek genitives, except one, the partitive genitive. This is the suggestion of at least one grammarian,[119] and it would make Jesus a member of creation.

NWT, COLOSSIANS 1 AND "ALL [OTHER] THINGS"

Apart from "a god" in John 1:1, the NWT rendering which has stirred up the most controversy is undoubtedly the inclusion of "other" in brackets in Colossians 1:16, 17 and 20. While many translations[120] render verse 15b as "the first-born of all creation," the inclusion of "other" in the following verses is, as far as I know, not found in any other Bible translation. There are several issues that need to be addressed before we can determine whether or not "other" indicates bias on the part of the NWT translators.

---

[119] N. Turner, *Grammatical Insights into the New Testament* (Edinburgh, T. & T. Clark, 1965), p. 124. While Turner advocates the partitive sense, he does not believe Christ is part of the created order. Rather, he believes that Christ is the new "Adam," and that he is the model after whom others would be patterned.

[120] For instance, NASB, NAB, NJB. A check of 155 modern translations found that 74 include Jesus in creation, 73 exclude him from creation, and 7 were neutral.

THE MEANING OF THE GREEK WORD PAS

When Paul, in 2 Timothy 1:15, wrote, "all the men in the [district] of Asia have turned away from me," he obviously did not have in mind every single inhabitant in Asia, but only those who claimed to be Christians. But even this qualification is not enough, because in verse 16 Paul said that Onesiphorus did not leave him, so the expression "all men" must refer to "most of the Christians in Asia."

This illustrates how the word *pas* and *pan* do not necessarily have an all-embracing meaning, but besides possibly having the meaning '(absolutely) all,' it may also mean, per the context, "all kinds of," "all sorts of," or "all other." One characteristic of NWT is that the translators endeavored to convey the most minute nuances of the text. For instance, they differentiate between *gnosis* ("knowledge") and *epignosis* ("accurate knowledge"), and between the words *anastasis* ("resurrection") and *exanastasis* ("the early resurrection"). Because it is difficult to know if, at a particular time in the past, the preposition in such words (*epi* and *ek*) does in fact represent a semantic difference compared to the forms used without a preposition, the different renderings of such words may be open to discussion. However, there is no doubt that NWT's treatment of these forms is a service to the readers, because they will likely realize that different words are used in the Greek text.

Regarding the word *pas/pan* we have no doubt that it has different meanings in different contexts. It is not possible to translate the word as "all" every time it occurs, because when it occurs before a word lacking the definite article it often means "every," thus stressing the individual member of the group. When the article occurs, many Bible translations render the word as "all" in every instance. At first sight, this may seem to be a service to the readers, allowing them to decide the meaning, and in some cases this does work well. If Luke 21:29 had been translated, "Note the fig tree and all trees" the reader would have no problem recognizing the meaning "the fig tree and all *other* trees."

However, the traditional translation of Acts 2:17 will undoubtedly mislead most readers. A comparison of NWT and 70 other translations reveals that NWT is the only one that has hit the target. It is quite obvious that God will not pour out his spirit upon *every* living man, including those who have committed sin against The holy spirit. Therefore, the TEV rendering, "I will pour out my Spirit upon all men" is misleading, while the NWT rendering, "I shall pour out some of my spirit upon every sort of flesh"[121] is illuminating. Blass-Debrunner, in discussing ellipses, says, "Further ellipses: (1) The omission of the notion 'other, whatever' (§306 (5)) is specifically Greek."[122] Two examples relevant to our discussion are given: 1 Corinthians 10:31 where the Greek word *ti* has the meaning "whatever else" and Hermas Mandates 4.3.7, 5.2.8, 8.12 where *kai pantes* mean "and all others."

Thus, there can be no doubt that from a linguistic point of view, the translation "all other" is perfectly legitimate in Colossians 1:16-17, 20. It is not mandatory, but it is possible. This means that the brackets that NWT uses around "other" may be removed, because the word "other" is no addition or interpolation, but in a given context it is a legitimate part of *pas*.

However, while there is no linguistic objection against using "other" in the aforementioned verses, this does not mean that an evaluation of all other factors will result in a recommendation for using the word in this context. We will take a closer look at this point, later.

THE MEANING OF THE GREEK WORD 'ARCHÊ

We will begin our examination with Colossians 1:18. It reads, "he is the beginning [*archē*], the first-born [*prōtotokos*] from the dead" (RSV). In addition to the word *prōtotokos*, which we have already examined, we also find another very important word, namely, *archē*. In John 1:1 we read "in the

---

[121] That different "sorts of flesh" are referred to in verse 16 also lends support to NWT's rendering.

[122] F. Blass and A. Debrunner, *A Greek Grammar of the New Testament and Other Early Christian Literature*, trans. Robert W. Funk (Chicago: University of Chicago Press, 1961), sec. 480, p. 254.

beginning [*archē*] was the Word," but in Colossians 1:18 we are told that Jesus *is* the *archē*. Tracking through both the classical and New Testament Greek usage of this word, we find the lexical meanings are as follows: 1) beginning, 2) origin/source and 3) ruler/authority.

In the NT *archē* occurs 53 times, and 26 of these must have the meaning "beginning," because they are preceded by a preposition (as "*from* the beginning"). In 8 instances[123] the word occurs in a genitive construction where the meaning is also, clearly, "beginning." In 6 instances[124] the meaning "beginning" is also appropriate. In 2 instances[125] it has the meaning "corner." In 11 instances[126] *archē* has the meaning "government" or "ruler." The final uses of this word are in Colossians 1:18 and Revelation 3:14, which are both theologically significant texts.

From the above it is clear that *archē*, in more than 75% of its occurrences, means "beginning." Apart from "corner," which also is a "beginning," the word is used in some sense connected with "government." The word *archē*, with the meaning "source," is nowhere attested in the NT, and 7 of the instances with the meaning "government" are in the plural. Also, the four singular occurrences with this meaning are qualified, either by "every" (1 Cor 15:24; Eph 1:21; Col 2:10) or by a genitive construction (Luke 20:20).

The word *archē* in Colossians 1:18 stands unqualified as a predication of Jesus, and the meaning "government" seems to be out of the question in this verse. In the next clause Jesus is said to be "the firstborn [*prōtotokos*] from the dead," and *archē* and *prōtotokos* occasionally occur together, expressing the concept "the first son" (compare Gen 49:3 and Deut 21:17 in the

---

[123] Matthew 24:8, Mark 1:1; 13:8, 19; Hebrews 5:12; 6:1; 7:3; 2 Peter 3:4.

[124] John 8:25; Jude 1:6; Hebrews 2:3; 3:14; Revelation 21:6; 22:13. In several of these texts there is a contrast between the "beginning" and the "end."

[125] Acts 10:11; 11:5

[126] TEV has the following readings, in parentheses: Luke 12:11 (governors); 20:20 (authority); Romans 8:38 (heavenly rulers); 1 Corinthians 15:24 (spiritual rulers); Ephesians 1:21 (heavenly rulers); 3:10 (angelic rulers); 6:12 (wicked spiritual forces); Colossians 1:16 (spiritual powers); 2:10 (spiritual leader); 2:15 (spiritual rulers); Titus 3:1 (rulers).

Septuagint). So *archē* and *prōtotokos* in verse 18 may express the same thought: Jesus is the first one to experience a resurrection from the dead with continuing life in view.

The application of *archē* to Jesus in Revelation 3:14 is parallel to its use in Colossians 1:15. In Revelation 3:14 *archē* is qualified by "God's creation," and this presents a problem for those who support the trinity doctrine. The sense "government, authority" is hardly fitting here, but if the translator chooses the only other meaning which is found in the NT, namely, "beginning," then Jesus is described as "the beginning of God's creation," and thus a part of creation.

To avoid including Jesus in creation, a meaning which is found in the Septuagint and in classical Greek (but not in the NT) is introduced, namely, "origin" or "source." It is interesting to note that only in Colossians 1:18 and Revelation 3:14 is "origin" or "source" used for *archē* in many translations. We cannot call this "bias" because "origin" or "source" is a lexical possibility, but the fact that this rendering is used *only* in the two above-mentioned passages in many translations shows that theology has exerted a strong influence upon the translators.

Getting back to Colossians 1:18, we have found support for rendering *archē* as "beginning" in other NT examples; even in Revelation 3:14, an important christological passage, the sense of "beginning" is strongly suggested. Additional support is found in the phrase "the firstborn of the dead" in verse 18. The meaning is evidently that he was the first to experience a resurrection.[127] The conclusion of the verse supports both "beginning" and "firstborn of the dead," because it gives a basis for these expressions, namely, "that he might become the one who is first in all things."

---

[127] Rgerading the resurrection, in 1 Corinthians 15:20, 23 Jesus is called the "first fruit" (*aparchē*). According to Acts 26:23 he was the "first to rise from the dead," and Revelation 1:5 uses the same phrase as Colossians 1:18, "firstborn of the dead."

JESUS AS MEDIATOR IN CREATION

Because *ta panta* is said to have been created "through him" in Colossians 1:16, Jesus is often viewed as the creator who is separate from the creation. But this is a misunderstanding of his role as mediator. In Colossians 1:16, 17 Jesus' role in creation is described by passive verbs. The agent in an active clause is the grammatical subject. If we transform an active clause into a passive one, the object of the active clause becomes the subject of the passive one (Examples are: "God created the world" [active] and "The world was created by God" [passive]). The agent of the passive clause may be identified by a preposition (in this case, *by* God), or the agent may simply be implied.[128] There is little semantic difference between the two clauses.

However, in a Greek passive clause more than the direct agent may be expressed; an *intermediate* agent may also be expressed. According to Robertson the direct agent is most commonly expressed by the Greek preposition *hupo* ("by"), and sometimes by *apo* ("from") and *ek* ("out of"). The intermediate agent is identified by *dia* ("through").[129] A literal rendering of Matthew 1:22 may illustrate some of these distinctions: "All this took place because what was spoken [aorist passive participle] by [*hupo*] the Lord through [*dia*] the prophet must be fulfilled [aorist passive subjunctive]." Here "the Lord" is the direct agent and "the prophet" is the intermediate agent.

What, then, is the position of Jesus in relation to creation? In Colossians 1:16 we find the preposition *en* ("in," "by means of"). This preposition governs *autō* ("him," in the dative case). Most of the 74 occurrences in the NT of *en autō* in the dative case are locative, that is, they refer to something or someone being in some place. Only one of the examples points to a *direct* agent.[130] In the last part of verse 16 we find the preposition *dia*,

---

[128] One reason why passive clauses are used is to avoid identifying the agent.

[129] Robertson, *Grammar*, p. 820.

[130] Grammatically speaking the phrase *en autō* in 1 Corinthians 6:2 could either refer to a direct agent or an indirect agent. It is explicitly said in this verse that the holy ones will judge the world, and therefore *en autō* must represent the direct agent. Each preposition can be used in a number of ways;

which governs *autou* in the genitive case. This is the typical marking of an *intermediate* agent, so this must be the proper way to view Jesus.

Does the context confirm that God is the direct agent of the passive verbs which speak about creation, and that Jesus is the intermediate agent? It certainly does! In Colossians 1:12 "the Father" is mentioned, and he is active through verse 20. This is seen in verse 19 where God is the implied subject for the verb, and it is particularly evident in verse 20, because here both the direct agent (God) and the intermediate agent (Jesus) are mentioned. It is said that the reconciliation is "through" (*dia*) Jesus and "to" (*eis*) God. The same thought is expressed in verse 22. The implied agent (grammatical subject) of the active verb "reconciled" is "God." The intermediate agent is Jesus, for it is said that reconciliation occurred "by means of" (*en*) his fleshly body and "through" (*dia*) his death.

The conclusion to this matter may be expressed in the words of one commentator: "It should be noted that ἐν (in), δία (through), and εἰς (for) are used, but not ἐκ (from). 'From whom are all things' (ἐξ οὖ τὰ πάντα) is said of God in 1 Corinthians 8:6. He is and remains the creator, but the pre-existent Christ is the mediator of creation."[131]

THE REFERENCE OF TA PANTA

Let us now return to the question about the relationship between Jesus and creation, by considering the reference of *ta panta*. As discussed above, God is the one who acts, the direct agent, and Jesus is the intermediate agent through whom *ta panta* was created. Therefore, it is obvious that Jesus is not a part of *ta panta*, but to use this fact as a basis for not including Jesus in "all creation" (*pasēs ktiseōs*) in verse 15 seems to be circular. As a matter of fact, *ta panta* may *linguistically* mean

---

we see particular patterns but nothing is fixed, so the context must be carefully considered in each case.

[131] Lohse, *A Commentary on the Epistles to the Colossians and to Philemon*, p. 50, note 125.

"all things" or "all other things," but to exclude the rendering "all *other* things" in Colossians 1—and this is very important—one must demonstrate that *ta panta* is identical with *pasēs ktiseōs* in verse 15.[132] But this is the very point under discussion, and cannot be presumed.

We will now compare various references to *ta panta* and compare them with references to with *pasēs ktiseōs*, and see if they are synonomous. The words *ta panta* occur 35 times in NT and of these 29 occur in the portion generally accepted as the Pauline corpus. Looking at the different passages, we see that it becomes clear that the words do not have fixed contents, and to understand them we must in each case find their reference. In fact, these words have fuzzy edges, and they serve as "signals" for thoughts, the contents of which can only be found by help of the context.

In Ephesians 3:9 and Revelation 4:11 the reference is to all that God has created, precisely the same reference as *pasēs ktiseōs* in Colossians 1:15. However, the reference may also be more restricted. In 1 Corinthians 12:19 the phrase *ta panta* refers to all the members of the human body, and by implication to all the members of the Christian congregation. In other instances the contents are abstract and it is more difficult to know exactly what is involved. Some examples include that which can be studied (1 Cor 2:15), all the operations of The holy spirit (1 Cor 12:6), all things in which a Christian may progress (Eph 4:15), and all the things that Christ represents (Col 3:11).

The words *ta panta* may also be used for negative things. In Philippians 3:8 the reference is to all the things offered by the world in contrast with Christian values, in Colossians 3:8 the

---

[132] One way to suggest identity would be to show that the lack of article before the noun *ktiseōs* occurring after *pasēs* means "every creature" and not "all creation." Jesus could hardly be "the firstborn of every creature," but he could be "the firstborn of all creation." In many instances the lack of the article before *pas* gives the meaning "every," but in Mark 13:19 and 2 Peter 3:4 the phrase *archē ktiseōs* (the beginning of the creation) without article is used in the inclusive sense. The lack of the article in Colossians 1:15 does not change the meaning from "all" to "every." See Nigel Turner, *A Grammar of New Testament Greek*, vol. 3, *Syntax* (Edinburgh: T & T Clark, 1963), pp. 199-200; Moule, *An Idiom Book of New Testament Greek*, pp. 94, 95; G. B. Winer, *Grammatik des neutestamentlichen Spachidioms* (Leipzig, 1862), sec. 18, p. 137.

reference is to all the bad things formerly practiced by the Colossians, and in Galatians 3:22 the reference is to all the things in which sin operates.

Returning to the use of *ta panta* in Colossians 1, we find it is clear that we cannot, at the outset, take for granted that *ta panta* in this chapter is all-inclusive and has the same meaning as *pasēs ktiseō* ("all creation"). In fact, we know for sure that this is not the case, at least not in verse 20. While *ta panta* in verses 16 and 17 evidently includes the angels of heaven, the same words in verse 20 do not include them, but must be restricted to those creatures who are sinners, and who are in need of reconciliation with God.[133] Thus, we cannot by the help of lexical evidence say that *ta panta* in verses 16 and 17 has the same meaning as *pasēs ktiseō* in verse 15.

THE TRANSLATION OF TA PANTA

In reviewing the evidence, we find that both lexically and grammatically a translation of Colossians 1:15 which includes Jesus Christ as part of the creation has strong support. Of particular importance is the lack of evidence that *prōtotokos* has a meaning other than "the one who is born first." Further, we found that, lexically speaking, *ta panta* could be translated as "all things" or as "all other things." The crucial point, therefore, in deciding between these two is not linguistics, but the context. Because the words *ta panta can* make different references— sometimes the reference is restricted, as in Colossians 1:20—we cannot presume that the use of these words in Colossians 1:16 and 17 have the same meaning as *pasēs ktiseō* in 1:15. Thus, there is nothing in the context that prevents us from including Jesus Christ as part of creation. In NWT the use of "all other" four times in Colossians 1 cannot be viewed as bias, and it is

---

[133] One could get the impression that creatures in heaven would also be reconciled with God through the blood of Jesus Christ, but such a thought is not articulated elsewhere in the Bible. I will not attempt to interpret the words, but I will point out that in Ephesians 2:5, 6 it is said that Christians are already seated in heaven, so the words of Colossians 1:20 need not apply to anyone other than those Christians still looking forward heavenly life.

not *interpolation*, since the very words of 1:15 reveal that Jesus Christ is a part of creation, which then implies the word "other" in these four places.

But what may we say about the interests of the readers? Are they best served by NWT's translation of Colossians 1:16-17? Both in the 1950 edition of NWT and in the NWTREF there is a footnote to Colossians 1:16 referring to Luke 11:41, 42, where *pas* is rendered "all other." However, this is not very helpful because only the lexical side of the issue is illustrated and the really controversial point is not addressed. The footnotes and appendices to John 1:1 and 8:58 are very informative to the reader, and an appendix would also have been of great help in this instance. But there is no such explanation.

Even though the rendering "all other" is linguistically and contextually justifiable, it is possible that the readers' interests may have been better served by not using "other." This is so, because the reader is hardly misled if *pas* is translated "all." In the case of The holy spirit, for instance, the translators had just two options, namely, to use capital letters or not, and either to add "the" or not; so they had to make the decision in behalf of the readers. But the verses with *pas* in Colossians 1 are not instances where the translators *must* make a similar decision in order to prevent a misunderstanding on the part of the readers. Colossians 1:15, on the other hand, is indeed an instance where translators must make a decision, either to include Jesus in the creation or not. When a linguistically sound translation of this verse is presented, as the one found in the NWT, the foundation is then laid for the readers to understand the meaning of *pas* in verses 16 and 17. Just as the readers will not be misled by the rendition "the fig tree and all trees," because they know that the fig is a tree, they will not be misled by the translation "all things" in Colossians 1:16, 17, when they read in verse 15 that Jesus is "the firstborn of all creation." Thus, by dropping "other" and translating *pas* with "all," very little is lost as far as meaning is concerned (compare 1 Cor 15:27). If a footnote and/or an appendix article with a complete discussion is provided, then the reader's interests are better served, and they are helped to make their own decision, thus having a part in translation process.

"SEIZURE" OR "BOOTY"?
THE MEANING OF PHILIPPIANS 2:6

The rendering of this verse, particularly the words that describe the relationship between Jesus and his Father, are different in NWT from most modern translations. Kubo and Specht describe the differences this way:

> A more subtle translation with the same theological motivation [as the rendering of "all other things" in Colossians 1] is the NWT rendering of Philippians 2:6 ". . . who, although he was existing in God's form, gave no consideration to a seizure, namely, that he should be equal to God." Compare this with the the translation of the JB: "His state was divine, yet he did not cling to his equality with God" Or the RSV: ". . . who, though he was in the form of God, did not count equality with God a thing to be grasped." The NWT implies simply that Jesus gave no consideration to being equal to God while the others assert that he did not cling to his equality with God but emptied himself. There is a vast difference of meaning and an important theological implication in these translations.[134]

The problem is nicely stated in this qoute, and we note that the choice of rendering may have important theological implications, and that the problem is what Jesus considered: either a decision to refrain from an attempt to make himself equal to God, or a decision to let go his of his equality with God, something which he already possessed. Our task is to find out whether the renderings of NWT and other translations are biased, and the role played by theology in the choice of rendering.

---

[134] Kubo and Specht, *So Many Versions?* p. 101.

THE MEANING OF THE GREEK WORD HARPAGMOS

The problem with this word is that it occurs only once in the NT. As Barr correctly argued, what counts in lexical semantics is to isolate the different uses of a word at the time when the NT was written, rather than finding its origin. But this is difficult when it only occurs in one context. Translators must, however, find a sense in which to render every word in the receptor language, and therefore we must look for clues as to the meaning of *harpagmos*. First, I will review the linguistic evidence, and then we will look for clues in the immediate context.

The verb *harpazō*, which comes from the same root as *harpagmos*, is found 14 times in the NT. According to NIDNTT it means "steal, carry off, drag away, lead away forcibly"[135]; and it is also used when the Spirit carries someone away. It never has the stative force of clinging to something one already possesses.[136] Another noun from the same root, *harpagē*, found only in Hebrews 10:34, means "plunder" or "robbery."

When a noun with the ending -*mos* was made from a verb, it became a verbal noun entailing the activity of the verb. Thus, *harpagmos* would mean "the act of snatching," from *harpazō* ("to snatch). Foerster gives this as the only meaning of *harpagmos* in pre-Christian Greek writings.[137] However, he also tells us that, in time, the meaning of the word changed somewhat, taking on a meaning similar to the related word *harpagma*, meaning "what is seized," that is, plunder or booty. This passive or stative meaning, however, is late. The aforementioned source cites the Homilies of the Church Father Chrysostom, from the fourth century CE, as evidence. And he may, of course, have been influenced by immature trinitarian thoughts of his day.

---

[135] C. Brown and E. Tiedtke, "ἁρπάζω," NIDNTT 3 (Grand Rapids: Zondervan, 1978), pp. 601-605.

[136] In Matthew 10:12; 12:29; 13:19; John 6:15; 10:12, 28, 29; Acts 23:10 and Jude 1:23 the use of force is evident; in Acts 8:39; 2 Corinthians 12:2, 4; 1 Thessalonians 4:17 and Revelation 12:5 the use of force is not so prominent.

[137] W. Foerster, "ἁρπαγμός," TDNT 1 (Grand Rapids: Eerdmans, 1964), pp. 473-474.

The material which suggests a meaning other than "snatching" is sparse, and modern authorities are divided. Martin wrote that the sense "robbery" is "next to impossible" in the Philippian context,[138] while Moule thinks that "snatching" is the right meaning in this context.[139] Many scholars, however, prefer the passive interpretation of "a thing seized," but from the view of lexical semantics, there was a clear preference for the meaning "a snatching" in the first century CE; according to Collange "plunder, booty" is an "exceptional interpretation."[140]

We should, however, consider a third suggestion, which has become popular since the publication of a thesis by R. W. Hoover[141] some 30 years ago, namely, that the word means "an advantage to be seized."[142] This meaning is also passive (or stative), and when applied to Philippians 2:6 it would cancel the active meaning of seizing from what Jesus did not consider. But there are several problems with Hoover's interpretation.

His principal witness is Eusebius of Caesarea. We should keep in mind that this church historian lived in the fourth century CE, and his use of *harpagmos* cannot straight away be used to interpret Paul's use of it three centuries earlier. Worse still is that Hoover seems to make a methodological blunder by overlooking the difference between what is semantic and what is pragmatic. Additionally, he offers a questionable translation of the verb in this passage from Eusebius. Let us take a close look at this passage: *ho petros* [Peter] *de* [but] *harpagmon* [the

---

[138] R. P. Martin, *Carmen Christi: Philippians 2:5-11 in Recent Interpretation and in the Setting of Early Christian Worship*, rev. ed. (Grand Rapids: Eerdmans, 1983), p. 134.

[139] C. F. D. Moule, "Further Reflexions on Philippians 2:5-11," in *Apostolic History and the Gospel: Biblical and Historical Essays Presented to F. F. Bruce on His 60th Birthday*, eds. W. W. Gasque and R. P. Martin (Exeter: Paternoster Press, 1970), pp. 264-276.

[140] J. Collange, *The Epistle of Saint Paul to the Philippians* (London Epworth Press, 1979), p. 99.

[141] Roy W. Hoover, "The Term Harpagmos in Philippians 2:6" (Th.D. thesis: Harvard, 1968).

[142] Roy W. Hoover, "The Harpagmos Enigma: A Philological Solution," *Harvard Theological Review* 64 (1971), p. 109.

word under discussion] *ton dia staurou thanaton* [the death by means of the stake] *epoieito* [make, bring about, imperfect] *dia tas sōtērious elpidas* [on account of the hope of salvation].[143]

Hoover offers the following translation of this text, "And Peter considered death by means of the cross *harpagmon* on account of the hope of salvation." The verb *hēgeomai* in Philippians 2:6 is basically static, having the meaning "consider," but it may also be used in the active or semiactive sense of "make plans." The verb *poieō* in his key text is primarily active, having the meaning "make," "bring about." However, Hoover translates it as "considered," giving it a stative meaning, but this rendition is strange and fails to account for the imperfective aspect of the verb.

Hoover makes the following comment on this text from Eusebius: "This statement cannot mean that Peter considered death by crucifixion to be a robbery, or something seized or to be seized by a violent self-assertion, or a treasure to be held fast . . . What he [Eusebius] wants to say, rather, is that because of the hope of salvation crucifixion was not a horror to be shunned, but an advantage to be seized." I do not deny that Peter may have viewed "crucifixion" as an advantage to be seized, but to say that "advantage" is a part of the meaning of *harpagmos*, thus being a semantic part of this word, without having considered whether this meaning is only pragmatic (due to the context), is questionable indeed. It is often difficult to distinguish between semantic and pragmatic factors in lexical semantics; especially is it difficult to make this distinction when a word occurs just a few times. Therefore, this text from Eusebius is not very convincing as a means of establishing a passive meaning for *harpagmos*.

I think it is better to take the verb *poieō* and *harpagmos* in this text in their normally active sense. I suggest the following translation: "But Peter made a seizure, namely, death on the stake, on account of the hope of salvation." Any translation of this text should fulfill at least two requirements: 1) It must not violate grammatical rules, and 2) there must be at

---

[143] Hoover, "The Harpagmos Enigma," p. 109. His reference is to Eusebius' Commentary on Luke 6.

least one context in which it is meaningful. Regarding the last point, I refer to Philippians 1:21-24. In Paul's view death was a gain (*kerdos*), because he would get a resurrection. But he did not know what to "choose." The meaning of the Greek word *haireō*, according to Liddell and Scott, is (active) "take with the hand, grasp, seize," and (middle) "take for oneself, choose." The verb is used three times in the NT[144] but whether the active sense of "seize," "take for oneself" or the passive "choose" is the most prominent notion is difficult to decide. In the Septuagint it is used twelve times with the same two possible meanings. In 2 Samuel 19:9 the middle form of the verb is translated as "rescue" (Brenton). In Jeremiah 8:3 we find a passage where death is the object of *haireomai* ("to choose death"), and this choice was active and not passive.

It seems that Hoover implicitly presumes that the alternative to a passive understanding of *harpagmos* is "robbery" or "violent seizure." However, as seen in note 135 (above) the verb *harpazō* is also used when the holy spirit seizes or leads someone (Acts 8:39). The notion of "violence," therefore, is not necessarily a part of *harpagmos* but only "using force." If we, therefore, only accentuate the element "to seize," there can be instances where *haireomai* can be synonymous with *harpazō*. If this is true, the noun *harpagmos*, which Peter "made," need not mean anything more than "choice," where the element of activity is stressed. When Eusebius wrote about Peter, he may very well have had Philippians in mind, not 2:6 but rather 1:21-23. When he wrote that Peter made a choice in which Paul was undecided, he could not choose the noun *hairesis* (corresponding to the verb *haireō* used by Paul) since this word was used with the meaning "sect."[145] But he could have chosen the word *harpagmos* from the next chapter, a word signaling the concept of "seizure," a meaning which would have been very close to a possible verbal noun made on the basis of the verb *haireō*.

---

[144] Philippians 1:22; 2 Thessalonians 2:13; Hebrews 11:25.

[145] The noun *hairesis* is occasionally used in the LXX with the meaning of "choice" (Gen 49:5; Lev 22:18, 21), but in the NT and in the early Church Fathers it has the meaning of "sect."

We therefore conclude that evidence for a passive meaning of *harpagmos* in Philippians 2:6 is almost non-existent. Thus, we should take it in the normal meaning of a verbal noun ending in -*mos*, namely, as "seizure."

THE SYNTAX OF PHILIPPIANS 2:6

The last part of the verse is the least problematic, because all agree that the meaning is "to be equal to God." The next clause begins with the word "but," indicating a contrast, "but he emptied himself and took a slave's form." The crucial point, then, is whether Jesus already was equal to God and did not cling to this equality, but instead emptied himself, or if he did not even consider making himself equal to God.

Jesus existed "in the form (*morphē*) of God." These words may, from a semantic point of view, be compatible with the translation suggesting that Jesus "was in essence God." And they may be compatible with the view that the "form" (external appearance) Jesus had before he came to earth was similar to that of God, just as the nature of a son is similar to the nature of his father, and is often manifested in the similarlities in their appearance (compare Hebrews 1:3). The words "took a slave's form" in verse 7 favor the later understanding, because they can hardly mean that Jesus was "in essence a slave." But this obviously indicates that Jesus had a human body, similar to the bodies of other humans. This is also indicated by the phrase "in the likeness of men" in the last part of verse 7.

Looking at the syntax of the crucial clause of verse 6, we find that the verb *hēgeomai* contains the subject and the predicate, and should, together with the negative, be translated "he did not consider." What did he not consider? Given that the sense of the noun *harpagmos* is active (which sense the data strongly suggest), Jesus did not consider a snatching. By recognizing this meaning of the verb and of the noun, we have taken the most important step. But we still need to discuss the syntactical meaning of the double accusative.

"TO BE EQUAL TO GOD"

Is this phrase a complement (predicate accusative) or should it be viewed appositionally? Verbs have different properties. Some are intransitive and do not take an object (for example, "Peter sings"). Some are transitive and take an object (for example, "Lena reads the Bible"). Others are ditransitive and take two objects, one direct and one indirect (for example, "Dad gave me [indirect object] a car [direct object]").

Still others take both an object and a complement (predicate accusative), and this group is important for this discussion because it includes verbs of opinion, such as "believe", "presume," "recon" and "consider." The role of such a complement is to describe the object, as is seen from the clause "They considered him [object] an embarassment [complement]."

In Philippians 2:6 we have in the Greek text a double accusative, that is, two phrases, both *harpagmon* ("snatching") and *to einai isa* [*theō*] ("to be equal [to God]), stand in the accusative case, indicating that one is object and the other has a relation to the object. The task of the translator is to decide whether we have a construction with object and complement (for example, *to einai isa* [*theō*] is object and *harpagmon* is complement) or we have a construction with an object and an apposition to the object (for example, *harpagmon* is object and *to einai isa* [*theō*] is in apposition to the object). Viewing the two accusatives as object/complement would give the literal translation: 1) "He did not consider equality with God a snatching." Viewing the accusatives as object/apposition would give: 2) "He did not consider a snatching, namely, to be equal to God." What is the best translation?

Robertson describes *harpagmos* as a "predicate accusative with *hēgēsato*"[146] and the infinitive construction as "accusative articular infinitive object of *hēgeomai*."[147] This accords with 1) above and against the NWT rendering, and and it seems to be confirmed by other similar examples from the NT. In the

---

[146] Aorist of *hēgeomai*.

[147] A.T. Robertson, *Word Pictures in the New Testament*, vol. 4, (Nashville: Broadman, 1931), p. 444.

sixteen examples[148] where we find a double accusative or an equivalent construction with *hēgeomai*, the thought is always to consider something/someone to be something, and never to consider something, and then add an apposition as an equivalent to what is considered. The two examples where the adjective "necessary"[149] is used accords with this as well.

The final word has not been said, however, because there is a possible difference between all these double accusatives in the NT, and the construction of Philippians 2:6. The side of the verb *hēgeomai* which is made visible by the sixteen double accusatives is the stative one, but if Paul used *harpagmon* with the sense of "a snatching," "a seizure," that is, in an active sense, this would make Philippians 2:6 different from the other constructions. This would mean that *hēgeomai*, in this verse, does not only mean "consider," in the sense of "believe," "regard," but rather in the sense of "cogitate," "make plans for." BAGD gives two principal meanings of *hēgeomai*, namely, "lead, guide" and "think, consider, regard." The context may help make visible different shades of meaning. In the Septuagint we find many examples with the same stative meaning of *hēgeomai* with a double accusative as we find in the NT. But let us consider one example which may throw some light on Philippians 2:6.

In 3 Maccabees 3:15[150] we find a letter from the king Ptolemy Philopator to his generals in Egypt, which says, in part: "We thought [aorist middle of *hēgeomai*] we would foster [aorist infinitive of *tithēneō*, "foster"] the inhabitants [accusative] of Coele-Syria [accusative] and Phoenikia [accusative], not by force of arms, but by kindness and great benevolence, conferring benefits on them willingly." Here the verb *hēgeomai* is not used in the sense of "lead, guide" but rather in the active sense "consider," which also is suggested by its plural form. The

---

[148] Acts 26:2; Philippians 2:3; 3:7, 8; 1 Thessalonians 5:13; 2 Thessalonians 3:15; 1 Timothy 1:12; 6:1; Hebrews 10:29; 11:11, 26; James 1:2; 2 Peter 1:13; 2:13; 3:9, 15.

[149] 2 Corinthians 9:5 and Philippians 2:25.

[150] Translated by H. Anderson in James H. Charlesworth, *The Old Testament Pseudepigrapha*, vol. 2 (Garden City: Doubleday, 1985), p. 521.

infinitive "to foster" is not stative; but the plural object indicates much work on the part of those who constitute the subject. We therefore have an example of an absolute (freestanding, not bounded) use of *hēgeomai* with an accusative object in an active setting. But is there a double accusative here? Not really, but the three commas after Phoenikia function as if a second accusative were used, since the words are coordinated with "foster."

Because of the instrumental nature of the three commas, the use of the accusative would not be natural. We can demonstrate this coordination by using the words of the three comma phrases instead of "foster." Then we could get the sentence: "We thought [planned] not to use force of arms, but by kindness and great benevolence, to confer benefits on the inhabitants[151] [accusative] of Coele-Syria [accusative] and Phoenikia [accusative] willingly." Thus the parallels between Philippians 2:6 and 3 Maccabbes 3:15 are:

1) Both use *hēgeomai* in an active sence. This sense is conveyed in 3 Maccabees by the Aktionsart of the infinitive "foster" and in Philippians 2 by the Aktionsart of *harpagmon*.

2) Both have accusatives which are either double or function as double accusatives.

The important conclusion to draw is that in 3 Maccabees the construction function as a double accusative where one is appositional to the other. Therefore, the same can be true in Philippians 2:6.[152]

---

[151] The antecedent of the English word "them" is "the inhabitants of Coele-Syria and Phoenikia," and therefore the substitution is justified. There is no word for "them" in the Greek text, but it is added to satisfy English idiom.

[152] Other examples containing an absolute use of *hēgeomai* include Job 35:2, "What is this [accusative object] (that) you [subject] have considered [*hēgeomai*, aorist (verb)] in the judgement [adverb]?" and Baruch 5:9, "For God [subject] will consider [verb] Israel [object] in joy by the light of his glory [adverb]."

Figure 6.3

Hēgeomai in 3 Maccabees 3:15 and Philippians 2:6

3 Maccabees 3:15	"We [subject] considered [*hēgeomai*, aorist] to foster [infinitive, accusative object] the inhabitants [accusative] of Coele-Syria [accusative] and Phoenicia, to show kindness willingly to them [apposition]."
Philippians 2:6	"He [subject] did not consider [*hēgeomai*, aorist (verb)] a snatching [accusative object] to be equal to God [apposition]."

Another example which may contain an absolute use of *hēgeomai* comes from Plutarch (*Aristeides* 2.4). This verse can be translated as follows:

On the occasion of Themistocles' giving opinion [*hēgeomai*] on a general's greatest[153] virtue, (namely his) understanding and anticipation of the plans of enemies.

The phrase "a general's greatest virtue" is the object and "understanding and anticipation of the plans of enemies," is in apposition to that object. This verse is therefore an example of another use of two accusatives, in addition to those we find in the stative NT examples. The verb that is used is *hēgeomai*, both here and in Philippians 2:6, and the appositional accusative phrase in both cases is preceded by the article *to* (accusative, neuter).

THE TRANSLATION OF PHILIPPIANS 2:6

Let us now return to Philippians 2:6 and take a closer look at how it can be translated. As has been shown, the most

---

[153] The word *megisten* ("greatest") is viewed as an adjective in attributive position to *aretēn* ("virtue") despite its separation from the noun it qualifies. In Matthew 4:16 we find a similar construction with the words "great light."

important question here is the meaning of the noun *harpagmos*, and there are three principal alternatives: 1) The noun is taken in the passive sense of "booty"; the prize was already in Jesus' possession, and he did not consider clinging to it. This is expressed by TEV, "He always had the nature of God, but he did not think that by force he should try to remain equal with God." 2) The noun is taken in the passive sense of "an advantage to be seized." This view is expressed by Hoover in his translation, "he did not regard being equal with God as something to take advantage of."[154] 3) The noun is taken in the active sense of "seizure"; Jesus did not want to use force to try to be equal to God. This is expressed by Scott's translation, "He did not regard it as a thing to be grasped at to rise to equality with God."[155]

The next question is how the syntax can help us decide which is the best rendering. In his discussion of the syntax of Philippians 2:6, Robertson describes *harpagmos* as "predicate accusative with *hēgēsato* [aorist of *hēgeomai*]" and the infinitive construction as "accusative articular infinitive object of *hēgeomai*."[156] The reason Robertson uses the words "articular infinitive" is because the article is used in front of the infinitive (*einai*). What is the function of this article? According to BDF, section 399, such an article is anaphoric, indicating that the phrase with the infinitive refers back to something previously mentioned.[157] Many commentators take it to refer to the first part of the verse, to the phrase "existing in God's form." This is a possible interpretation, but there is another possibility as well, namely, that it refers to a word which is both closer and in the same case, *harpagmos*. Regardless of what it refers to, this article also prevents us from automatically concluding that the syntax of Philippians 2:6 is similar to the other NT examples, because they lack the article.

---

[154] Hoover, "The Harpagmos Enigma," p. 118.

[155] C. A. A. Scott, *Footnotes on St. Paul* (Cambridge: n.p., 1935), p. 192.

[156] Robertson, *Word Pictures in the New Testament*, p. 444.

[157] It may also refer to something well known.

What, then, are the translation possibilities for this verse? The sense in which *harpagmos* is taken will greatly influence the translation. Almost all of the evidence points to an active meaning which includes force, and all the English translations on the Gramcord CD (NAB, ASV, Darby, NASB, YNG, NIV, NJB, NKJV, RSV and TEV), except NRSV, which uses "exploit," translate it with an active meaning. But if this is correct, we have to consider an important question asked by R. P. Martin, "What exactly was it that our Lord refused to plunder?" Martin answers, "There is no satisfactory answer to that question, which presses for a reply if an active signification is given to the key-term."[158] This means that if *harpagmos* is understood in an active sense, its complement (accusative predicate) cannot be a state which already holds.

We can illustrate this by two sentences expressing a permanent and a temporary state, respectively:

1) "He did not consider being as tall as his father a seizure."

2) "He did not consider being president that year a seizure."

If Paul wanted to convey that Jesus already was equal to God, this would have been a permanent characteristic, and Philippians 2:6 would be close to sentence 1); a stative accusative predicate would in this case have been impossible. Sentence 2) is also strange, because "a seizure" is performed to obtain something which one does not have; "to be president" would hardly collocate with "seizure" as would "to become president."

The most natural way to understand the two accusatives occurring with *hēgeomai* from a syntactical point of view, if the active/passive nature of the clause is not considered, is to take one as object and the other as its complement. But to use this construction in an English translation to convey the thought that Jesus already was equal to God, requires that *harpagmos* be taken in the passive (stative) sense of "booty," or something similar. This is Martin's preferred view.

---

[158] Martin, *Carmen Christi*, p. 135.

We therefore have two different ways in which to translate this verse:

a) "[he] did not consider a snatching in order to be [or, become] equal to God."

b) "[he] did not regard it as booty [this] being equal with God"; or "he did not regard being equal with God as something to take advantage of."

In favor of a) there is strong evidence for the active meaning of *harpagmos* as "snatching." In favor of b) there is strong evidence for taking one accusative as object and the other as complement where *hēgeomai* occurs with a double accusative. The NT examples do, however, express states. They conform with and bolster b) but they do not necessarily speak against a), which is active and not stative. The examples from 3 Maccabees and the one from Plutarch about an absolute use of *hēgeomai* with a double accusative establish the syntactic construction of a). We must therefore conclude that the lexical and syntactical information we have are not decisive, and that the translators' theology must play an important role in the translation process.

What, though, does the context have to say? In particular, verse 9 seems to contain some important clues. Consider the verb *charizomai*, which has the meaning "to grant as an act of grace."[159] Also, we have the verb *huperupsoō* ("highly exalt"). In his large grammar,[160] Robertson shows that he understands the verb in a comparative sense, that Jesus received a higher position than he had before he came to earth, but almost all other commentators take it in the superlative sense of the most high position. In any case, God is the subject. He put Jesus in the highest position next to himself, and kindly gave Jesus the exalted name. It is the superior who gives his subjects something out of grace; it is not given to a co-equal person.

---

[159] J. Loh and E. Nida, *A Translators Handbook on Paul's Letter to the Philippians* (Stuttgart: United Bible Societies, 1977) p. 61.

[160] Robertson, *A Grammar of the Greek New Testament*, p. 445.

Thus, the element of grace in the verb *charizomai* clearly indicates that the Father and the Son are not equal. Verses 10 and 11 also support this conclusion: All must acknowledge that Jesus is Lord "to the glory of God the Father."

Returning to the rendition of Philippians 2:6 in NWT, we must conclude that it is based on sound linguistic evidence and cannot be viewed as biased. We have seen that the linguistic evidence is not decisive, so theology must play an important role in the translators' choice, and the NWT translators have evidently used their theology in a legitimate way.

THE HOLY SPIRIT
"HE" OR "IT"?

Even those who believe in the trinity doctrine admit that descriptions of The holy spirit's nature are much less frequent than is the case for Jesus Christ. This is evidently one of the reasons why The holy spirit was hardly mentioned at the council of Nicaea. Even at the council in Constantinople 56 years later it was not explicitly stated that The holy spirit was God. Jesus is called *theos* three times in the NT and once in the OT, but nowhere in the Bible is The holy spirit called *theos*!

Countess discusses "The Deity of the Holy Spirit," and criticizes NWT for its translation of passages relating to The holy spirit, though he does not produce any lexical or grammatical arguments against the NWT renderings.[161] We have already shown that more than half of the passages mentioning The holy spirit do not have the Greek article and the words may be rendered as "holy spirit" in English. Because the treatment of the trinity doctrine in this book is meant to cover only those sides which directly relates to Bible translation, we will not discuss, point by point, the trinitarian views held by Countess and others, as they relate to The holy spirit. But we will discuss Countess' argument concerning the translation of the demonstrative pronoun *ekeinos* in passages about The holy spirit.

---

[161] Countess, *The Jehovah's Witnesses' New Testament*, p. 70.

Before we do that, I would like to state my agreement with Countess that passages such as Matthew 28:19, 20, from an objective point of view, strongly suggest that The holy spirit is divine. The phrase "the Father, the Son and The holy spirit," thus a co-ordination of three, just as strongly suggests personality on the part of The holy spirit. The same is also true of the passages Countess mentions on page 71 about the role of The holy spirit in teaching, guiding, hearing and helping, and we may add Ephesians 4:30 about "grieving The holy spirit."

Just as the above passages speak in favor of the personality of The holy spirit there are an ample number of passages not compatible with such a view. For example, the words of Acts 2:17 say that God's holy spirit would be poured out upon men. Also, there are all the anarthrous occurrences of "holy spirit," and passages where impersonal expressions are used in reference to The holy spirit.

These two groups of data are not necessarily mutually exclusive, but they must be viewed in the light of how the Biblical writers express themselves. Here are some important points that should be carefully considered: In the Bible there are scores of impersonal things that are personified, but hardly any person that is de-personified. Middleton, Greek grammarian of the last century, had a point when he said, "there being but one Holy Spirit, he could not be spoken of indefinitely." But this does seem to remove the force from his statement that in those passages where the personality of The holy spirit is stressed by ascribing personal acts to him, "πνεῦμα and ἅγιον invariably have the article."[162]

In Romans 6, for instance, there is rich imagery where impersonal things are personified. In Romans 5:21 sin and death are described as kings ruling over mankind. In chapter 6 men are described as soldiers either in the army of King Sin and King Death or in the army of King Grace. The acts of men are described as weapons, and in 6:23 the Greek word for a soldier's pay is used. Men will either get their reward as soldiers

---

[162] T. F. Middleton, *The Doctrine of the Greek Article Applied to the Criticism and Illustration of the Greek New Testament*, A New Edition with Prefatory Observations and Notes by Hugh James Rose (Cambridge: J. & J. J. Deighton, 1833), p. 126.

from King Sin, and that payment is death; or the free gift through the King Jesus Christ, and this gift is everlasting life.

At this juncture we may draw a point from our earlier discussion, namely, that human words do not adequately describe heavenly things, but they do provide a hazy outline of such things. If there is evidence that The holy spirit is not God, nor even a person or an individual, the only alternative is that The holy spirit is a force. The NWT takes this position, as shown in its translation of Genesis 1:2, where *rûaḥ 'elōhîm* is translated as "God's active force."[163]

Given the connotations of the word "force," it is a very unfortunate description of The holy spirit. Scientifically speaking all the different forces operating in the universe can be traced back to the four fundamental forces, the strong and weak forces of the atom, electro-magnetism and gravity. But these four primary forces, and all the secondary ones, have one thing in common: they are blind! They just work in one way according to the laws of nature. To use the words "God's active force" as a description of The holy spirit, therefore, leaves much to be desired. But they are the best words we have. The holy spirit has scores of operations, but the most important is that it conveys some of God's personality to us, some of the personal warmth and love of God. A *blind* force cannot do that! Still, applying the word "force" to The holy spirit, from the imagery of our material world, seems to be the best tool at our disposal. But, in using this word we must keep in mind that it is a unique force which cannot be compared with anything else.

In view of the OT practice of personifying impersonal things we might be in a better position to understand certain words about The holy spirit as *parakletos* ("advocate," "helper") in John 14-16. Countess presents the following argument: "That the Holy Spirit is personal may be observed further by Jesus referring to Him as ἐκεῖνος three times in John 16:7-14. The neuter of this demonstrative is ἐκεῖνο and grammatically would

---

[163] The footnote in NWTREF reads, "'And . . . **active force (spirit)**.' Heb., *weru 'ach*. Besides being translated 'spirit,' *ru 'ach* is also translated 'wind' and by other words that denote an invisible active force."

agree with τὸ πνεῦμα τῆς ἀληθείας ['the spirit of truth'] of verse thirteen."[164]

Countess tries to prove that The holy spirit is a person by means of grammatical gender, but this is a futile exercise. In the Greek language nouns and pronouns have grammatical gender. For example, the word for "spirit," *pneuma*, is neuter, whereas *parakletos* is masculine and *harmartia* ("sin") is feminine. When such nouns are replaced with pronouns, demonstrative and personal ones, the same gender and number is used. The consequence of this is that a demonstrative or a personal pronoun cannot tell us the real sex of its antecedent, only its grammatical gender. A neuter demonstrative referring back to *pneuma* does not prove that the particular spirit referred to is impersonal, and a masculine demonstrative referring back to *parakletos* does not prove that the "helper" is a man or even a person.

Countess' observation that the masculine demonstrative *ekeinos* is three times used in reference to The holy spirit is correct. This occurs in John 16:7 where NWT has "him" and in John 16:13, 14 where NWT has "that one" and "he." The footnote says, "'That one'; in the masculine gender to agree with with 'helper' in verse 7.'"

This is an illuminating footnote. In verse 7 the masculine *parakletos* is used. To satisfy the grammar the personal pronoun "him" is used in this same verse, and in verse 8 the demonstrative *ekeinos* is used, which NWT translates as "that one." Thus, The holy spirit is portrayed as an advocate or helper, and because The holy spirit is personified and in view of the necessary grammatical agreement, the demonstrative in the masculine gender is used.

But we should also consider John 14:17, where "the spirit of truth" is mentioned and is referred to by the neuter relative pronoun, translated "which" by NWT, but twice it is translated with the neuter personal pronoun, "it." Interesting are also the two references to The holy spirit in John 14:16 because of the difference in gender. The relative pronoun immediately following *pneuma* is neuter because the antecedent is neuter;

---

[164] Countess, *The Jehovah's Witnesses' New Testament*, pp. 71-72.

however, the demonstrative pronoun a little further into the verse is masculine, because it refers to *paraklētos* at the beginning of the verse. Two such references with a gender difference in the same verse clearly reveal that we cannot use the grammatical gender to show personality versus impersonality, or to point out the real sex of an object of reference. A final reference that drives home this point is 1 John 5:16, where *ekeinēs* (the feminine demonstrative) is used with reference to *harmartia* ("sin"). But sin is certainly not a feminine person!

So, in conclusion, John 14-16 cannot be used to prove that the trinity doctrine should be used as a translation principle. NWT has rendered the relative and personal pronouns referring to The holy spirit without bias.

"COMING" OR "PRESENCE"?

The Greek word *parousia* occurs 24 times in the NT, and the different renderings of it provide good examples of the role played by theology in lexical semantics. Regarding the rendering "presence," Kubo and Specht say, "The word has this meaning, but surely in the majority of the cases, especially where it refers to the second advent, it should be translated 'coming.'"[165] The words "second advent" express the view of many evangelical Christians that, suddenly, at a certain point in time, Jesus will return and he will be visible to all men. This belief is an important reason for the rendering "coming." Two renderings of Matthew 24:3 may give us a helpful approach to the problem:

---

[165] Kubo and Specht, *So Many Versions?* p. 108.

Figure 6.4

Two Translations of Matthew 24:3

NWT	"what will be the sign of your presence, and of the conclusion of the system of things?"
TEV	"and what will happen to show that it is time for your coming and the end of the age?"

The NWT renders the word as "presence" in all cases, while TEV uses the noun "coming" or the verb "come" in 22 cases, and an expression which is a synonym for "presence" in only 2 cases. In 16 NT passages the *parousia* of Jesus Christ is mentioned, and the question in these instances is whether the meaning is punctual, referring to a sudden advent, or whether the meaning is stative and durative, referring to the presence of Jesus Christ. Or, to put it differently, we might ask, did the apostles ask for a sign that would be seen *before* Jesus came, or did they ask for a sign showing that he *had* come? These are, of course, theological questions, but they must be considered by the translator.

Etymologically speaking, *parousia* is a compound of the preposition *para* ("beside") and *ousia* (present participle of the verb "to be"). Etymology is not what is most important, but this word was evidently still used with its "compound" meaning of "being beside, being present" in the first century CE. In BAGD we find the meanings "(1) *presence* . . . (2) *coming, advent* as the first stage in presence." Nobody denies that *parousia* has the sense "presence" in the NT. Even TEV, in 2 Corinthians 10:10, translates it as "(when) he is with us" and as "am with (you)" in in Philippians 1:26. But in none of the other 22 instances is there anything in the context forbidding the rendering "presence."

The sense "coming" is primarily theologically conditioned, but what is the evidence for this meaning? According to TDNT the word was used in Hellenism for the presence of the gods and for the visit of a ruler or high official. It is not found in the Septuagint, but occurs in the extra-canonical books of Judith (10:18), 2 Maccabees (8:12; 15:21) and 3 Maccabees (3:17), all with the meaning "presence." Josephus uses the word for the presence of God in the Shekinah.[166]

The problem with the sense "coming" when used for *parousia* is that it is very difficult, from the context alone, to know that only what is punctual and momentary is meant. This can be illustrated with the three passages given by Braumann for the meaning "arrival" or "coming," namely, 2 Corinthians 7:6, Philippians 1:26 and 2:12.[167] In the first and second instances we cannot know whether the *arrival* or the *visit* of Titus and Paul is stressed, but in the third instance there is a strong case for the sense "presence," because *parousia* is used in contrast with *apousia* ("absence"). Turner gives us another example, when he quotes Philocetetes 276, "Would one of you announce our arrival?" But there is no reason why we could not translate this passage as, "Would one of you announce our presence?"[168]

Regarding the use of *parousia* as a technical term for the return of Jesus, there are some problems:

First, in none of the 16 instances is there anything in the context demanding a punctual understanding of the word, but in Matthew 24:37, 39 the *parousia* of the Son of man is seen as parallel to "the days of Noah" and not "the day of Noah," which strongly suggests the durative "presence" rather than "coming."

Second, all the things the NT says Jesus will do at his *parousia*, and how it will affect the holy ones and his enemies, are hardly compatible with a punctual coming. The resurrection of "those who belong to the Christ" will occur "in [or, during]" his *parousia* (1 Cor 15:23). At his *parousia* they will be "gathered together to him" (1 Thess 4:14). According to Paul's words in 1 Thessalonians 4:15 some will survive until his *parousia*. The Lord will descend from heaven, the dead will rise *first*, and afterwards the living will *meet* the Lord in the air (verses 16, 17). Thus, there is a sequence of events. However,

---

[166] *Antiquities of the Jews* 3.8.5 (202), 9.4.3 (55).

[167] G. Braumann, "παρουσία," NIDNTT 2 (Grand Rapids: Zondervan, 1976), p. 899.

[168] Nigel Turner, *Christian Words* (Nashville: Thomas Nelson Publishers, 1981), p. 404.

more important to our discussion is that 1 Thessalonians 3:13 tells us that his presence will be *with* the holy ones. Jesus can hardly come to meet the holy ones and at the same time come together with them.

Also, 2 Thessalonians 1:10 refers to a time when Jesus comes to be glorified "in" (Greek: *en*) his holy ones. This time is identical with his revelation (*apokalupsis*) from heaven together with his angels, when his enemies will be destroyed. This, however, is hardly compatible with Matthew 25:31-33, which tells us that Jesus comes (Greek: *erchomai*) in his glory with his angels to separate the people of the earth. In view of all the different events connected with the *parousia*, Turner's comments are to the point:

> There is no alternative but to understand that the *parousia* of Christ takes place in two distinct phases, each separated from the other by an interval of time. The victorious revelation of Jesus in great power is evidently not the whole *parousia*, but it is the more dramatic aspect of it.[169]

In speaking of "the manifestation" (*epiphaneia*) of his *parousia*, 2 Thessalonians 2:8 confirms Turner's remarks, because this expression suggests that the *parousia* is made manifest only at a certain point of time.

Third, even the Greek verb *erchomai* ("come," "go") used in reference to Jesus may be durative rather than punctual. In Matthew 24:30 the present participle of the Greek verb is used, "they will see the Son of man *coming* on the clouds of heaven." This coming must be durative and take a certain amount of time. The reason for the choice of participle is evidently due to the Aramaic text in Daniel 7:14, which has a perfect together with an active participle, a construction which may be viewed as durative.[170]

---

[169] Turner, *Christian Words* , p. 405.

[170] Aramaic uses participles as predicates, both alone and together with finite verbs to a much greater extent than does Hebrew. It is very difficult to insist that a particular Aramaic verb is punctual.

The above discussion has shown that the consistent rendering of *parousia* by NWT has a sound foundation; the traditional rendering "coming" is also possible, but because of lexical evidence and contextual matters it is less likely. To a great degree it builds on a theological opinion. It does not serve the interests of the readers because it forces upon them a religious view without informing them of the alternative. NWT's consistent renderings, together with footnotes and an appendix, are of much greater benefit to the readers.

However, the Appendix in NWTNT (page 779) is of more benefit to the reader than the Appendix 5B (page 1576) in NWTREF, as it helps the reader to make a more informed choice. This is so because NWTNT mentions Deissmann's alternative data for *parousia* being used with the sense of "arrival" in extra-Biblical papyri. It is always good to inform the reader of alternative meanings and uses for a term. It is also unfortunate that the important principle of lexical semantics that we find in NWTNT, and which Barr stressed eleven years later, is left out in NWTREF. This principle has to do with synchronic word study (an analysis of a word's meaning in documents from the same time period) being superior to diachronic word study (the analysis of a word's meaning through time).

"GOD AND SAVIOR"
TITUS 2:13 AND 2 PETER 1:1

Of the ten passages which may or may not call Jesus God, we find two that are very similar in Titus 2:13 and 2 Peter 1:1. Different translations have been offered for each of these texts:

Figure 6.5
Translations of Titus 2:13 and 2 Peter 1:1

NWT	"of the great God and of our Savior Christ Jesus"
TEV	"of our great God and Saviour Jesus Christ"

NWT	"by the righteousness of our God and [the] Savior Jesus Christ."
TEV	"the righteousness of our God and Saviour"

The disagreement between these translations has to do with whether or not one or two individuals are mentioned. If there is one, Jesus is called "God and Savior," but if there are two, Jesus is called Savior but not God. There is no quarrel about the lexical meaning of the words, but what must be taken into account by the translator are syntactical rules, the context, and the theology of the author of the passage.

Beginning with the context, we note that in Titus 1:3, 4 both God and Jesus Christ are called "savior" and in 2:10 God is again referred to as "savior." According to John 3:16 *God* sent forth his *Son* to save mankind, so there is no problem in referring to either one of them as "savior." In fact, since the Bible presents God as the author of salvation and Jesus is said to be the medium through which salvation is administered (compare Joh 3:16; 1 Joh 4:14), it is quite natural to refer to both of them as "savior."

One commentator believes that while Titus 2:13 is "an uncertain passage, . . . it is probable that Christ is called 'God' here."[171] In favor of this he points out that "savior" is applied to God six times[172] in the pastoral epistles, and that Titus 2:14 ascribes acts to Jesus which are normally ascribed to God. According to Cullmann, 2 Peter 1:1 also calls Jesus "God," and as confirmation of this view he points to the fact that Jesus is called "Lord and Savior" four times[173] in the epistle.

Against this it may be pointed out that God and Jesus are described as different individuals 10 times in 2 Peter and in the pastoral epistles.[174] Indeed, one of these distinctions is made in 2 Peter 1:2, the verse immediately following 2 Peter 1:1. Dibelius

---

[171] Oscar Cullmann, *The Christology of the New Testament*, Study Edition (London: SCM Press, 1973), p. 313.

[172] 1 Timothy 1:1; 2:3; 4:10; Titus 1:3; 2:10; 3:4.

[173] 2 Peter 1:11; 2:20; 3:2, 18.

[174] 2 Peter 1:2; 1 Timothy 1:1, 2; 2:5; 6:13; 2 Timothy 1:1, 2; 4:1; Titus 1:1; 3:6.

and Conzelmann disagree with Cullmann regarding Titus 2:13,[175] and speak of a "clear subordination." As a matter of fact, neither view can be definitely established, because there is nothing in the context which is decisive.

Countess uses a syntactical argument, namely, the rule of Granville Sharp,[176] which says, in part, that when two nouns in the same case are connected with *kai* ("and"), when only the first noun has the article, both nouns refer to the same person. Sharp formulated this as an absolute rule, which, with certain qualifications (such as plurals and proper names), is without exception, but Countess himself refers to Matthew 17:1 as a possible exception, though it would not qualify as a legitimate exception since Sharp excluded proper names from his rule. But it is precisely due to the presence of a proper name ("Jesus Christ") that the article is not necessary in the second instance of several passages.[177] Thus, these christologically significant passages are not governed by Sharp's rule, since the restrictive force of the proper name creates a semantically similar situation to the use of proper names in passages like Matthew 17:1. This rule, then, is not a decisive guide for interpreting Titus 2:13 or 2 Peter 1:1.[178]

---

[175] M. Dibelius and H. Conzelmann, *The Pastoral Epistles* (Philadelphia: Fortress Press, 1972), p. 143.

[176] Countess, *The Jehovah's Witnesses' New Testament*, p. 69.

[177] Other examples where this is the case include Ephesians 5:5; 2 Thessalonians 1:12; 1 Timothy 5:21; 6:13; 2 Timothy 4:1. Acts 13:50 and 15:22 are two other examples where proper names are involved in article-noun-*kai*-noun constructions.

[178] In his book, *Jehovah's Witnesses Defended: An Answer to Scholars and Critics*, 2d. ed. (Huntington Beach, CA: Elihu Books, 1999) Greg Stafford has an Excursus wherein he discusses all the issues surrounding the use and limitations of the Granville Sharp rule. The first edition of his book (1998) contains the Excursus on pages 221-248, but his second edition contains a very illuminating chart which tabulates the use of the term "God" in the Pauline and Peterine writings, as well as an important discussion of the description "the great God" as used in Titus 2:13. His conclusion is that the Septuagint, the Dead Sea Scrolls, Philo and the writings of Josephus provide a basis for recognizing the description ("the great God") as a semantic signal for YHWH the Father, as distinct from Jesus. But he also acknowledges that if "the great God" were used of Jesus in this verse, that the Greco-Roman use of

The translator, therefore, is in a situation where neither the lexical contents of the words nor the context are decisive, and the syntax is not decisive. The only thing left is the translator's theology. So in the case of Titus 2:13 and 2 Peter 1:1, the theology of the translator plays a legitimate role. In fact, it plays the most important role. He or she has but two possibilities, either to choose a rendering that makes Jesus identical with God or to adopt a rendering that differentiates between the two. Thus, when Countess says that NWT "interpolates the preposition 'of' before 'our Savior,'" he is wrong. In view of all the information considered, this is a legitimate way of translating the verse, which includes use of the disputed preposition.

ACTS 20:28
WHOSE BLOOD?

The problem involved in translating this passage is the *reference* of the word "blood." Translations of this verse do differ, as seen in the following comparison:

Figure 6.6

Translations of Acts 20:28

NWT	"the congregation of God, which he purchased with the blood of his own [Son]."
RSV	"the Church of the Lord which he obtained by his own blood."

this expression would provide another source from which Paul could have borrowed the description. It is possible that Paul, against the Greco-Roman religious usage of this expression, referred to Jesus as "the great God" in a manner consistent with the Biblical presentation of Jesus as subordinate to the one who is his "God and Father" (compare Eph 1:3, 17; Rom 15:5, 6).

Wainwright gives his view of the problem: "If the reading θεοῦ ["god," in the genitive case] is accepted, does the verse mean that God purchased the church with his own blood? It is difficult to imagine that the divinity of Christ should have been stated in such a blunt and misleading fashion."[179]

In trying to find a solution to the problem, the first point we have to consider is a textual one. Some Greek manuscripts have the rendering "the congregation of the Lord" while others have "the congregation of God." The first alternative would completely remove the problem because "the Lord" could either refer to the Father or to the Son. However, two important codices, Sinaiticus (א) and Vaticanus 1209 (B), have the rendering "of God," and because NWT seldom uses renderings other than those found in the Greek text of Westcott and Hort, they have chosen "of God."

This Greek *tou haimatos tou idiou* (word for word, "the blood of the [or 'his'] own") may be understood in two different ways. One way is to view the last two words "his own" as referring to "his blood," thus giving the meaning "his own blood." The other way is to view "his own" as an ellipsis, referring to another person who is his own, which can be no other than his Son; this is the basis for the rendering "the blood of his own Son."

Countess says that NWT "by interpolating 'Son' in brackets, has taken a liberty with the text,"[180] but this simply is not true! Countess himself quotes Metzger to substantiate that "his own" as an ellipsis for "his own son" is without NT parallel.[181] Yet Metzger's reference to such a use in the Greek papyri is more than enough to show that the NWT translators followed sound translation principles when they made their choice. The example involving sparrows in Matthew 10:29, quoted in this book on page 151, namely, "not one of them fall to the ground without your Father's knowledge," where

---

[179] A. W. Wainwright, *The Trinity in the New Testament* (London: S. P. C. K., 1962), p. 74.

[180] Countess, *The Jehovah's Witnesses' New Testament*, p. 60.

[181] Metzger, *A Textual Commentary on the Greek New Testament*, p. 481.

"knowledge" is not in the Greek text but is implied, is parallel to "his own" and well illustrates the principle of ellipsis.

Let us now look at two other passages in the NWT which have been criticized by Kubo and Specht.

"MEANS" OR "IS" in 1 Corinthians 11:24, 25?

Kubo and Specht criticize the rendering, "This means my body" because the Greek word *estin* normally has the meaning "is."[182] This verb form (present, third person singular) occurs 966 times in the NT, and NWT translates 48 of these by "mean" or "means" (and one by "stand as"). Thus in 5% of the 966 occurrences this alternative meaning is used.[183] Lexically speaking, the rendering, "This means my body" is quite legitimate.

But what about the interests of the readers? Are they properly cared for in this matter? The footnote to 1 Corinthians 11:24, 25 says, "Lit., 'is' Gr., *estin*. See Mt 26:26 ftn." The footnote to Matthew 26:26 refers to the Greek word *estin* and then adds, "in the sense of signifying, importing, representing." The reader is informed that a literal rendering of the word is "is," and the sense of the rendering "means" in the verse is elucidated. But he or she is not informed that the reason for the choice of *means* is entirely theological, because there is nothing linguistic or contextual which demands this rendering.

These verses, and the three other, similar verses are, theologically speaking, very important, and the meaning of *estin* has been widely debated since the days of Luther and Calvin. Thus, the Catholic Church believes in transubstantiation, the belief that the wine and the bread literally *become* the flesh and blood of Jesus during mass, while Lutherans believe in consubstantiation, the view that the wine and the bread do indeed become Jesus' blood and flesh, though they ascertain this

---

[182] Kubo and Specht, *So Many Versions?* pp. 102-103.

[183] The 8 instances where *estin* refers to bread or wine are not included in this percentage.

in a heavenly way. Because the interpretations of this verse are so diametrically opposed, and because the interests of the readers are best served by making as few choices as possible in their behalf, it would have been better to use "is" in the main text and "means" in the footnotes, together with any additional explanations that the translators deem necessary.

"BAPTIZED FOR THE PURPOSE OF [BEING] DEAD ONES"—1 CORINTHIANS 15:29

Kubo and Specht says there is no justification for this translation, particularly not for putting the word "being" in brackets.[184] This verse is difficult to translate regardless of how we understand it, so it well illustrates how translators may serve the interests of the readers in difficult situations.

There can be no question that the most natural rendering of *baptizomenoi huper tōn nekrōn* would be "being baptized for the dead" or "being baptized in behalf of the dead." In almost every other context, such a rendering would have been chosen. However, several translators and commentators have held the opinion that such a rendering is problematic in this context. As far back as 1889 Godet wrote: "Somewhere about thirty explanations are reckoned of the expression: *to be baptized for the dead.* This diversity is due, on the one hand, to our ignorance of the usage to which Paul alludes, and on the other, to the absence of any parallel expression to guide us in the explanation of it."[185]

We must never forget that translation is communication, and that the task of the translator is to help the reader to grasp the author's meaning. (We remember the example of the word *chairein*, which literally means "to rejoice" but must be translated as "to say a greeting.") A translator who works with the interests of the reader in mind will translate the text so that

---

[184] Kubo and Specht, *So Many Versions?* p. 102.

[185] F. L. Godet, *Commentary on First Corinthians* (Grand Rapids: Kregel, 1985 [1889]), p. 811.

the reader can make as many choices as possible, refraining, as much as possible, from introducing interpretative elements into the text. But in particular instances the reader will be mislead without such elements. In passages such as 1 Corinthians 15:29, where the translators are faced with a dilemma, they cannot deviate from the text, but neither can they use the most natural rendering if that would prove to be misleading. So the question becomes, How can translators best help the readers to understand the message?

In connection with the problem at 1 Corinthians 15:29, Lenski made some linguistic comments which closely approach the reasonings of the NWT translators. He translated the phrase "with a view to the dead" and said that the preposition *huper* could indicate the motive for the reception of baptism, a use attested to both in classical and NT Greek.[186] Furthermore, he stated that "the dead" cannot refer to actual dead persons, for then it would have been without article; so it must refer to living persons. Even though such reasonings have a linguistic foundation, they must be classified as theological interpretations rather than philological reasons. But in verses like this such interpretations are unavoidable, because otherwise the reader is left in the dark, and could be completely mislead.

What is interesting, though, is that if Lenski's comments are accepted, even the bracketed word "being" before "dead ones" is *implied* by Paul. Because of the nature of the verse, the NWT rendering is perfectly legitimate. The footnote says: "Or, 'baptized by reason of.'" To better serve the reader's interests, however, the footnote should also have contained the more linguistically satisfying renderings, "baptized for" and "baptized in behalf of."

---

[186] R. C. H. Lenski, *Interpretaion of I and II Corinthians* (Minneapolis: Augsburg Publishing House, 1963), p. 690.

CHAPTER 7

THE READERS AND THEIR "INFORMED CHOICE"

In the first philosophy lecture I attended at college, one of the definitions given for *truth* was "the opinion of the experts." My reaction to this definition was negative, and I still do not accept it. However, it is not completely beyond sense, because to a large extent all of us build our lives on informants or experts; we depend on them and put our trust in them. In fact, we simply cannot achieve much at all without knowledge accumulated by others.

Take for instance the Bible: 1) We are dependent upon those who wrote it, and we trust that they did a faithful job; 2) we are dependent upon the Masoretes and those who made the modern critical editions of the original texts of the OT and NT. We trust that they were sincere and had the expertise that was necessary; 3) we are dependent upon those who have done Greek and Hebrew word studies which inform the different lexicons. We trust that their results generally are reliable; 4) we depend upon grammarians, upon those who have studied the Greek and Hebrew text to present us with grammatical and syntactical rules. We believe that their grammars are reliable; 5) we trust in the Bible translators—those who work hard to convey the thoughts of the authors to modern persons; 6) we trust that the texts that are used in the different Bible versions we read are reliable; 7) we trust our religious teachers and believe that their teaching is sound and helpful.

So wherever we turn, we have to build on informants and authorities; we simply cannot live without them. However, our dependence is not absolute. Those who are not able to work with the original languages on their own are dependent upon the first four groups of informants mentioned above, but when we come to the fifth and the sixth, to Bible translation into our own language, and to explanations of the Bible, we are not so dependent. Therefore this book has used the medical principle of "informed consent" as an illustration applied to Bible translation. The point is that the Bible student should be given the tools to check the Bible translator. But it cannot be taken for granted that this is what automatically happens, because there is a fight for the souls, as it were.

Given that the Bible has a uniform teaching as to the basics of Christianity, some, or even many must have been misinformed by their informants. Among those who consider themselves Christians or Evangelical Christians, there is a wide variety of opinion, even as to the basics of the Bible's teachings. Obviously Jesus cannot both be the God of eternity and a creature at the same time, the soul cannot be both mortal and immortal, and sinners cannot be both tormented forever and be annihilated. Yet these diametrically opposite beliefs are variously held by persons claiming to be the followers of Jesus. This fact underscores the importance of being able to work with the text of the Bible on one's own.

Even though it is not the task of the Bible translator to teach people the Christian faith, he or she is deeply involved in this through the different translation choices that must be made. And that is what this book has tried to point out, namely, that teachings which are held by the majority are read into the very text of most translations. Thus, the interested reader begins with a handicap when he or she opens the Bible for study. There is, therefore, a need for literal Bible translations with extensive footnotes and appendices, so as to inform the reader of the different choices that have been made on his or her behalf. Because the NWT is just such a translation, it was chosen as the object of our study.

But before we draw the different lines together for a final evaluation of NWT from the viewpoint of theology and bias, and make some suggestions for the readers, we should draw some conclusions as to the criticisms of the NWT.

AN EVALUATION OF NWT'S CRITICS

In contrast with the medical doctor, who may not have any personal interest in the patient's choice of treatment, the religious world is filled with emotions, and the desire to defend one's religious views is strong. So the Bible student, even before he or she starts the study of the Bible, is influenced by theology. This is readily seen in the following three books that discuss the NWT.

KUBO and SPECHT
So Many Versions?

A positive side of Kubo and Specht's review of the NWT is that their criticisms are followed by several quotes from the NWT, which allow the readers get a good idea of the issues under consideration. They should also be commended for their use of the word "denominational" rather than "cultic" or "sectarian." Their view of the NWT as a Bible translation, however, is very negative. We find such expressions as "biased," "arbitrarily," "especially objectionable," "no justification," "no consistency," "special pleading," "this obscurity," "repulse the reader," "poor quality," and "at the expense of literary beauty." The few good points they find, such as the rendition of Greek verbs, the Greek text used, and the avoidance of archaic language is neutralized by "the theological bias and the inconsistent quality of the translation."[1] Thus their negative evaluation is not primarily based on linguistics and translation theory, but rather on theology.

The forty-year-old quote they present from OT scholar H. H. Rowley[2] is especially interesting as it accents the rather negative light in which they review the NWT. Rowley wrote: "The jargon which they use is often scarcely English at all, and it reminds of nothing so much as a schoolboy's first painful beginnings of translating Latin into English."

Such a quote sows doubts in the minds of the readers because it conveys the thought that the translators did not master the Biblical languages which they translated, nor the

---

[1] Sakae Kubo and Walter F. Specht, *So Many Versions? 20th Century English Versions of the Bible*, Revised and Enlarged ed. (Grand Rapids: Zondervan, 1983), p. 110.

[2] H. H. Rowley, "How Not to Translate the Bible," *Expository Times* 65 (1953-54), pp. 41-42.

English language.[3] What the reader is not told is that Rowley uses the particular premise that only idiomatic translations are warranted. But it is bad methodology to use such a premise when evaluating a literal translation, particularly when the premise is not stated. A translation should be judged on the basis of its own merits, and not on the basis of personal viewpoints as to what a Bible translation should look like.

A translation which follows the sentence structure of the source language rather than the receptor language *must* be somewhat wooden and unidiomatic, and this is also the case with the NWT. But this is completely different from what Rowley is talking about. On can only wonder why Kubo and Specht, who know the NWT translaton principles, which are stated in its Preface, would offer such a quote to their readers.

R. H. COUNTESS
The Jehovah's Witnesses' New Testament

We have already shown that Countess' book is apologetic in nature; this fact being underlined by his words that the NWT is so biased that its text can be compared with "milk with an admixture of arsenic" and reading it "could very well be injurious to one's health."[4] His account of the NWT, therefore, is not a balanced, scholarly presentation; rather, it surrenders both to emotionally inspired caricature and a partisan spirit.

His intention, evidently, is to defend the trinity doctrine and other doctrines held by evangelical Christians. He shows a good understanding of Greek grammar, making several instructive observations regarding the Greek article, though he misapplies Colwell's rule and makes an inaccurate comment regarding an alleged exception to Sharp's rule, which does not

---

[3] Incidentally, it may be mentioned that this is an often repeated claim which evidently is totally unfounded.

[4] Robert Countess, *The Jehovah's Witnesses' New Testament* (Phillipsburg, NJ: Presbyterian and Reformed, 1982), p. xiv.

apply to proper names.[5] His appendix is valuable because of its data content.

The book has two principal weaknesses. First of all, Countess ascribes to the NWT translators rules for translation which they have never expressed, and then he shows how inconsistently the translators have followed these rules. Second, he overlooks the fact that context plays an important role for the one doing the literal Bible translation; instead, he makes unreasonable demands on the translators, which can only be fulfilled by an interlinear translation.

However, I appreciate his comment on page xiv. "I solicit from the readers *their* insights, data, and counter-arguments on the major positions taken herein, because I regard highly the reasoned disagreements that come from the community of scholars." I hope my book will be a contribution towards fulfilling his solicitation.

R. M. BOWMAN, Jr.
Jehovah's Witnesses, Jesus Christ, and the Gospel of John

In his book, Bowman both states and shows that his position is primarily theological and that his principal intention is to defend the trinity doctrine. To a large extent he correctly presents the position of Jehovah's Witnesses, but his attempts to show the inconsistency of different Witnesses he has met with in person is less than convincing.

The treatment he gives John 1:1 is on the whole very good. His "Definition of terms" is to the point and illuminating, and his linguistic arguments are sound. A major blunder, however, is the confusion of *reference* and *meaning* in the word *theos*. His insight on Colwell's rule is exceptional, and his application of it in relation to John 1:1 is a useful pattern for other studies. But his claim that Colewell did not apply his rule on John 1:1 is wrong. His basic conclusions are also untenable because of faulty premises.

---

[5] On page 69 of his book Countess says that Matthew 17:1 may be an exception to Sharp's rule, but since this text involves the proper names "Peter" and "James" it would not fall under the constraints of Sharp's rule.

His discussion of John 8:58 leaves much to be desired as far as linguistics is concerned. He is not in touch with the conclusions of modern aspectual studies of Greek verbs and confuses *Aktionsart* and aspect. Because of his theological approach, he makes some propositions which are linguistically quite dramatic, but which cannot be upheld. His book is, however, unabashedly theological in its avowed purpose of defending the trinity doctrine, and as such it is a useful contribution.

THEOLOGY, BIAS, AND BIBLE TRANSLATIONS

Any Bible translation will be influenced by the theology of the translators. This is so because the Bible is a book about God, and its text cannot be translated if it is not understood. Additionally, a translator's horizon of understanding will influence the translation, as will the translation principles in which he or she believes. Let us now collect the data we have discussed in order to make a final evaluation of the NWT, from the reader's point of view.

According to the definition in this book, bias in Bible translation is characterized by *renderings that either 1) contradict lexicon, grammar or syntax; or 2) definitely weaken or distort the meaning by addition or subtraction of unwarranted semantic elements, in order to promote the translator's own theology.*

We have discussed two important sides of the NWT, and have found the claim that it violates its own translation principles to be without substance. Actually, we found that its non-trinitarian[6] renderings of particular verses have a sound linguistic and grammatical foundation. Thus in no instance have I found *bias*, in the sense discussed above, in the renditions of NWT, and I agree with the words of the Israeli professor Benjamin Kedar:

---

[6] We should use the term "non-trinitarian" instead of "anti-trinitarian" because the first term is neutral and descriptive, the second one may presume that the trinity doctrine has some authority.

Several years ago I quoted the so-called New World Translation among several Bible versions in articles that dealt with purely philological questions (such as the rendition of the causative hiphil, of the participle qotel). In the course of my comparative studies I found the NWT rather illuminating: it gives evidence of an acute awareness of the structural characteristics of Hebrew as well as of an honest effort to faithfully render these in the target language. A translation is bound to be a compromise, and as such its details are open to criticism; this applies to the NWT too. In the portion corresponding to the Hebrew Bible, however, I have never come upon an obviously erroneous rendition which would find its explanation in a dogmatic bias. Repeatedly I have asked the antagonists of the Watchtower-Bible who turned to me for a clarification of my views, to name specific verses for a renewed scrutiny. This either was not done or else the verses submitted (e.g. Genesis 4:13, 6:3, 10:9, 15:5, 18:20 etc.) did not prove the point, namely a tendentious translation.[7]

I myself have compared the entire Hebrew OT text with the English text of the NWT verse by verse, and it is evident to me that the translators have done a very good job. Several times, after first reading the Hebrew text and then the English, I asked myself, "Is this nuance really in the Hebrew text?" And it certainly was! The translators have been extremely careful to render the text as exactly as possible, even if the result is a wooden translation.

Often when NWT is accused of bias, the reason is that it has not preferred the traditional Christian dogmas, such as the trinity doctrine, as translation principles. This means, however,

---

[7] This quote is from a general letter that professor Kedar sends out to those who inquire about his views of the NWT. Regarding his view of religious bodies, Kedar says in this statement: "I beg to make clear that I do not feel sympathy for any sect and this includes Jehovah's witnesses. Of course, my mistrust is not directed against the individual member of such sect but rather against the organisation that manipulates him and puts forward its dogmas and rules as ultimate truth. It should be conceded, however, that the groups and organisations that fiercly oppose the Witnesses do not behave any better. On the whole, synagogue, church and mosque also tend to exhibit dogmatic arrogance coupled with intolerance of and enmity with other confessions."

that the bone of contention is hardly "bias or not bias," but, rather, whether the NWT translators have used *their theology* in a legitimate way. Regarding this, the following view was previously given in this book: *A word, phrase or sentence of doctrinal importance, where there are more than two translation choices, and there are no compelling linguistic reasons to choose one before the others, is liable to criticism if the chosen rendering represents a particular theological view and this is not brought to the reader's attention together with the alternatives.*

Proposed Interpolations. A debated feature of NWT is the name Jehovah in the NT. It is a weakness that the name is found in no Greek NT manuscript, but the evidence suggesting its legitimate place in the NT is so strong that it is, from a philological point of view, more than enough to justify its inclusion in the text. The footnotes and the appendices serve the interests of the readers. The other supposed interpolations turned out rather to be implicatures.

Word Studies. Regarding *stauros* ("stake") NWT should be commended for not using the word "cross," which is loaded with modern connotations that are not found in the Bible, and which ascribes an unwarranted form to the instrument involved in Jesus' death. However, the rendition "torture stake" represents a reference rather than a sense, and it implies that "torture" is a part of the word meaning. Thus, it would have better served the interests of the reader to use "stake."

Regarding the Greek word *parousia* ("presence"), the NWT uses its compound meaning *presence*, a meaning that accords both with its etymology and with the evident sense of several examples found in the NT. The "technical" meaning "coming," which is applied to the word in most Bible translations, is based on theology, on the majority view of how Jesus will return. Thus, the NWT rendering has a much stronger backing, philologically speaking.

The Translation of "To Be." The NWT rendition of John 8:58, "Before Abraham came into existence I have been" is ungrammatical in English, but that is also the case with the familiar translation, "Before Abraham was, I am," which is much less desirable because of its mysticism. There is no way to fully convey both the Greek sense and grammar in an English translation of this text without adding words, but there is no doubt that the NWT conveys the sense of the Greek in an understandable way. The NWT rendition "this means my body" in 1 Corinthians 11:24 accords with the lexical meaning of the word, but this rendition is entirely based on theology and may be criticized. The NWTREF has a footnote pointing out that the normal meaning of the word is "is," but aside from this the footnote is not very illuminating.

Jesus as God. Of the 10 examples in the NT where Jesus is allegedly called *theos*, only two are certain, namely, John 1:1 and 1:18. In John 1:1 both grammar and context give a clear preference to the NWT rendering "a god," or even "divine" or "a divine being," and in 1:18 both textual evidence and the context give a preference for "the only-begotten/uniquely derived god" rather than "the only-begotten/unique, who is God." In Romans 9:5 it is likely that the Father is called God, not Jesus. In Titus 2:13 and 2 Peter 1:1 there is no preference, but theology is the decisive factor. In all of these instances the NWT translators have legitimately applied their theology, the interests of the readers have been served by footnotes and appendices, and the NWT renditions have a strong philological backing.

Jesus as a Creature. In several instances related to Jesus the traditional translations use words in a special (technical) sense for which it is difficult to find evidence, while the NWT often uses these same words in their everyday sense. We see this in John 8:58, and we see it again in Philippians 2:6 where the NWT reads "seizure" while other translations use words indicating that Jesus did not choose to cling to equality with God. There can be no doubt that almost all the evidence of lexical semantics favors the NWT reading. We have the same situation in Colossians 1:15 where NWT uses "firstborn" with the meaning "one who is born first" and translates the genitive construction in accordance with this meaning. Other translations with very little linguistic evidence have renditions placing Jesus above or before the creatures. Philologically speaking, the NWT position is strong. The NWT's use of "all other" four times in Colossians 1 is grammatically possible and is justified by the translation "firstborn of all creation" in verse 15. The premise of the counterargument which posits that *ta panta* has the same meaning as *pasēs ktiseōs* is unjustified. While the translation "all other" has a sound philological backing, the interests of the reader are not adequately served because the NWT footnote to this verse gives little information, and there is no Appendix explaining the basis for the reading.

The points mentioned above, which are the primary points of contention raised by the three aforementioned, critical books, reveal some instances where the interests of the readers could have been better served, but only one instance where a reading in NWT is based entirely on theology. From a philological and linguistic point of view, therefore, the NWT is a very accurate and scholarly translation.

BIBLE STUDENTS AND BIBLE TRANSLATIONS

To understand the basic message of the Bible any translation can be used. There are several differences between the translations, but these differences usually do not affect the overall message, only nuances and details. In reading a book like this, one may get the impression that there is little agreement on anything when it comes to Bible translation. But that is not the case at all. This book has discussed some important passages, and, for theological reasons, there is much dispute about how these should be translated. However, such passages cover a very small part of the biblical text, and there is little dispute about what the rest of the text means.

We have shown that words and ideas in our mind have fuzzy edges, and very often when we speak about a subject we do not carefully review all its details in our mind. If we, for instance, speak of "the resurrection of the dead," the only thing we may have in mind is that dead persons will receive life again. However, the Bible speaks of the "first resurrection" (Rev 20:6), thus implying a second one. It says that each one will be resurrected "in his own rank" (1 Cor 15:23) and that there will be a resurrection "on the last day" (Joh 11:24), in addition to many other details. But our attention is usually not focused on all of these details.

The message of the Bible, therefore, can be said to have different levels which are different as to detail. The "upper level(s)" can be learned by reading any Bible translation, the deeper ones require a particular kind of translation. For Bible students who want to have as big a share as possible in the translation process, idiomatic translations will only be of limited help. Literal translations, including NWT, will only be truly helpful to the reader if they contain footnotes that help the reader along the way.

However, the NWTREF is an excellent help. Its extensive use of footnotes,[8] its appendices, and the system of cross references are very helpful to the reader. Important words are often transliterated,[9] and it has made good use of the ancient versions, often citing their alternative readings. For those who want to go to an even deeper level, there is an interlinear version of the NWT called *The Kingdom Interlinear Translation of the Greek Scriptures* (KIT [2nd ed. 1985]), which can provide even finer nuances to the student of the Scriptures. There are also several other interlinear Bibles both for the OT and the NT, and all of these can be useful.

We may illustrate this with the words of John 17:3: "This means everlasting life, their taking in knowledge of you, the only true God, and of the one whom you sent forth, Jesus Christ." The rendering of the verb in this verse may teach us a lesson. In Greek it is *ginōskō*, having the stative meaning "to know," or the active meaning "to learn, ascertain, find out." The difference in meaning is simply one of stress, because even the active process of aquiring knowledge leads to the state where one "knows." When translating, however, it is not possible to focus on both the action and the state at the same time, but one has to choose. NWT takes the verb in the active sense,

---

[8] As opposed to most other "Study Bibles" the footnotes of NWTREF basically are of a textual nature, rather than exegetical.

[9] From the reader's point of view, the system of transliteration in NWT is too cumbersome. The letter "h" is used too extensively. Above Psalm 112:4, for instance, we find the transliteration "Chehth" for the second letter in the Hebrew alphabet. The word contains "h" three times, and the reader will have difficulties both in pronouncing it and in understanding the "h's" purpose. By using such a system, Hebrew seems to be much more difficult than it really is. The system of modern Hebrew grammars is much easier and is recommended; instead of "Chehth" such a system would give "het" (with a point beneath the "h" to differentiate it from "h," pronounced without a guttural sound).

translating it as "taking in knowledge." This *could* be construed to mean that the very *process* of acquiring knowledge means everlasting life. Obviously, though, what means everlasting life is the *result* of this ongoing process, namely, an increase in the knowledge of God and his Son; not a stative knowledge, acquired once and for all, but a knowledge that becomes fuller and fuller because the active process is continuing, resulting in a relationship with both the true God and his Son.

Looking at KIT we find the words "they may be knowing" beneath the Greek verb. To "know" is normally not used in continuous tenses because it is a state which by definition continues without any input of energy. The use of "know" rather than "knowledge" indicates that Jesus includes the state in his words, and the choice of the participle indicates that this state is semi-active, suggesting a continuous development of it. Thus, the NWT stresses the process while KIT stresses the state, and both may be consulted to get an accurate knowledge of the passage.

DIFFERENT KINDS OF LITERAL TRANSLATIONS

One additional reason for using interlinear bibles is that "literal translation" may mean different things to different people. Yes, even "strictly literal" translations may be quite different. This is because such translations are also influenced by their purpose and their target group. The strictly literal *Schocken Bible I, The Five Books of Moses* (1995), translated by Everett Fox, is an interesting example of this. This version is meant to be read aloud and thereby convey the rhythm and sound of the Hebrew text. It therefore mimics the syntax of the Hebrew text, scrupulously preserving its repetition, allusion, alliteration and wordplay (Translator's Preface, p. ix).

Compared with the NWT, which stresses meaning rather than sound or music, it is a different form of communication. Fox correctly observes (page xii), "Clearly there is a difference between translating what the text means and what it says." The Schocken Bible stresses word form and the rhythm and music of the original, thus communicating less information to its readers than does the NWT, which stresses meaning. The

302

Schocken Bible therefore stands between an interlinear Bible, which communicates little or nothing, and the strictly literal NWT which communicates much to the reader.

We may use the Hebrew *Infinitive absolute* as an example of the difference between these two strictly literal translations. This infinitive is often made from the same root as the main verb of the clause, and is then used for emphasis. Genesis 2:17 says (word for word), "because on day of your eating from it dying [infinitive absolute] you will die." The *Schocken Bible* says, "for on the day that you eat from it, you must die, yes die." NWT reads, "for in the day you eat from it you will positively die." Both renditions are literal but they serve different purposes. The *Schocken Bible* is only concerned with the words, and the grammatical fact that the infinitive absolute modifies the verb is ignored; but its repetition will, of course, indicate some stress. The NWT, which is concerned both with the words and the grammar, modifies the verb by help of an adverb, thus conveying the meaning.

A good example of where several verb forms are rendered differently in the two translations is Exodus 22:21-23. In verse 21 we find the single verb "afflict," and both versions are quite similar. The *Schocken Bible* reads, "Any widow or orphan you are not to afflict." NWT (verse 22) says, "You people must not afflict any widow or fatherless boy." In verse 22 we find three infinitive absolutes. *Schocken* says: "Oh, if you afflict, afflict them . . . ! For (then) they will cry, cry out to me, and I will hearken, hearken to their cry." NWT (verse 23) says: "If you should afflict him at all, then if he cries out to me at all, I shall unfailingly hear his outcry." The emphasis signaled by the three infinitive absolutes in this verse is expressed by repetition in *Schocken*, and this musical way of doing it is readily felt when the text is read aloud. NWT, on the other hand, expresses the emphasis semantically by using "at all" twice and by using "unfailingly" once.

In verse 23, however, *Schocken* has not been able to convey the Hebrew melody in an adequate way, while the NWT continues to show the emphasis, thus carrying the thought to its logical end. *Schocken* says, "my anger will flare up, and I will kill you with the sword, so that your wives become widows, and your children, orphans." NWT (verse 24) says, "And my anger

303

will indeed blaze, and I shall certainly kill YOU with the sword, and YOUR wives must become widows and YOUR sons fatherless boys." The *Schocken Bible* has no emphasis in verse 23, which is strange, particularly because of the repetition of "hearken" at the end of verse 22. Why should only God's hearing be stressed, and not his actions as a result of this hearing?

The basic problem with the *Schocken Bible* is a faulty grammatical theory, but it also illustrates some weaknesses with its method of translating "what the text says" rather than "what it means," especially when this is taken to the extreme. All three verbs in verse 23 are perfects, with future meaning preceded by *waw*. According to traditional grammars, there is no semantic difference between these perfects (perfect consecutives) and a normal imperfect, pointing to the future. Therefore, the *Schocken Bible* uses a normal English future. Viewing the Hebrew conjugations as aspects rather than tenses, these perfects portray the future action as a whole while an imperfect simply stresses a part of it. The NWT is sensitive to this aspectual difference, and conveys it by using the adverbs "indeed" and "certainly" and the verb "must." In this way some of the verbs' real force is communicated to the readers, without any deviation from the strictly literal translation method.

BEYOND LITERAL AND INTERLINEAR TRANSLATIONS

The circumstances for Bible students differ, and even if our interest is great we may not have time to proceed to the deeper levels on our own. A Bible with many footnotes and appendices, such as NWTREF, will be a great help to the reader in this situation. To learn a little more about the original words on the basis of English alone, there are some basic tools available, such as W. E. Vine's *An Expository Dictionary of New Testament Words*, and A. Pick's *Dictionary of Old Testament Words*.

If we want to proceed further, the first natural step is to learn the Greek and/or the Hebrew alphabet. This is not very difficult. A good exercise for Greek is to get a copy of the United Bible Society's Greek New Testament or the 27th edition of the

Nestle-Aland Greek Text and an interlinear NT. Then start reading John 1 and 2 from whatever Greek text you choose, and occasionally look at the interlinear text to find the meaning, until you master the letters. The Hebrew letters can be learned in a similar way by using the Genesis volume of the Biblia Hebraica Stuttgartensia, together with an interlinear Bible. Read Genesis 1 and 2 until you master the Hebrew letters.

There are several advantages in mastering the script. First of all, there is a great satisfaction in doing so, which often triggers a desire to learn more. By knowing the letters, we are also able to use those lexicons which are organized on the basis of the Hebrew and Greek alphabet.[10] We will also be able to identify the words in interlinear Bibles and be able to look up and understand the grammatical forms by help of books such as *The Analytical Greek Lexicon* by Samuel Bagster and Sons (other editions by other publishers are also available) and B. Davidson's *The Analytical Hebrew and Chaldee Lexicon*. Both are very helpful for the beginner. We may also be able to use electronic Greek and Hebrew texts, such as those found in the Logos Library System.[11]

Once the student obtains a good knowledge of the letters of each language, he or she may proceed with learning some basic Greek or Hebrew grammar. Introductory grammars, such as C. L. Seow's *A Grammar for Biblical Hebrew* and J. A. Hewett's *New Testament Greek: A Beginning and Intermediate Grammar*, may suffice to teach some of the basics of each language. If a beginning student of the biblical languages wishes to proceed with their studies, or if they have a question about the grammar

---

[10] For Greek: W. Bauer, W. F. Arndt, F. W. Gingrich *A Greek-English Lexicon of the New Testament and Other Early Christian Literature*; G. Kittel, *Theological Dictionary of the New Testament*, 10 volumes; and C. Brown, *Dictionary of New Testament Theology*, 3 volumes. For Hebrew: L. Koehler, W. Baumgartner *Lexicon in Veteris Testamenti Libros*, 2 volumes; and G. J. Botterweck and H. Ringgren, *Theological Dictionary of the Old Testament*, 10 volumes. These are advanced works that will really only be useful for one who knows the letters of each language well enough to look up words as they are written in those languages.

[11] This text is based on the Gramcord modules, which is the best tool available. However, to use this tool one needs to have a working knowledge of Hebrew and/or Greek.

of the language, he or she may consult A. T. Robertson's *A Grammar of the Greek New Testament in the Light of Historical Research* for Greek; E. Kautzsch and A. E. Cowley *Gesenius' Hebrew Grammar*; B. K. Waltke and M. O'Connor, *An Introduction to Biblical Hebrew Syntax* for Hebrew. But we should remember that none of these books can be trusted in everything. The student should be particularly cautious about a grammar's discussion of the verbs. However, before learning Hebrew or Greek there is an important step which must be taken, namely, to learn the grammar of our mother tongue. A good knowledge of both the English verbal system and of how sentences should be analyzed is essential in order to properly learn the grammar of the biblical languages.

A few persons may want to proceed even further and take an introductory course in Greek or Hebrew. There are teach-yourself books and courses for both languages, but if you have the opportunity it is better to be taught in the classroom. I know a few persons who have taught themselves the biblical languages, but it can be a hard road to travel. In any case, the more we know about the original languages, the more we are able to have a part in the translation process of the Bible. But never forget that you, as any translator, also have a horizon of understanding and a set of beliefs. So be careful not to make faulty judgements because of irrational forces in your own mind!

CONCLUSION

A principal thought of this book has been that bias should not be defined on the basis of orthodox religion—that any rendition that does not bolster the traditional faith of the majority is biased. But it should rather be defined on the basis of language—any rendition violating normal translation principles or linguistic rules is biased. On this basis, my investigation of the NWT has resulted in a conclusion completely different from those reached by Countess, Bowman, and Kubo and Specht. Taking into account its target group and translation principles, NWT is an excellent piece of work. In particular, the NWT study edition is a good tool for Bible study, because it helps the readers to make informed choices. Professor Kedar correctly observed that any Bible translation is bound to be a compromise, and NWT also has its weaknesses.

We started with a question about the reliability of English Bible translations, that is whether or not they faithfully render the original text. We have seen that by and large they do. But in some instances, particularly when important doctrinal questions such as the trinity are at stake, they are colored by theology, and this is rarely brought to the attention of the readers.

In recent years the rights of medical patients have been strengthened and there is no longer any reason for the doctor to make decisions over the authority of the patients. The patients should make use of their right of informed consent. In a similar way, there is no longer any reason for Bible translators to make all the decisions for the readers. The readers should be given a share in the translation process, and be helped to make informed choices. The conclusion, therefore, is that bias has no place in Bible translation, but theology certainly has. Your task, as a Bible reader, is to make sure that theology plays a *legitimate* role in the Bible translations you decide to use.

EXPLANATIONS OF WORDS AND EXPRESSIONS

ANAPHORIC – Pointing backwards. A word pointing back to another word, for instance, a relative pronoun pointing back to a substantive is anaphoric.

ANARTHROUS – A substantive without the Greek article.

ANTHROMORPHISM – To ascribe human shape or attributes to gods, objects, animals, etc.

APOCRYPHA – The word means "hidden," "concealed" and refers to different books which occur in Roman Catholic Bibles, but which are lacking in Protestant Bibles.

APOLOGETIC – The work of a branch of theology having to do with the defense and proofs of the Christian faith.

a priori – Conclusions made on the basis of theory rather than experiments are made *a priori* . Such conclusions are taken for granted without any demand for evidence.

ARGUMENTS OF THE VERB – The subject and/or object in a clause.

ARTICULAR (or *ARTHROUS*) – Words that are used with the (Greek) article.

BASIC TRANSLATION UNIT – The smallest part of the text which, as a unit, can be directly transmitted into another language.

CLOSEST NATURAL EQUIVALENT – The words in the target language that best convey the message of the source language. These are obtained when the lexical meanings of the words of the source language are taken into consideration, and this meaning is adjusted so that it can be understood by the receivers. This is not the same as simply translating the text word for word, which is called "semantic equivalence."

CONCEPT – This word is used in two ways: 1) The total understanding of a word as it is stored in the minds of people sharing the same presupposition pool, and 2) the label used to designate an abstract notion, an idea, a viewpoint or a theory.

CONNOTATION – An idea suggested by or associated with a word or phrase. The words "prostitute," "whore," "harlot," "lady of the night," and "courtesan" can all translate the Greek word *pornē*. They imply the same kind of behavior or action(s), but their connotations are different from each other.

COPULA – The small word, usually a form of "to be," occurring between a verb and its complement (and which binds them together) in a stative clause, such as, "And the Word was a god."

COUNT NOUN – A noun that can be counted and which has a plural form. Words such as "bread" and "body" are count nouns"; words such as "water" and "blood" are noncount nouns.

CLASSICAL HEBREW – Includes the language found in the Bible, in the old inscriptions, and in the writings from Qumran.

DEFINITE – A particular individual or exemplar is meant. While "articular" (or "arthrous," indicating that the article occurs) is a grammatical term, "definite" is a pragmatic term. This means that it is the context that decides whether or not a noun is definite. The article has different roles as a signal for definiteness, in different languages.

DOXOLOGY – A praising or uttering of praise.

ECCLESIASTICUS – Another name for the book "The Wisdom of Ben Sira."

ECLECTIC – The word comes from the Greek *kaleō* ("to call out"). An eclectic use of a text means that one single manuscript is not used, but that words from different manuscripts are chosen on the basis of the author's judgement, and then they are put together as one text.

EGRESSIVE – "Going out." A term meaning that the end is approached or reached.

ELLIPSIS – Meaning "omission." An element in a clause can be invisible (it is just implied), but when translated to another language, this element must, because of the structure of the target language, in many instances be explicitly translated.

EMPIRICAL – Something that is based on experience.

EPITHET – An adjective, noun, or phrase expressing some characteristic quality of a thing.

EUPHEMISM – The use of a word or phrase that is less expressive or direct than another word, but which is considered less distasteful or offensive. The phrase "to walk," in both English and in Hebrew, is used for "to die."

ETYMOLOGY – The origin and development of a word; tracing it back as far as possible, often by the help of comparative linguistics.

FINITE VERB – A verb which can be parsed in person and number, in contrast to nonfinite forms such as the infinitive.

FREQUENTATIVE – Something done over and over again.

GENERIC – Referring to a kind, class or group; inclusive or general, opposed to specific or special.

GNOMIC – A word, for instance, a verb, which expresses a general thought that can be applied to any time.

GRAMMATICALIZED – If a particular semantic nuance, such as aspect, is expressed by a particular morphosyntactic form in a language, this nuance is grammaticalized, as opposed to nuances which are pragmatic, that is, they must be construed by a study of the context.

HABITUAL – A verb expressing a habitual or customary action, such as "each year he went up to Jerusalem."

HORIZON OF UNDERSTANDING – The totality of concepts and attitudes that we have at a given moment, conscious and unconscious, toward which our attention is not directed.

IDIOMATIC TRANSLATION – A translation which is more free than a literal translation. The principle informing an idiomatic translation is that the idioms and expressions of the target language should completely dominate the translated text, and any construction in the source language should be completely transformed into the equivalents of the target language.

INDEFINITE – As opposed to definite; having no exact limits. In a linguistic context the term is often pragmatic; that is, it refers to general objects and not to one or more clearly identifiable objects.

INGRESSIVE – Where the beginning and first part of an event or the entering into a state is stressed.

INNOVATION – A change in the established order, creating something new.

INTERLINEAR TRANSLATION – A translation where the text of the target language is placed beneath the text of the source language, line by line and word by word. Each word in the source language is given its equivalent in the target language. Grammar, syntax and context are ignored.

ITERATIVE – To repeat an action or performance, such as in "she was knocking at the door."

LACUNA – A blank space in or missing portion of a manuscript.

LEXICAL MEANING – The meaning given to words in a lexicon.

LEXICAL EQUIVALENCE – The most frequently used sense(s) in the target language of a word in the source language.

LINGUISTICS – The study of language from the point of view of the structure of language, in contrast to philology, where extralinguistic information is used to establish and understand the text of a particular manuscript.

LITERAL TRANSLATION – Translation which closely follows the words of the source text, as opposed to an idiomatic translation. The principle behind a literal translation is that the original words must be translated as faithfully and uniformly as possible. Often the sentence structure of the source language will also be followed.

MEANING – In this book "meaning" is used in two ways: 1) to indicate the sum of all the senses we ascribe to a word. This is the general use of the word, and it indicates that "sense," as it is used in this book, covers a smaller area than does "meaning." 2) To indicate the minimum number of English words which are necessary to signal to the English mind the same comprehension as a native Greek or Hebrew would get from all the uses of a particular word in the Bible. This is the technical use of the word, particularly in connecteion with the triangles of signification.

MISHNA – A book not much smaller than the Bible, which contains expressions from Jewish sages. It is supposed to have been written in the first part of the third century CE, and is written in Mishnaic Hebrew, with elements of Aramaic.

MISHNAIC HEBREW – A dialect of Hebrew which developed in the first few centuries CE. The aspectual nature of Classical Hebrew is lost and a tense system is used with perfect as past tense, participle as present tense and imperfect as future tense. The language structure is closer to modern Hebrew than to Classical Hebrew.

MORPHOLOGICAL – Pertaining to form. A morphological difference between two words is a difference in the form of each word.

MORPHOSYNTACTIC – A word with a certain morphology seen from a grammatical point of view, as when distinctions are made in an inflectional paradigm (= a systematic arrangement of a word according to its grammatical features).

NOMINA SACRA – Names or designations referring to or having connections with God. Some of these are abbreviated in manuscripts of the Septuagint and the New Testament; *theos* occurs as θς and *kurios* occurs as κς.

ONTOLOGY – The branch of metaphysics dealing with the nature of being and reality. An ontological difference or similarity refers to a similarity or difference in being or nature.

PARAMETER – A constant with variable values used as a referent for determining other variables.

PARTICIPLE – A word which participates in the nature of both verb and adjective or verb and substantive. Present participles in English end with - ing (singing), past participles include "made" and "mentioned."

PHONEME – A class of closely related speech sounds regarded as a single sound and represented in phonetic transcription by the same symbol. For example, the sound of "r" in "bring," "red" and "round."

PHILOLOGY – The use of extralinguistic information to establish and understand the text of a particular manuscript, in contrast to linguistics, which represents the study of language from the point of view of the structure of language.

PHYLACTERIES – A small leather case holding slips inscribed with scriptures. The case was fastened to a person's forehead or to the left arm.

PREDICATE NOMINATIVE – Verbs indicating action often take objects, while stative verbs, such as "to be," do not take objects but take predicate nominatives instead. In the clause, "John built a house," "built" is verb, "John" is the subject and "a house" is the object. In the clause, "John is tall," "is" is the verb, "John" is the subject and "tall" is predicate nominative.

PREFERENCE – A rendering which is to be preferred because of language (linguistics), meaning (semantics) or context.

PREFIX – A syllable or group of syllables joined to the beginning of a word, in order to alter its meaning or create a new word.

PRESUPPOSITION POOL – The common knowledge and understanding of the world which a particular group has built on their language, their culture, their religion and their everyday life. While this word only entails knowledge and understanding as they relate to a group, the word "horizon of understanding" involves motives and attitudes as they relate to an individual.

PROBLEM OF INDUCTION – This problem means that if we have a hypothesis which predicts something, and what is predicted turns out to be true, the hypothesis is not proved to be true because there may be many other circumstances in which the same result might also occur.

PSEUDEPIGRAPHAL BOOKS – Books which falsely ascribe their authorship to certain well-known persons, such as Enoch or Abraham. Some of these books, or parts of them, are pre-Christian. Most of them were written from the first century CE onward.

PUNCTUAL (or *PUNCTILIAR*) – Verbs expressing actions which occur instantly and which do not have any inner constituency, such as "knock" and "fall."

QUALITATIVE – Normally applied to adjectives. When it is applied to generic substantives, it signals that in this particular context the quality or attributes of the subject are stressed, rather than its membership in the class. But the substantive is still generic and as such either definite or indefinite, also.

RECEPTOR LANGUAGE – The language into which the text is translated.

REFERENT – The person or thing referred to.

RESULTATIVE – A verb form which is used to express that the object is lead through the end of the action and into a resultant state. The English expression "Sit down!" formally expresses an action, but what is stressed is the resultant state of being seated.

SABELLIANISM – Sabellius was a religious leader in the fourth century CE who taught that God the Father and the Son were the same person and were identical in every respect. Viewpoints along these same lines are typically referred to as Sabellianism.

SEMANTIC EQUIVALENT – A correspondence between the words of the source language and the target language on the lexical plane. The closest natural equivalent, in contrast, refers to a correspondence between the message in the source language and the target language.

SEMANTICS – The science of meaning.

SENSE – In this book "sense" covers a smaller area than "meaning": The sum of all the senses we moderns ascribe to a Greek or Hebrew word that constitutes its meaning.

SOURCE LANGUAGE – The language from which a text is translated.

SYNTAX – Laws and rules governing the relationship between the different parts of a clause or sentence.

SOURCE LANGUAGE – The language from which the translation is done. The OT is translated from Hebrew, with some texts in Aramaic, namely, Ezra 4:8-6:18; 7:12-26 and Daniel 2:4-7:28. The NT is translated from Greek.

SPECIFIC – The opposite of "generic." The word refers to a particular individual who is clearly distinguished or identified.

STOCK OF PHONEMES – A class or family of closely related speech sounds (phones) regarded as a single sound. For example, the "r" in "bring," "red," and "round" constitutes phoneme. The stock of phonemes is the total number of phonemes in a language, and this can differ from language to language.

SUBORDINATIONIST – The view that the Son was/is subordinate to the Father.

SUBSTANTIVIZED ADJECTIVE – A word which is formally an adjective but which syntactically functions as a substantive. The word "elder" is, for instance, an adjective in the comparative form, but it is used as a substantive.

TALMUD – This work is supposed to have been written down in the fifth or the sixth century CE. It was written in Aramaic with elements of Mishnaic Hebrew, and it exists in a Babylonian version of thirty volumes and in a shorter Palestinian version. It contains the Mishna and comments on it.

TARGUM – Translations or paraphrases of the books in the Old Testament into Aramaic.

TARGET LANGUAGE – The language into which the translation is done.

THEOPHORIC ELEMENTS – Names consisting of elements from YHWH, *'ēl* or other designations of God, such as Nathana*el*, *Jeho*shaphat or Isa*iah*.

TOSEFTA – A collection of traditions related to Jewish oral law. It was produced later than the Mishna and can be viewed as a complement to it.

BIBLIOGRAPHY

Abbot, T. K. *A Critical and Exegetical Commentary on the Epistles to the Ephesians and to the Colossians.* Edinburgh: T & T Clark, 1990 (1909).

Aitchison, J. *The Articulate Mammal: An Introduction to Psycholinguistics.* Third Edition. London: Routledge, 1989.

————. *Words in the Mind: An Introduction to the Mental Lexicon.* Oxford: Blackwell, 1993.

Ali, Z., and L. Koenen. *Three Rolls of the Early Septuagint: Genesis and Deuteronomy.* Papyrologische Texte und Abhandlungen. Band 27. Bonn: Rudolf Habelt Verlag GMBH, 1980.

Archer, G. L., H. Laird, and B. Waltke. eds. *Theological Wordbook of the Old Testament.* Vol. 1. Chicago: Moody Press, 1980.

————., and G. Chirichigno. *Old Testament Quotations in the New Testament.* Chicago: Moody Press, 1983.

Backe, C. *Verbal Aspect: A General Theory and Its Application to Present-Day English.* Odense: Odense University Press, 1985.

Barnes, O. L. *A New Approach to the Problem of the Hebrew Tenses and its Solution Without the Recourse to Waw Consecutuve.* Oxford: J. Thornton and Son, University Booksellers, 1965.

Bauer, W. *A Greek-English Lexicon of the New Testament and Other Early Christian Literature.* Revised by F. W. Gingrich and F. W. Danker. Translated into English by W. F. Arndt and F. W. Gingrich. 2d ed. Chicago: University of Chicago Press, 1979.

Barr, J. *Semantics of Biblical Language.* Oxford: Oxford University Press, 1975.

————. (1992). "Hebrew Lexicography: Informal Thoughts." In *Linguistics and Biblical Hebrew.* Edited by W. R. Bodine. Winona Lake: Eisenbrauns, 1992.

Barthélemy, D. "Redécouverte d'un chainon manquant de l'histoire de la Septante." *Revue Biblique* 60 (1953), pp. 18-29.

————. *Les devanciers d'Aquila.* Supplement to Vetus Testamentum 10. Leiden: Brill, 1963.

Beekman, J. and J. Callow. *Translating the Word of God.* Grand Rapids:: Zondervan Publishing House, 1975.

Bertram, G. "Theologische Aussagen im Griechischen Alten Testament, Gottesnamen." *Zeitschrift der deutschen morgenländischen Gesellschaft* 3.4 (1978).

Bethune-Baker, J. F. *An Introduction to the Early History of Christian Doctrine.* London, 1933.

Bibelen Guds Ord. *Det Gamle og Det Nye Testamente med bibelordbok Den norske King James-oversettelsen av.* Oslo: Bibelforlaget A/S, 1997.

Bickerman, E. *The Jews in the Greek Age.* Cambridge, Mass.: Harvard University Press, 1988.

Blass, F., and A. Debrunner. *A Greek Grammar of the New Testament and Other Early Christian Literature.* Translated by Robert W. Funk. Chicago: University of Chicago Press, 1961.

Bowman, R. M. *Jehovah's Witnesses, Jesus Christ, and the Gospel of John.* Grand Rapids: Baker, 1989.

Brandenburger, E. "σταυρός." NIDNTT 1. Grand Rapids: Zondervan, 1979.

Bratcher, R. G., and E. A. Nida. *A Translators Handbook on Paul's Letters to the Colossians and to Philemon.* Helps for Translators 10. Stuttgart: United Bible Societies, 1977.

Bratsiotis, N. P. "אֱנוֹשׁ." TDOT 1. Grand Rapids: Eerdmans, 1974.

Braumann, G. "παρουσία." NIDNTT 2. Grand Rapids: Zondervan, 1976.

Brown, C., and E. Tiedtke. "ἁρπάζω." NIDNTT 3. Grand Rapids: Zondervan, 1978.

Brown, R. E. *Jesus: God and Man.* New York: Mackmillan, 1967.

Brouw, R. O. D. "The Problem of the Missing Article in the Use of 'God.'" *Religious Studies* 30 (1994), pp. 17-27.

Büchsel, F. "μονογενής." TDNT 4. Grand Rapids: Eerdmans, 1967.

Byatt, A. "The Holy Spirit: A Further Examination." *The Expository Times* 100 (1989), pp. 3, 215-216.

Charlesworth, J. H. *A Graphic Concordance to the Dead Sea Scrolls.* Tübingen: Mohr, 1991.

———. *The Old Testament Pseudepigrapha.* Vol. 2 . Garden City: Doubleday, 1985.

Chomsky, N. *Syntactic Structures.* The Hague: Mouton, 1957.

———. *Aspects of the Theory of Syntax.* Cambridge, Mass.: M. I. T, 1965.

Cohon, S. S. "The Name of God: A Study in Rabbinic Theology." *Hebrew Union College Annual* (1951), pp. 579-604.

Collange, J. *The Epistle of Saint Paul to the Philippians.* London: Epworth Press, 1979.

Colwell, E. C. "A Definite Rule for the Use of the Article in the Greek New Testament." *Journal of Biblical Literature* 52 (1933), pp. 12-21.

Comrie, B. *Tense.* Cambridge: Cambridge University Press, 1985.

———. *Aspect: An Introduction to the Study of Verbal Aspect and Related Problems.* Cambridge: Cambridge University Press, 1976.

Cotterell, P., and M. Turner. *Linguistics and Biblical Interpretation.* Downers Grove: InterVarsity Press, 1989.

Countess, R. H. *The Jehovah's Witnesses' New Testament.* Phillipsburg: Presbyterian and Reformed, 1982.

Cullmann, O. *The Christology of the New Testament.* Study Edition. London: SCM Press, 1973.

Curtis, J. J. "An Application of the Syntax of Hebrew Verbs to the Writings of Amos." Ph.D. dissertation, Southern Baptist Theological Seminary, 1943.

Davidson, B. *An Analytical Hebrew and Chaldee Lexicon.* Grand Rapids: Zondervan, 1980 [1850].

Delisle, J. *Translation: An Interpretative Approach.* Translation Studies 8. Ottawa: University of Ottawa Press, 1988.

Dibelius, M., and H. Conzelmann. *The Pastoral Epistles*. Hermeneia. Philadelphia: Fortress Press, 1972.

Dixon, P. S. "The Significance of the Anarthrous Predicate Nominative in John." Th. M. thesis, Dallas Theological Seminary, 1975.

Driver, S. R. *A Treatise on the Use of the Tenses in Hebrew*. 3rd ed. Oxford: Clarendon, 1892.

Dunand, F. *Papyrus Grecs Biblique*. Recherches d'archeologie, de philologie et d'histoire 27. Etudes de papyrologie. T.9, Cairo, 1966.

Eddleman, L. "Waw Consecutive and the Consecution of Tenses as Reflected by Eight Century Hebrew." Ph.D dissertation, Southern Baptist Theological Seminary, 1943.

Ehrman, B. D. *The Orthodox Corruption of Scripture: The Effect of Early Christological Controversies on the Text of the New Testament*. New York, Oxford: Oxford University Press, 1993.

Fanning, B. M. *Verbal Aspect in New Testament Greek*: Oxford, Clarendon Press, 1990.

Finkelstein, L. *New Light on the Prophets*. London: Vallentine, Mitchell, 1969.

Fitzmyer, J. A. *A Wandering Aramean*. Monograph Series 25. Society of Biblical literature, Missoula: Scholars Press, 1979.

Foerster, W. "ἁρπαγμός." TDNT 1. Grand Rapids: Eerdmans, 1964.

Fortman E. J. *The Triune God: A Historical Study of the Doctrine of the Trinity*. Grand Rapids: Baker, 1972.

Fox, E. *The Schocken Bible*. Vol. 1. The Five Books of Moses. New York: Schocken Books, 1995.

Fowler, J. D. *Theophoric Personal Names in Ancient Hebrew: A Comparative Study*. Journal for the Study of the Old Testament. Supplement Series 49. Sheffield: Sheffield Academic Press, 1988.

Franks, R. S. *The Doctrine of the Trinity*. London: Gerald Duckworth, 1958.

Furuli, R. "Imperfect Consecutive and the Verbal System of Biblical Hebrew." Mag. Art thesis: University of Oslo, 1995.

Gesenius, H. W. F. *Gesenius' Hebrew Grammar*. Edited by E. Kautzsch. Translated into English by A. E. Cowley. 2d ed. Oxford: Clarendon Press, 1980.

Gibson, A. *Biblical Semantic Logic*. Oxford: Basil Blackwell, 1981.

Godet, F. L. *Commentary on First Corinthians*. Grand Rapids: Kregel Publications, 1985 [1889].

Grant, R. M. *The Apostolic Fathers IV*. New York: Nelson, 1966.

———. *Gods and the One God*. Library of Early Christianity. Philadelphia: Westminster Press, 1986.

Grillmeyer, A. *Christ in Christian Tradition*. Vol. 1. From the Apostolic Age to Chalcedon (451). Atlanta: John Knox Press, 1975.

Guthrie, D. *The New Bible Commentary*. Revised ed. London: InterVarsity Press, 1970.

Hanson, R. P. C. *The Search for the Christian Doctrine of God*. Edinburgh: T. & T. Clark, 1988.

Harnack, A. *History of Dogma*. New York: Dover Publications, 1961.

Harner, P. B. "Qualitative Anarthrous Predicate Nouns: Mark 15:39 and John 1:1." *Journal of Biblical Literature* 92 (1973), pp. 75-87.

Harris, M. J. *Jesus as God: The New Testament Use of* Theos *in Reference to Jesus.* Grand Rapids:: Baker, 1992.

Hatch, E. *The Influence of Greek Ideas and Usages on the Christian Church.* Edited by A. M. Fairbairn. 5th ed. Peabody, Mass.: Hendrickson, 1995 [1895].

Herford, R. T. *Christianity in the Talmud and Midrash.* Library of Religious and Philolosophical Thought. New Jersey: Reference Books Publishers, 1966.

Holmquist, H., and J. Nørregård. *Kirkehistorie I.* København: J. H. Schultz Forlag, 1966.

Hjelmslev, L. *Omkring sprogteoriens grundlæggelse.* København: Akademisak Forlag, 1966.

Hewson, J., and V. Bubenik. *Tense and Aspect in Indo-European Languages.* Current Issues in Linguistic Theory. Amsterdam: J. Benjamins, 1997.

Hoover, R. W. "The Term Harpagmos in Philippians 2:6." Th.D. thesis, Harvard University, 1968.

———. "The Harpagmos Enigma: A Philological Solution." *Harvard Theological Review* 64 (1971), pp. 95-119.

Howard, G. "The Tetragram and the New Testament." *Journal of Biblical Literature* 96 (1977), pp. 63-84.

Joüon, P., and T. Muraoka. *A Grammar of Biblical Hebrew.* Subsidia Biblica—14.2. 1991, Roma: Editrice Pontificio Istituto Biblico, 1991.

Kahle, P. *The Cairo Geniza,* Oxford: Basil Blackwell, 1959.

Kasher, M. M. *The Encyclopedia of Biblical Interpretation.* New York: American Biblical Enmcyclopedia Society, 1967.

Kedar-Kopfstein, B. "The Interpretative Element in Transliteration." *Textus* (1973), pp. 55-77.

Kelly, J. N. D. *Early Christian Doctrines.* Revised ed. New York: Harper & Row, 1978.

Kennedy, H. A. A. *Sources of New Testament Greek.* Edinburgh: T & T Clark, 1895.

Kilpatrick, G. D. *Etudes de Papyrologie Tome Neuvieme.* Le Caire. Imprimiere de L'Institut Francais d'Archaéologie Orientale (1971), pp. 221-226.

Kim, Y. K. "Palaeographical dating of P^{46} to the Later First Century." *Biblica* 69 (1988), pp. 248-257.

Kohler, K. "The Tetragrammaton and its Uses," *Journal of Jewish Lore and Philosophy* 1 (1919), pp. 26, 27.

Kubo, S., and W. F. Specht. *So Many Versions? 20th Century English Versions of the Bible.* Revised and Enlarged ed. Grand Rapids: Zondervan, 1983.

Kustar, P. "Aspekt im Hebräischen." Ph.D. dissertation, Universität Basel, 1972.

Køhn, R. *Hebraisk Grammatikk.* Oslo: Universitetsforlaget, 1972.

Lake, K. *The Apostolic Fathers.* In 2 volumes. The Loeb Classical Library. Cambridge, Mass.: Harvard University Press, 1975.

Lenski, R. C. H. *Interpretations of I and II Corinhians.* Minneapolis: Augsburg Publishing House, 1985.

Leivestad, R. *Nytestamentlig Gresk Grmmatikk.* Oslo: Universitetsforlaget, 1972.

Liddell, H. G., and R. Scott. *A Greek-English Lexicon*. 9th Edition with Supplement. Revised by H. S. Jones and R. McKenzie. Oxford: Clarendon Press, 1968 and 1996.

Lipinski, E. *Semitic Languages: Outline of a Comparative Grammar*. Orientalia Lovaniensia Analecta 80. Leuven: Uitgivei Peeters en Departement Oosterse Studies, 1997.

Loh, J., and E. A. Nida. *A Translator's Handbook on Paul's Letter to the Philippians*. Helps for Translators Vol. 19. Stuttgart: United Bible Societies, 1977.

Lohse, E. *A Commentary on the Epistles to the Colossians and to Philemon*. Hermeneia Series. Philadelphia: Fortress Press, 1971.

Lomheim, S. *Omsetjingsteori*. Oslo: Universitetsforlaget, 1995.

Louw, J. P. *Semantics of New Testament Greek*. Chico, CA.: Scholars Press, 1982.

————., and E. A. Nida, eds. *Greek-English Lexicon of the New Testament Based on Semantic Domains*. In 2 volumes. 2d ed. New York: United Bible Societies, 1989.

McFall, L. *The Enigma of the Hebrew Verbal System*. Sheffield: The Almond Press, 1982.

McKay, K. L. *A New Syntax of the Verb in New Testament Greek*. New York: Peter Lang, 1994.

Marmorstein, A. *The Old Rabbinic Doctrine of God*. Jew's College Publications no. 10 [and 14 (1969)]. London: Oxford University Press, 1927.

Martin, R. P. *Carmen Christi: Philippians 2:5-11 in Recent Interpretation, and in the Setting of Early Christian Worship*. Revised ed. Grand Rapids: Eerdmans, 1983.

Martínez, F. G. *The Dead Sea Scrolls Translated: The Qumran Texts in English*. Translated by W. G. E. Watson. 2d ed. Leiden: Brill; Grand Rapids: Eerdmans, 1994.

Meijering, E. P. *Orthodoxy and Platonism in Athanasius: Synthesis or Antithesis?* Leiden: Brill, 1974.

Metzger, B, M. "The New World Translation of the Christian Greek Scriptures." Book review in *The Bible Translator* 15.4 (1964), pp. 150-152.

————. "The Jehovah's Witnesses and Jesus Christ: A Biblical and Theological Appraisal." *Theology Today* 10 (1953), pp. 65-85.

————. A Textual Commentary on the Greek New Testament. Stuttgart: United Bible Societies, 1971.

Michel, D. Tempora und Satzstellung in den Psalmen, Ph.D. dissertation, Rheinischen Friedrich-Wilhelms-Universität, Bonn, 1960.

Middeldorpf, H. *Codex Syriaco-Hexaplaris*, Berolini: Th. Chr. Fr. Enslin, 1835.

Middleton, T. F. *The Doctrine of the Greek Article Applied to the Criticism and Illustration of the New Testament*. New ed. Revised by H. J. Rose. London: J. G. & F. Rivington, 1833.

Moore, G. F. *Judaism in the First Centuries of the Christian Era: The Age of the Tannaim*. Vol. 1. Cambridge: Cambridge University Press, 1955.

Moule, C. F. D. *The Epistles of Paul the Apostle to the Colossians and to Philemon*. The Cambridge Greek Testament Commentary. Cambridge: Cambridge University Press, 1968.

————. "Further Reflexions on Philippians 2:5-11." In *Apostolic History and the Gospel: Biblical and Historical Essays Presented to F. F. Bruce on His 60th Birthday*. Edited by W. W. Gasque and R. P. Martin. London: Exeter, 1970.

————. *An Idiom Book of New Testament Greek*. Cambridge: Cambridge University Press, 1975.

Newman, B. M., and E. A. *A Translator's Handbook on Paul's Letter to the Romans*. Helps for Translators 14. Stuttgart: United Bible Societies, 1973.

Newmark, P. *A Textbook of Translation*. New York: Prentice Hall, 1988.

Newton, B. H. *The Altered Translation of Genesis ii,5*. (1888).

Nida, E. A. *Toward a Science of Translating*. Leiden: Brill, 1964.

————., and C. R. Taber. *The Theory and Practice of Translation*. Leiden: Brill, 1974.

Ogden, C. K. *The Meaning of Meaning*. International Library of Psychology, Philosophy and Scientific Method. London: Kegan Paul, Trench, Trubner & Co, 1923.

O'Collins, G. G. "Crucifixion." In *The Anchor Bible Dictionary*. Vol. 1. Edited by David Noel Freedman. New York: Doubleday, 1992.

Olsen, M. B. *A Semantic and Pragmatic Model of Lexical and Grammatical Aspect*. New York and London: Garland Publishing, 1997.

The Oxyrhynchus Papyri. Vol. 50. Graeco-Roman Memoirs no. 70. Published for the British Aacademy by the Egypt Exploration society. London, 1983.

Parsons, P. J. *Discoveries in the Judean Desert 9*. Cave 4. Oxford: Clarendon Press, 1992.

Peterson, S. "Media Papyri: An Examination of Carsten Thiede's Rediscovered Fragments." Electronically published by the author (http://ccat.sas. upenn.edu/~petersig/theide2.txt). (1995).

Pietersma, A. "Kyrios or Tetragram: A Renewed Quest for the Original Septuagint." In *De Septuaginta. Studies in Honour of John William Wevers on His Sixty-Fifth Birthday*. Edited by A. Pietersma and C. Cox, pp. 85-101. Toronto: Benben Publications, 1984.

Pick, A. *Dictionary of Old Testament Words for English Readers*. Grand Rapids: Kregel, 1979.

Pitt, F. D. "The Holy Spirit A Statistical Inquiry." *The Expository Times* (1989), pp. 136, 137.

Porter, S. E. *Verbal Aspect in the Greek of the New Testament, with Reference to Tense and Mood*. New York: Peter Lang, 1993.

Prestige, G. L. *God in Patristic Thought*. London: S. P. C. K., 1975.

Roberts, B. J. *The Old Testament Text and Versions: The Hebrew Text in Transmission and the History of the Ancient Versions*. Cardiff: University of Wales Press, 1951.

Roberts, C. H. *Manuscript, Society and Belief in Early Christian Egypt*. The Schweich Lectures for 1977.

Robertson, A. T. *Word Studies in the New Testament*. In 6 volumes. Nashville: Broadman Press, 1931.

————. *A Grammar of the Greek New Testament in the Light of Historical Research*. Nashville: Broadman Press, 1934.

Rosin, H. "Translating the Divine Names." *The Bible Translator* 3.4 (1952), pp. 180-187.

Rowly, H.H. "How Not to Translate the Bible." *Expository Times* 65 (1953-54), pp. 41-42.

de Saussure, F. *A Course in General Linguistics*. London: Duckworth, 1972.

Scanlin, H. P. "The Study of Semantics in General Linguistics." In *Linguistics and Biblical Hebrew*. Edited by W. R. Bodine. Winona Lake: Eisenbrauns, 1992.

Schiffmann L. H. *Who is a Jew? Rabbinic and Halakhic Perspectives on the Jewish Christian Schism*. New Jersey: Ktav Publishing, 1985.

Schubart, W. *Papyri Graecae*. Papyri Graecae Berolinensis/Collegit, 1911.

Schuller, E. M. *Non-Canonical Psalms from Qumran: A Pseudepigraphic Collection*. Harvard Semitic Studies 28. Atlanta, Georgia: Scholars Press, 1986.

Scoggin, E. B. "Application of Hebrew Verb States to a Translation of Isaiah 40-55." Ph.D. dissertation, Southern Baptist Theological Seminary, 1955.

Scott, C. A. A. *Footnotes on St Paul*. Cambridge, 1935.

Septuaginta. *Susanna - Daniel - Bel et Draco*. Vetus Testamentum Graecum Auctoritate Societatis Litterarum Gottingensis editum. Vol. 16. Göttingen - Vandenhoeck & Ruprecht, 1954.

Seleskovitch, D. *Language Learning and Professional Training in Interpretation*. National Resource Center for Translation and Interpretation, Washington D.C., 1978.

Silva, M. *Biblical Words and Their Meaning: An Introduction to Lexical Semantics*. Grand Rapids: Zondervan, 1983.

Skehan, P. W. "The Qumran Manuscripts and Textual Criticism." In *Volume du congrès, Strasbourg 1956*.VTSup 4, pp. 148-160. Leiden: Brill, 1957.

————., and A. A. DiLella. *The Wisdom of Ben Sira*. The Anchor Bible 39. New York: Doubleday, 1987.

————., Ulrich, E., and J. E. Sanderson. *Qumran Cave 4*. Discoveries in the Judean Desert 9. Oxford: Clarendon Press, 1992.

————. "The Divine Name at Qumran, in the Masada Scroll, and in the Septuagint." *Bulletin for the International Organization for Septuagint and Cognate Studies* 13 (1980), pp. 14-44.

Stafford, G. *Jehovah's Witnesses Defended: An Answer to Scholars and Critics*. 2d ed. Huntington Beach, CA: Elihu Books, 1999.

Stegemann, H. ΚΥΡΙΟΣ Ο ΘΕΟΣ *und* ΚΥΡΙΟΣ ΙΗΣΟΥΣ *Aufkommen und Ausbreitung des religiösen Gebrauchs von* ΚΥΡΙΟΣ *und seine Verwendung im Neuen Testament*. Ph.D. dissertation (Habil. Masch.), Bonn., 1969.

The Translator's New Testament. London: The British and Foreign Bible Society, 1973.

Thiede, C. P. "Papyrus Magdalen Greek 17 (Gregory-Aland P 64): A Reappraisal." *Tyndale Bulletin* 46.1 (1995), pp. 29-42.

Tov, E. *The Greek Minor Prophets Scroll From Nahal Hever (8HevXIIgr)*. Discoveries in the Judean Desert 8. Oxford: Clarendon Press, 1990.

Turner, N. *A Grammar of New Testament Greek*. Vol. 3. *Syntax*. Edinburgh: T. & T. Clark, 1963.

————. Grammatical Insights into the New Testament. Edinburgh: T. & T. Clark, 1965.

————. *Christian Words*. Nashville: Thomas Nelson Publishers, 1981.

de Waard J., and E. A. Nida. *From One Language to Another: Functional Equivalence in Bible Translating*. Nashville: Thomas Nelson Publishers, 1986.

Vine, W. E. *An Expositionary Dictionary of New Testament Words*. Old Tappan, New Jersey: Fleming H. Revell Company, 1966.

Waddel, W. G. "The Tetragrammaton in the LXX." *Journal of Theological Studies* 45 (1944), pp. 158-161.

Wainwright, A. W. *The Trinity in the New Testament*. London: S. P. C. K., 1962.

Wallace, D. B. *Greek Grammar Beyond the Basics*. Grand Rapids:: Zondervan, 1996.

Waltke, B. K., and M. O'Connor. *An Introduction to Biblical Hebrew Syntax*. Winona Lake: Eisenbrauns, 1990.

Watts, J. W. *A Survey of Syntax in the Hebrew Old Testament*. Grand Rapids: Eerdmans, 1964.

Webster's Encyclopedic Unabridged Dictionary of the English Language. New York: Gramery Books, 1989.

Wiener, G. B. *Grammatik des neutestamentlichen Sprachidioms*. Leipzig, 1867.

Wootton, R. W. F. "'Spirit' and 'Soul' in The New Testament." *The Bible Translator* 26.2 (1975), pp. 239-244.

Wolfson, H. A. *The Philosophy of the Church Fathers*. Cambridge Mass.: Harvard University Press, 1970.

AUTHOR INDEX

326

SCRIPTURE INDEX